IMAGES
of America

BRADLEY COUNTY

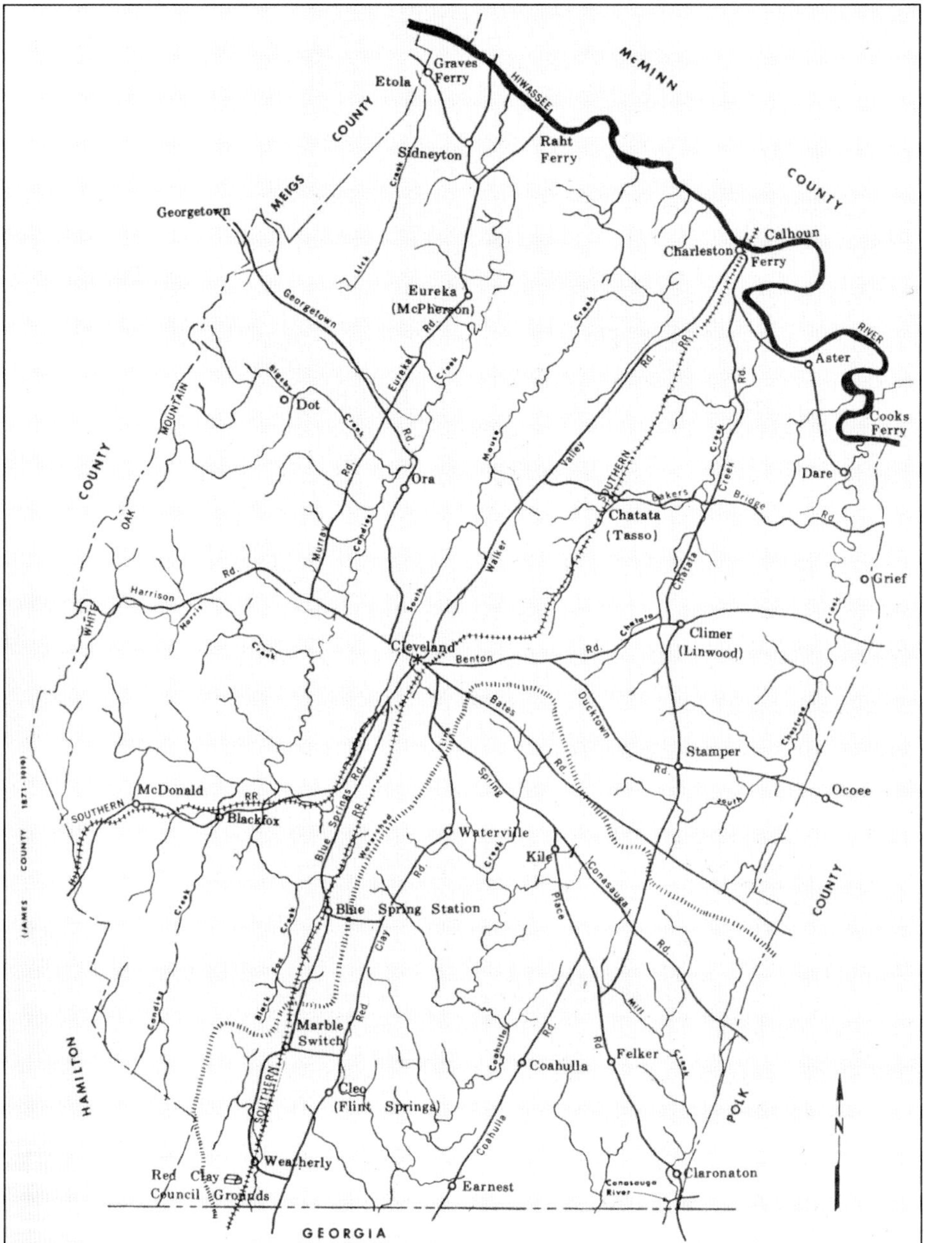

This early map of Bradley County shows the towns and communities as they existed in 1901–1902.

ON THE COVER: The third courthouse constructed by Bradley County was a majestic edifice and served the county for over 70 years. It is warmly referred to as the "old' courthouse.

IMAGES
of America

BRADLEY COUNTY

Robert L. George and Mitchell T. Kinder

ARCADIA
PUBLISHING

ISBN 978-0-7385-4387-1

Published by Arcadia Publishing
Charleston, South Carolina

Printed in the United States of America

Library of Congress Catalog Card Number: 2006934563

For all general information contact Arcadia Publishing at:
Telephone 843-853-2070
Fax 843-853-0044
E-mail sales@arcadiapublishing.com
For customer service and orders:
Toll-Free 1-888-313-2665

Visit us on the Internet at www.arcadiapublishing.com

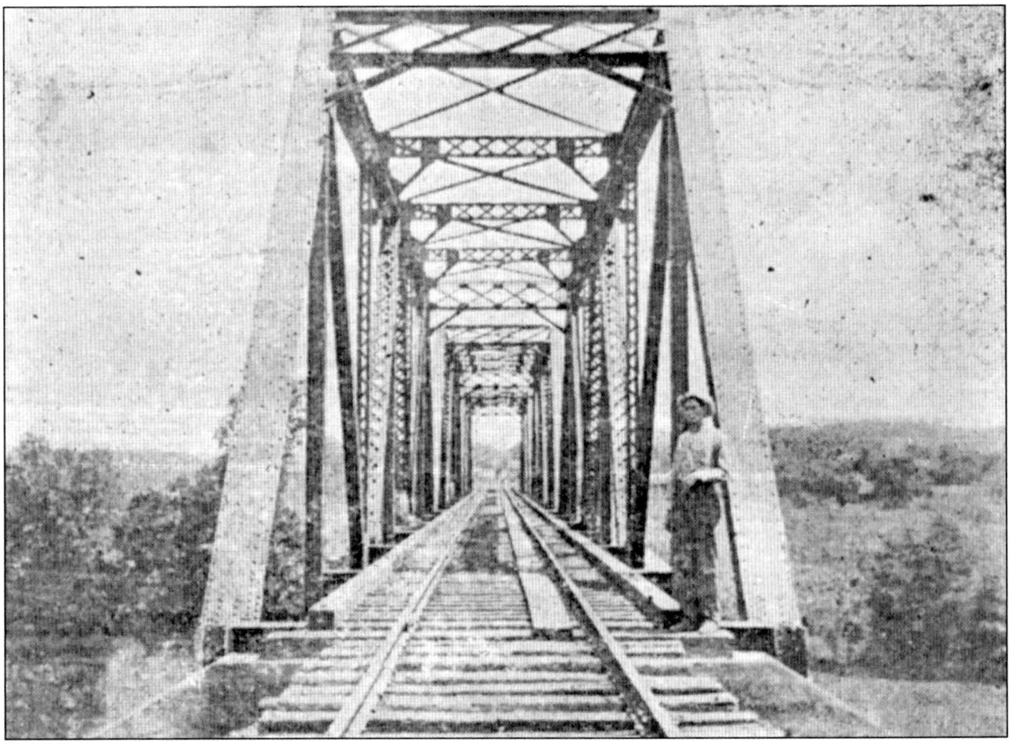

On January 11, 1842, a bridge was opened at Charleston across the Hiwassee River. It was used for rail traffic beginning in 1851. The railroad brought many visitors to Bradley County from 1851 to 1960.

CONTENTS

ACKNOWLEDGMENTS

The authors wish to thank their wives, Mary Lou Cooke George and Sherra E. Shroyer Kinder, for all of their help, guidance, and understanding in making this book a reality. In addition, thanks for sharing photographs and information are due Ruba Parks Allen, Cletis Bailey, Bradley County Historical Society, V. O. "Pete" Bryant, Dot Campbell, Ellen Ann Campbell, David Carroll, Jean Cochran, John Conner, Florence Cooke, Jimmy and Ann Cooke, Elaine Dillard, Elizabeth Cooke Disney, Martha Dooley, Betty Edmondson, James D. Finley, Sarah Elizabeth George, Lynn Gobble, Becca Goins, Gerald Goins, Jack Hall, History Branch of the Cleveland Public Library, Gaynelle Humberd, Johnnie Humberd, Reginald Hyberger, David Ingram, Summerfield Johnston Jr., Wyleen Jones, Harold and Betty Kelley, Lee University Alumni Office, Jean Malone, Ed and Pat Martin, Joan May, Billyfrank Marrison, Museum at Five Points, Bess Neil, Phil Newman, Ocoee Odd Fellows Lodge No. 97, Tommie Olsson, Adrian Ownby, Pleasant Grove United Methodist Church, Becky Smith, Jan and Bill Snell, Patricia A. Spencer, United Christian Church, Suzanne Wallace, Lyle and Eloise Wikre, and Joyce Womac.

INTRODUCTION

Bradley County embraces an area of 340 square miles. It consists of rolling hills in several valleys at the base of the Smoky Mountains. Bradley County was created by the Tennessee Legislature on February 10, 1836. It was formally organized on June 1, 1836. It is named for Col. Edward Bradley, a friend of Andrew Jackson and a veteran of the War of 1812. Cleveland is the county seat and is named after Col. Benjamin Cleveland, a revolutionary leader at the Battle of King's Mountain in the Revolutionary War. Other major towns and communities include Charleston, Tasso, McDonald, Georgetown, and Flint Springs.

The earliest recorded European visitor was Hernando DeSoto, who traveled through Bradley County in 1540. The Yuchi Indians fell to the Cherokee in 1711, and the area became part of the Cherokee Nation. The Cherokee Indian Agency was established in Charleston in 1819. Return Jonathan Meigs, known as White Eagle, was the first Indian agent to serve this post.

The Cherokees welcomed mission schools to teach their children. Brainerd Mission, founded in 1817, on Chickamauga Creek, helped establish three mission schools, which also served as churches, in Bradley County. Candy's Creek Mission was founded in 1824 and closed in 1839. Amohee Mission was founded in 1831 and closed in 1833. Red Clay Mission and school were founded in 1835 and closed in 1839.

The Cherokee Indians called themselves the Principal People. Their language is of the Iroquois family. At one time, the Cherokee Nation encompassed land in eight states. In 1827, the Cherokee Nation passed a constitution. A series of treaties with the U.S. government decreased the Cherokee Nation to land in parts of Alabama, Georgia, North Carolina, and Tennessee. The capital of the Cherokee Nation was New Echota in Georgia. Due to oppressive Georgia laws that decreed that the Cherokees could not meet except to cede lands, the Cherokee Council meetings were moved in 1832 out of Georgia to Red Clay, Tennessee. Chief John Ross moved his home to Flint Springs, Tennessee. Despite the new capital in Bradley County, 100 pro-removal Cherokees met in 1835 in New Echota to negotiate a new treaty. Several prominent Cherokees were in the treaty party, including The Ridge, Elias Boudinot, and Andrew Ross. The Treaty of New Echota was signed December 29, 1835, and by it, the Cherokee relinquished all lands in the Ocoee District in exchange for land in the West and $5 million. Fifteen thousand Cherokees signed a petition to protest the treaty, but the U.S. Senate ratified the treaty by a majority of one vote on May 23, 1836. The deadline for final removal of the Cherokee to the West was set as May 23, 1838.

The first permanent white settlement had begun by 1835 at Cleveland, which was known originally as Taylor's Place after Andrew Taylor, whose house was a favorite stopping place for travelers. The first county courthouse, a log structure, was built during the summer of 1836 on the southwest corner of the present courthouse square. The log building was replaced in 1840 by a plain brick building, which in turn was replaced by a majestic structure in 1892. The present courthouse was built in 1964. On August 10, 1852, the East Tennessee and Georgia Railroad entered the county, replacing dirt roads and the Hiwassee River as the main trade and transportation routes. In its heyday, trains carried passengers, mail, and freight to the county several times a day. Today trains are used only for industrial use.

Although Bradley County voted against secession of Tennessee from the Union, the majority of Tennessee residents voted for Tennessee to join the Confederacy. The vote in Bradley County saw the rural voters primarily supporting the Union, while the citizens of Cleveland supported the Confederacy. Soon after the War Between the States started, the county was occupied by Confederate troops. Union sympathizers had to go to Kentucky to join units supporting the North. Bitterness reigned on both sides. When the Union forces were victorious at the Battle of Missionary Ridge in Chattanooga, the occupying forces changed from Confederate to Union. Two blockhouses were constructed to secure the railroad bridge across the Hiwassee River. Large numbers of troops were camped in the Blue Springs area. Cleveland was under constant Union army rule. Although no major battles were fought in Bradley County, the impact of the war was severe.

Farming dominated the local economy until the late 19th century. Corn, wheat, tobacco, and vegetables were the main crops, with some farmers specializing in peaches and strawberries. Dairy farms are predominant today with broilers and beef also being raised. With the close of the Civil War, the local economy started to diversify with the founding of Hardwick Stove and Hardwick Clothes. Eventually industry would provide manufacturing jobs for about 15,000 employees. This provided a stimulus for prosperity in the retail sector.

There are more springs in Bradley County than any other East Tennessee county. The McDonald community and surrounding areas became well-known for their summer resort hotels, springs, and cabins. The springs were all widely used resorts from the late 1880s to about 1933.

After the mission schools closed, the Oak Grove Male Academy was the first institution to be chartered in the Ocoee District. Red Hill Academy, Chatata Seminary, the Masonic Female Institute, and Flint Springs Academy were early private educational institutions in the county. In the 1880s, Cleveland started its own public school system. The county landscape was dotted with one- and two-room public schools like Center Point School, Bunker Hill, Eureka, Hopewell, Blue Springs, and Georgetown. Centenary Female College was sponsored by the Methodist Church and was open from 1884 until 1929. Bob Jones College moved from Florida to Cleveland in 1933, having purchased the Centenary campus. Bob Jones College remained until 1947 when the Church of God Training School purchased the campus and moved here from Sevierville. Upon arrival, the school was named Lee College and in 1994 became Lee University. Cleveland State Community College commenced classes in 1967.

The church has been at the foundation of the county, and today the county is the international headquarters for seven denominations: Church of God, the Church of God of Prophecy, the Church of God at Jerusalem Acres, the United Christian Church, The Church of God, Zion Assembly Church of God, and the Church of Jesus Christ (Apostolic).

The first federal census of Bradley County in 1840 reports that 7,441 persons were residing in the county, including 450 slaves and 19 free blacks. By 1850, the county population had reached 12,259 and included 744 slaves and 37 free blacks. In 1900, the county reported a total population of 15,757, including 2,085 blacks. The 1970 census showed 50,686 with 2,280 blacks and 97 others. As of the census of 2000, there were 87,965 people residing in the county.

One

In the Early Days

The custom of the Indians was to annually burn the leaves, which kept down the young growth, hence the bushes being kept down, grass grew luxuriantly, and the entire county had more the appearance of a well kept park than a forest.

—R. M. Edwards
Moved to Bradley County in October 1835

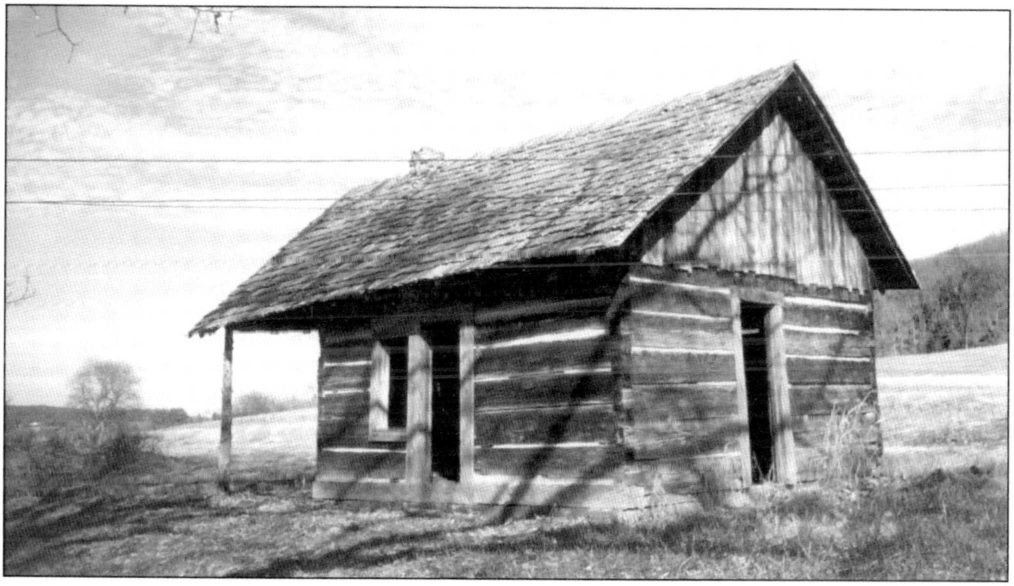

Located at Flint Springs, this log cabin was the last home, east of the Mississippi, of John Ross, principal chief of the Cherokee Nation. Here Chief Ross and John Howard Payne, author of *Home Sweet Home*, were arrested by Georgia deputies for violating a Georgia law forbidding the Cherokees to meet and were taken to Spring Place, Georgia, where they were imprisoned November 7, 1835.

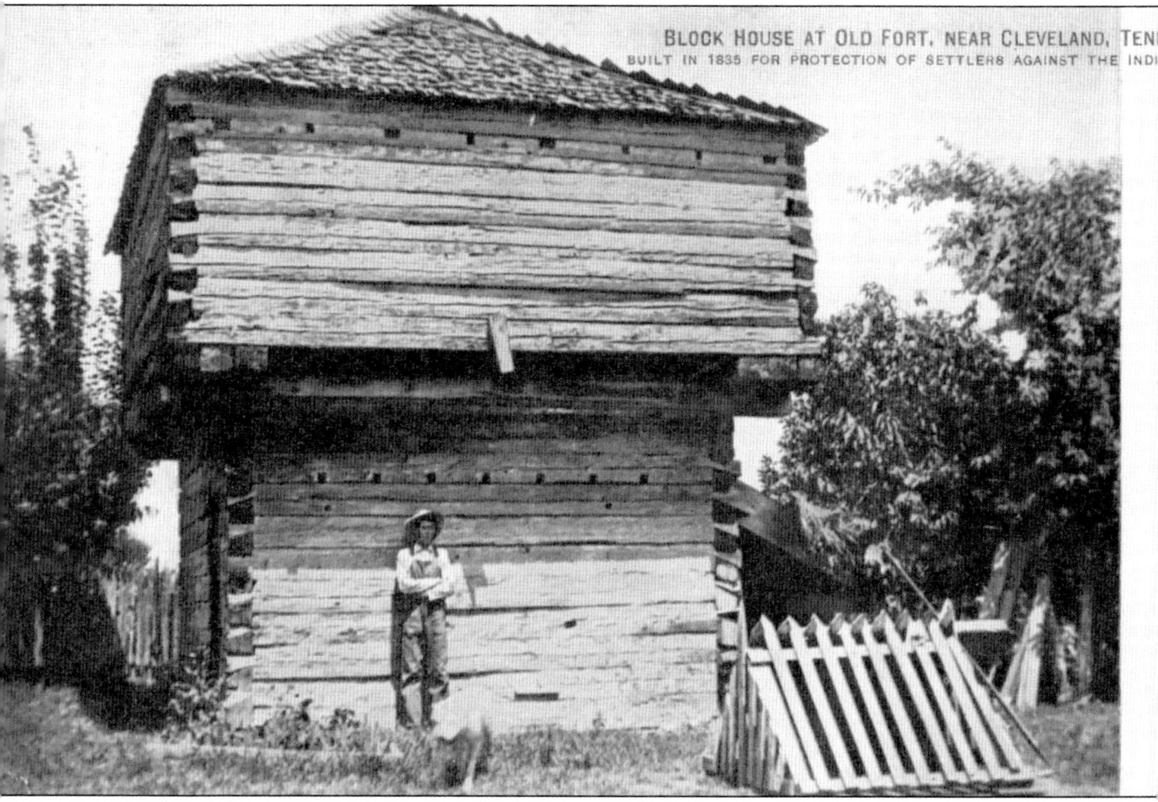

The block house at Old Fort was built in the 1830s near McNair's Stand just north of the Conasauga River to protect settlers from the Cherokee Indians. The building was moved to Benton around 1920. The area now known as Polk County was originally part of Bradley County until November 29, 1839.

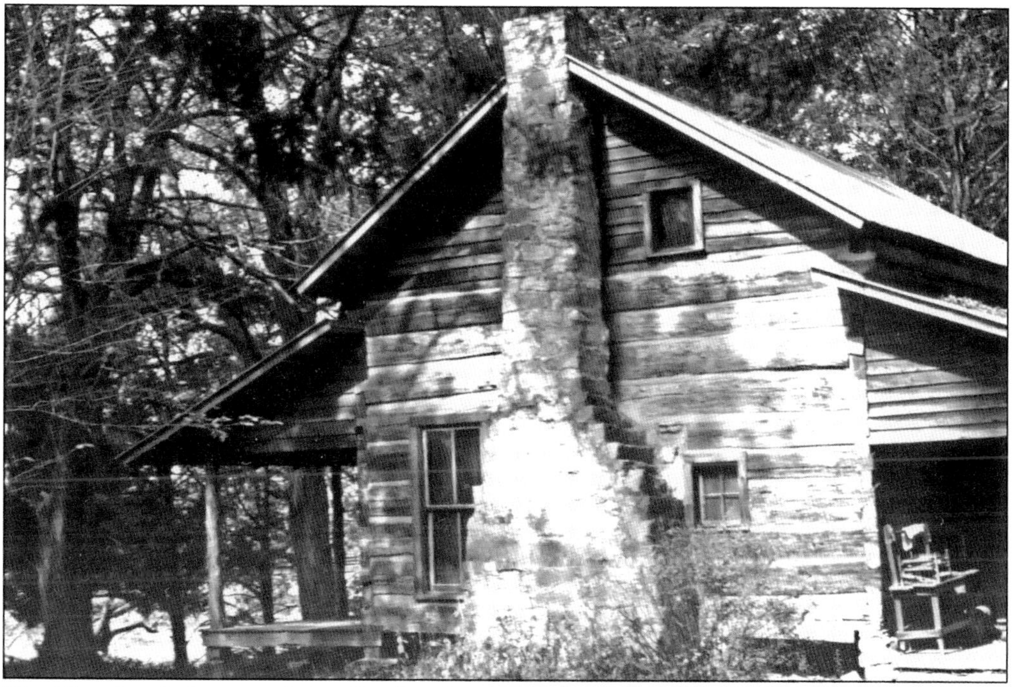

The Cherokee Indians settled in Bradley County in the 1700s. Shown is the Hair Conrad cabin dating from the early 1800s. Hair Conrad was a leader of the Cherokee people, raising seven children in this cabin. The Cherokee left for Oklahoma on the Trail of Tears in 1838. The cabin is located on Blythewood Farms and is on the National Register of Historic Places.

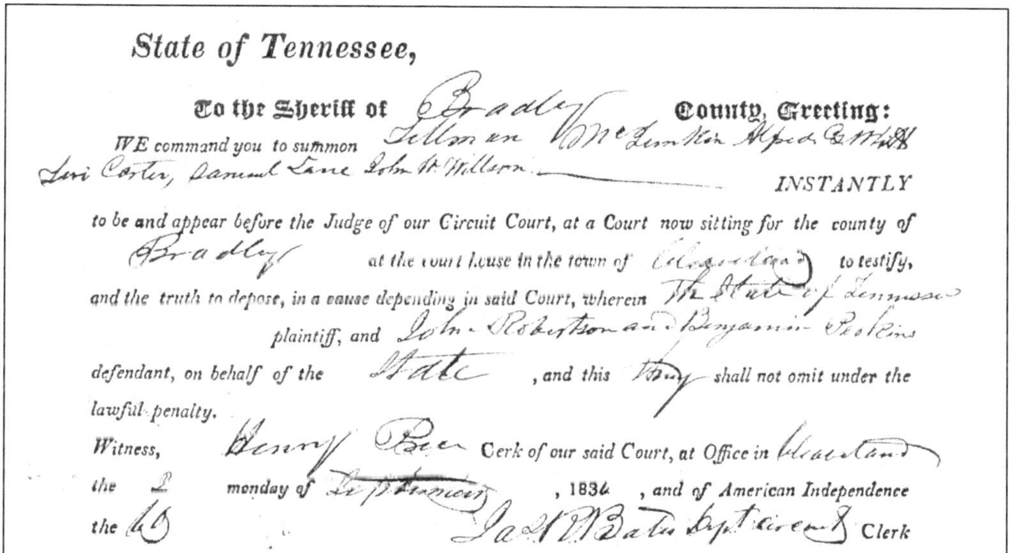

State of Tennessee,

To the Sheriff of Bradley County, Greeting:

WE command you to summon Tillman ... Levi Carter, Samuel Lane John W. Willson INSTANTLY to be and appear before the Judge of our Circuit Court, at a Court now sitting for the county of Bradley at the court house in the town of Cleveland to testify, and the truth to depose, in a cause depending in said Court, wherein The State of Tennessee plaintiff, and John Robertson and Benjamin Perkins defendant, on behalf of the State, and this they shall not omit under the lawful penalty.

Witness, Henry Price Clerk of our said Court, at Office in Cleveland the 2 monday of September, 1836, and of American Independence the 60

... Dep't Clerk

This 1836 Bradley County court document was issued the year the county was founded. Henry Price was elected the first Circuit Court clerk of Bradley County. Price also served as a Methodist evangelist. A tribute paid to him in the *Cleveland Herald* many years after his death stated he was the most popular man in the county in his day. He was friends with the Cherokees as well as the white settlers who occupied the area.

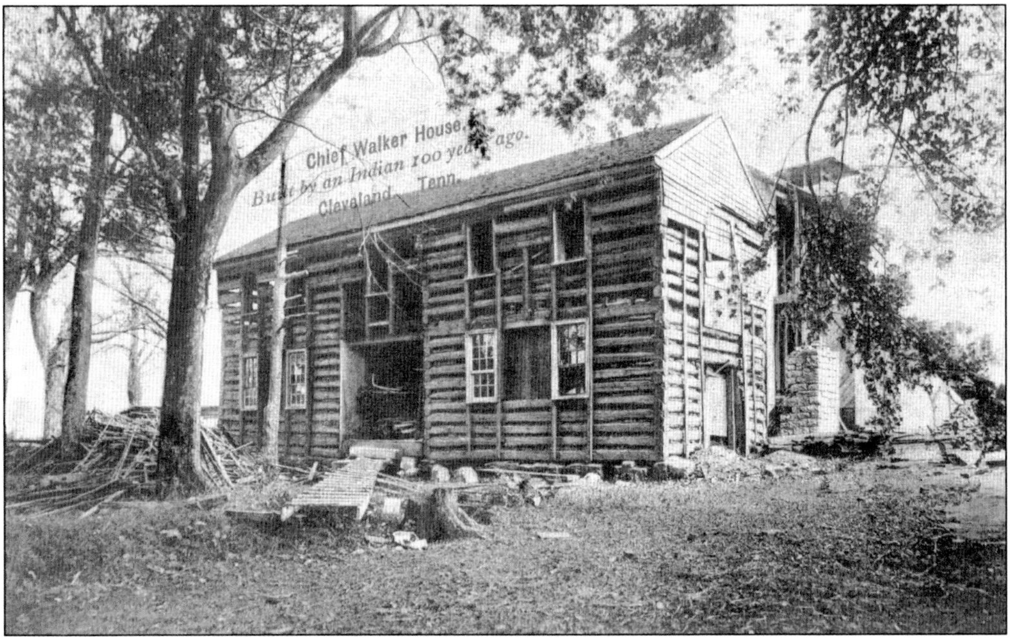

Chief Jack Walker was a member of the pro-treaty party of the Cherokee Nation. Before he was murdered in 1834, his home was located on present-day North Lee Highway.

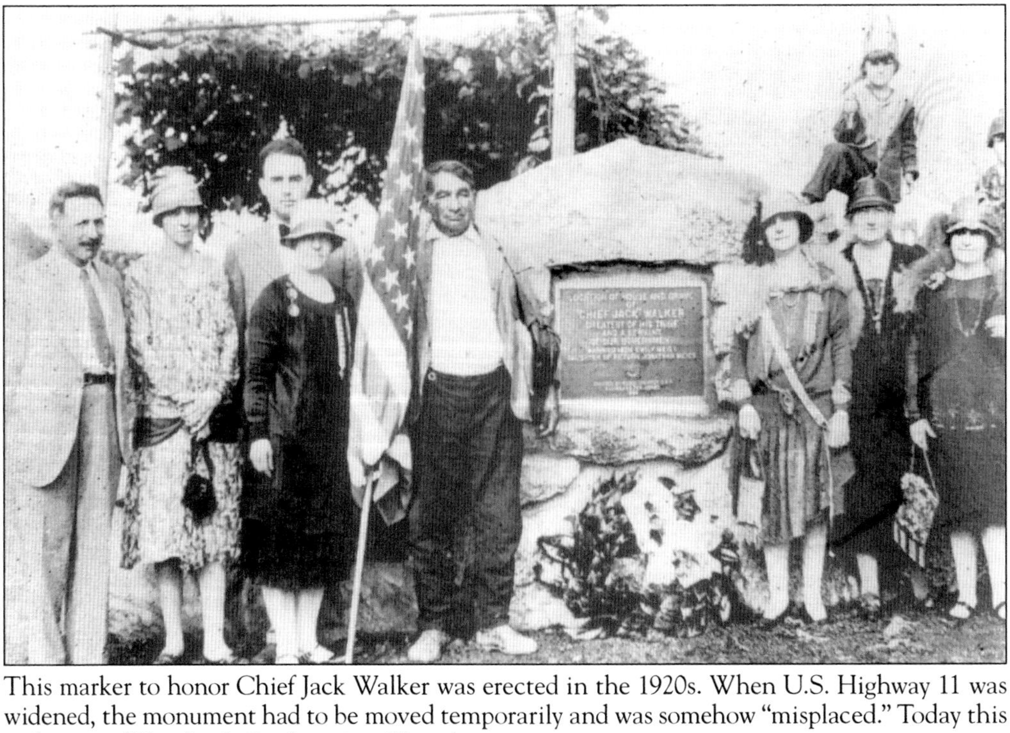

This marker to honor Chief Jack Walker was erected in the 1920s. When U.S. Highway 11 was widened, the monument had to be moved temporarily and was somehow "misplaced." Today this is the site of Northside Presbyterian Church.

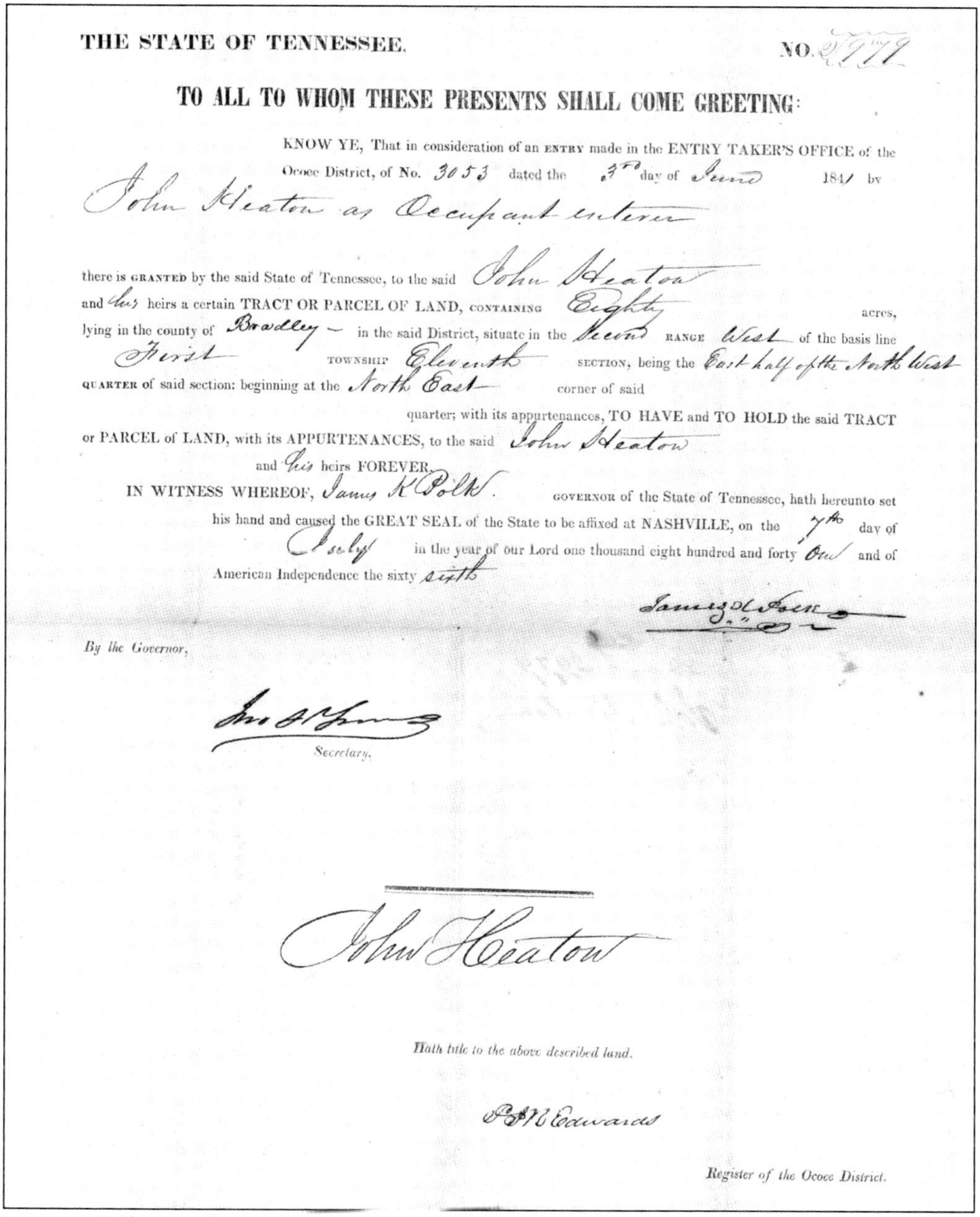

THE STATE OF TENNESSEE. NO. 2779

TO ALL TO WHOM THESE PRESENTS SHALL COME GREETING:

KNOW YE, That in consideration of an ENTRY made in the ENTRY TAKER'S OFFICE of the Ocoee District, of No. 3053 dated the 3rd day of June 1841 by John Heaton as Occupant enterer

there is GRANTED by the said State of Tennessee, to the said John Heaton and his heirs a certain TRACT OR PARCEL OF LAND, CONTAINING Eighty acres, lying in the county of Bradley in the said District, situate in the Second RANGE West of the basis line First TOWNSHIP Eleventh SECTION, being the East half of the North West QUARTER of said section: beginning at the North East corner of said quarter; with its appurtenances, TO HAVE and TO HOLD the said TRACT or PARCEL of LAND, with its APPURTENANCES, to the said John Heaton and his heirs FOREVER.

IN WITNESS WHEREOF, James K Polk. GOVERNOR of the State of Tennessee, hath hereunto set his hand and caused the GREAT SEAL of the State to be affixed at NASHVILLE, on the 7th day of July in the year of our Lord one thousand eight hundred and forty One and of American Independence the sixty sixth

James K. Polk

By the Governor,

Jno S. Young

Secretary.

John Heaton

Hath title to the above described land.

P. H. Edwards

Register of the Ocoee District.

James K. Polk served as governor of Tennessee before he became president of the United States. This is a document of the Ocoee District dated June 3, 1841, for a land grant of 80 acres in Bradley County. It is signed by Gov. James K. Polk.

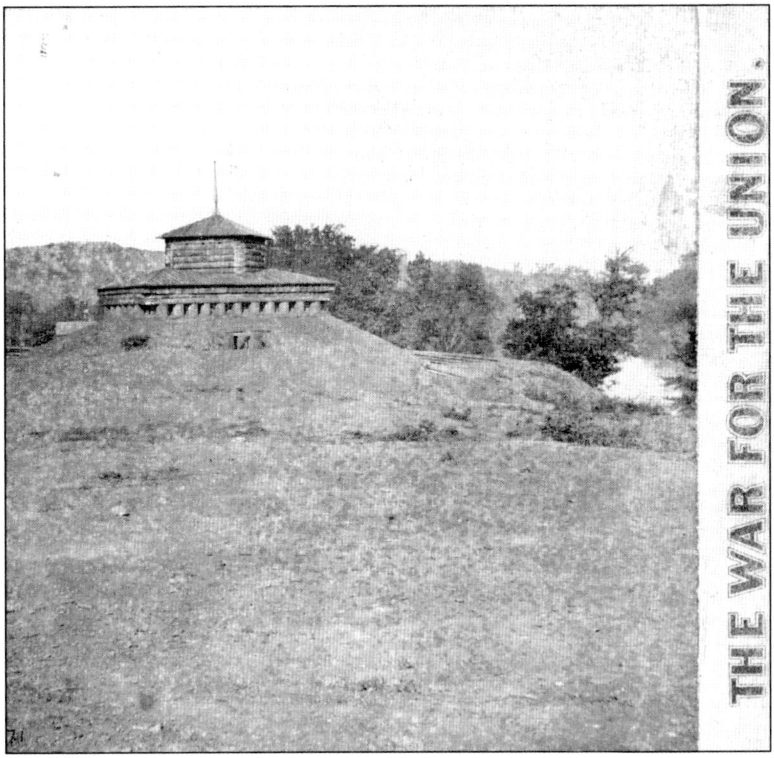

During the War Between the States, the railroad bridge at Charleston was of strategic importance to both North and South. The Confederacy had secured it with foot soldiers in trenches. As seen in this stereoscope picture, the Union constructed two blockhouses on the bluff overlooking the Hiwassee River bridge to secure this vital transportation link.

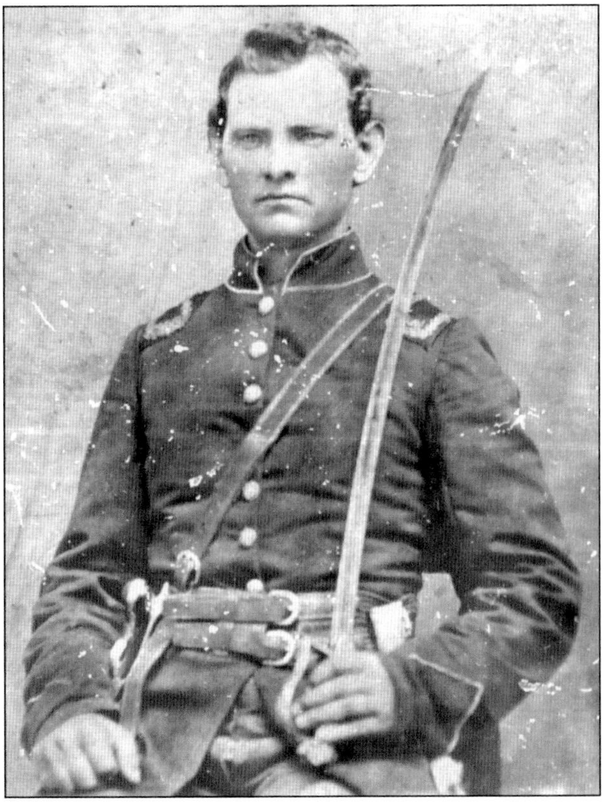

Bradley County was almost evenly split on Tennessee's secession from the Union. By a slim majority, the actual vote in the county was for Tennessee to remain in the Union. Voters in the rural areas tended to vote for the Union while city voters supported the Confederacy. Shown here, young William "Billy" Bain (November 28, 1823–July 5, 1892) was a soldier of the Confederate States of America.

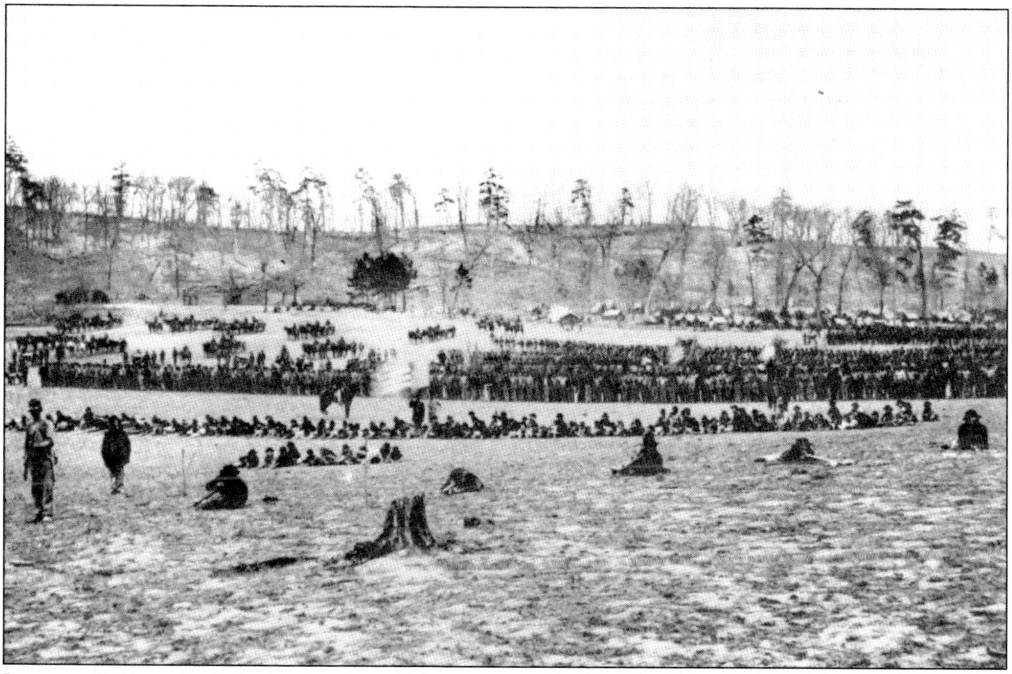

January 1864 marked the beginning of Union control of Bradley County. In February 1864, there were 7,582 Union troops quartered at Blue Springs, south of Cleveland. The troops trained here in anticipation of the Union assault on Atlanta. Shown are skirmishers lying in the front, the skirmish reserve behind them, and a battery in support.

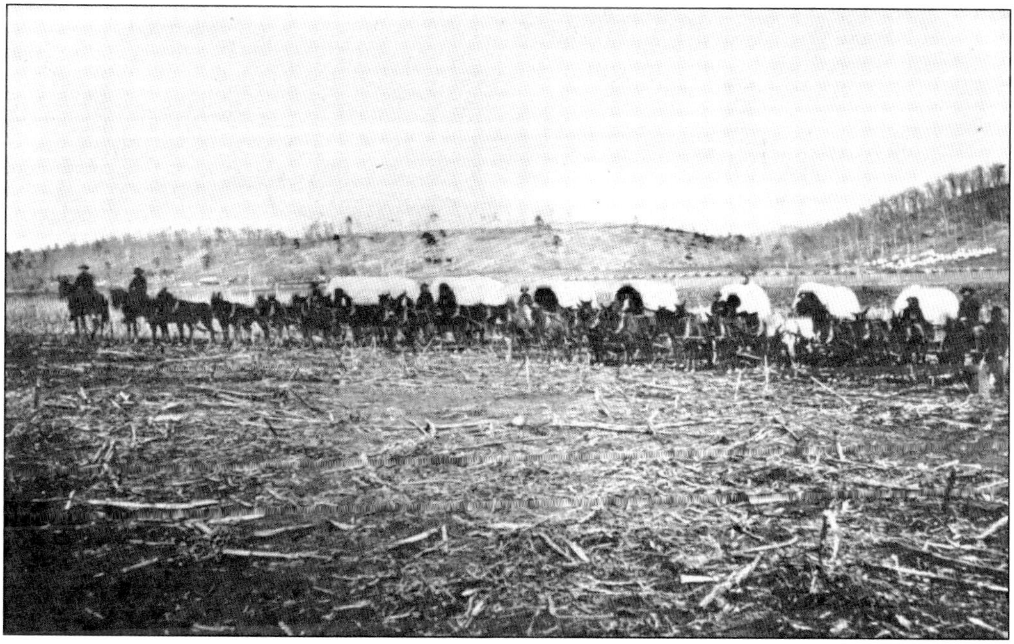

The 3rd Brigade, 1st Division, IV Corps, Army of the Cumberland, occupied an old campground at Blue Springs from January to May 1864. Col. William Grose of the 36th Indiana Infantry Regiment was commander of this brigade. This photograph shows the 36th Indiana Infantry wagons at Blue Springs.

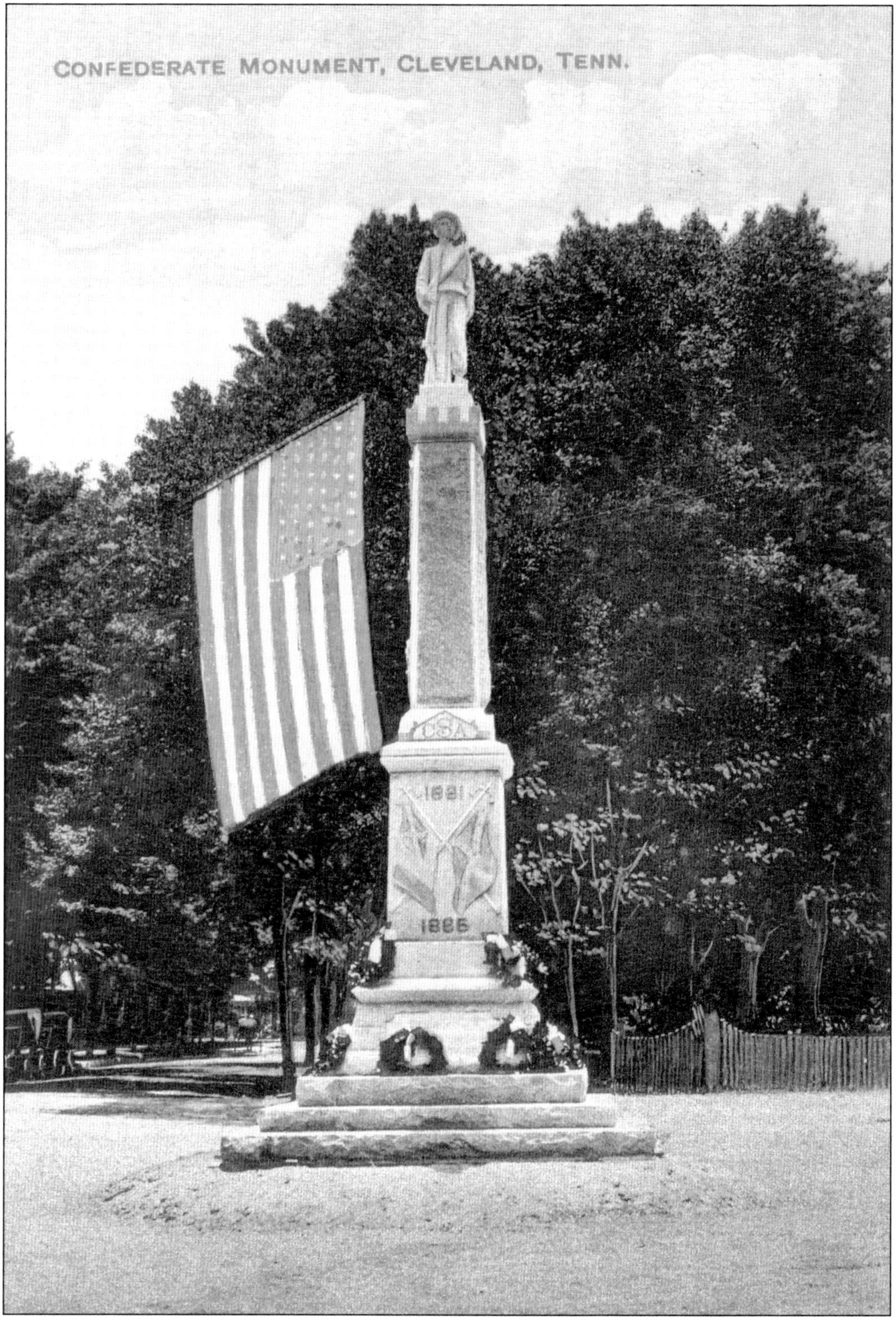

"Lest we forget" was taken to heart by members of the United Daughters of the Confederacy by their erection of this Confederate monument in 1911.

Two

FARM LIFE

Let the farmer forevermore be honored in his calling, for they who labor in the earth are the chosen people of God.

—Thomas Jefferson

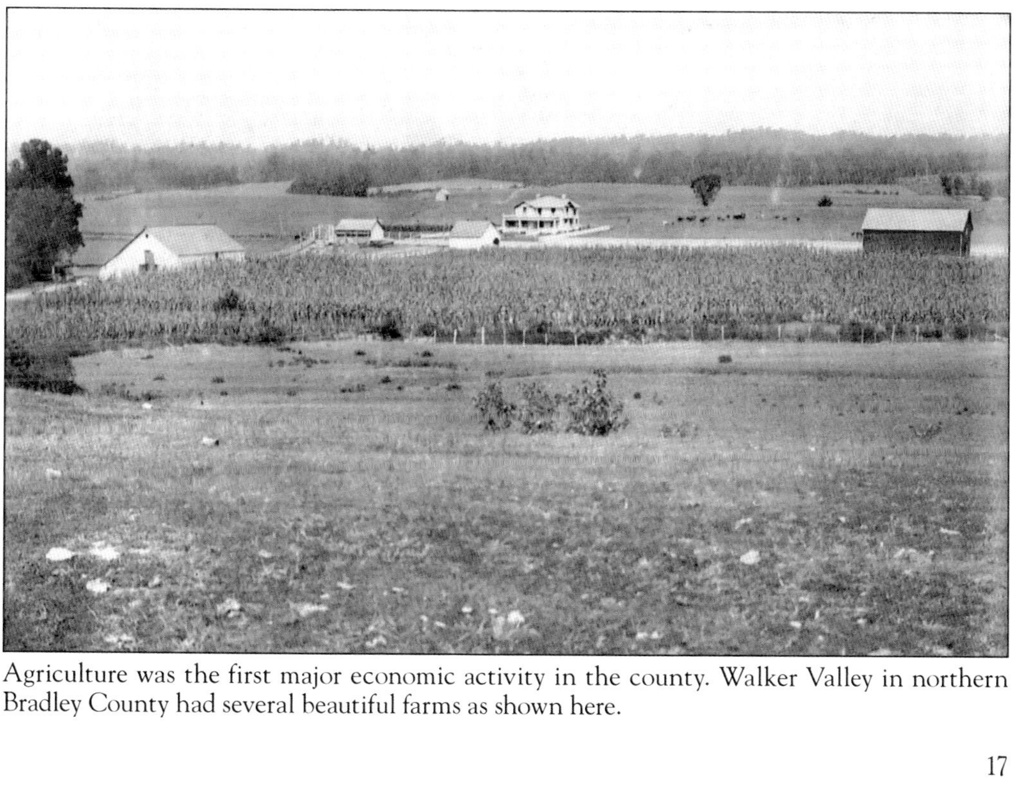

Agriculture was the first major economic activity in the county. Walker Valley in northern Bradley County had several beautiful farms as shown here.

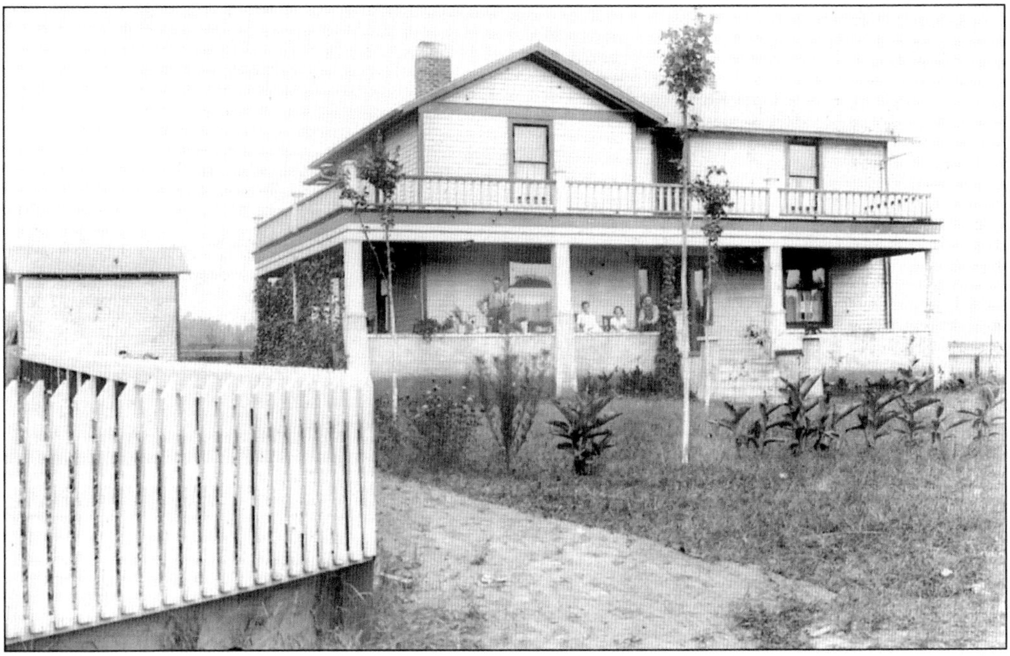

This is a beautiful country home on a farm in Bradley County. The wide porches around the house were nice work areas on a rainy day or comfortable places to relax on a hot, sunny day. The house remains today and is located on Walker Valley Road.

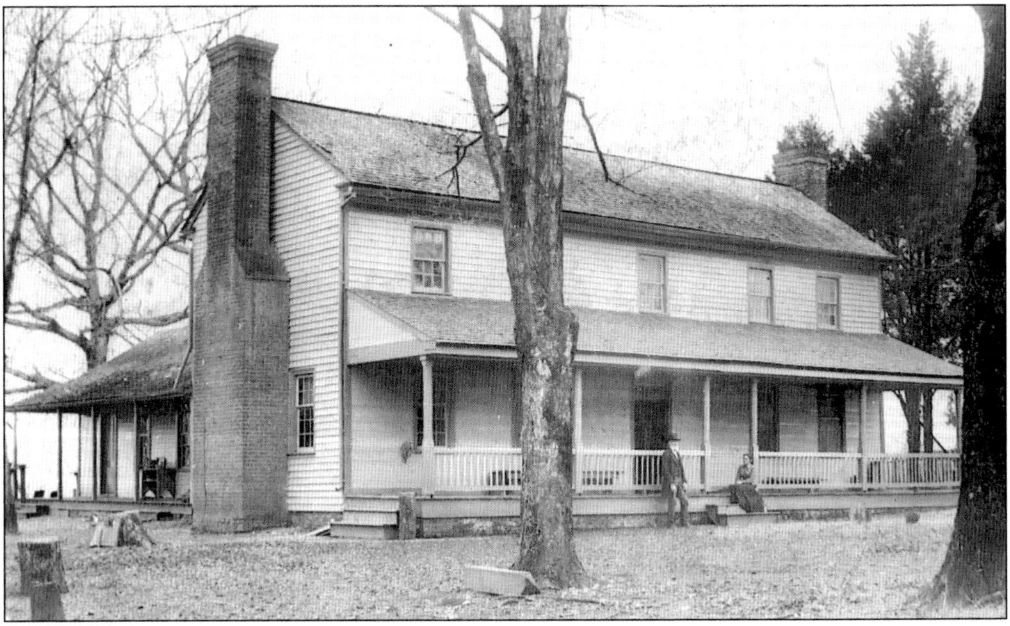

This house was originally built of logs and later covered with boards. It was built by the Clingan family from whom Baldwin Harle III bought the farm along Candies Creek. The Clingans were half Cherokee Indian. In the front of the house were two rooms downstairs and two rooms upstairs joined by a stair-hall. The dining room, kitchen, and storerooms were in an ell at the back of the house. The Wattenbargers bought the farm after the deaths of J. H. and L. L. Harle, tore the house down, and replaced it with a brick bungalow.

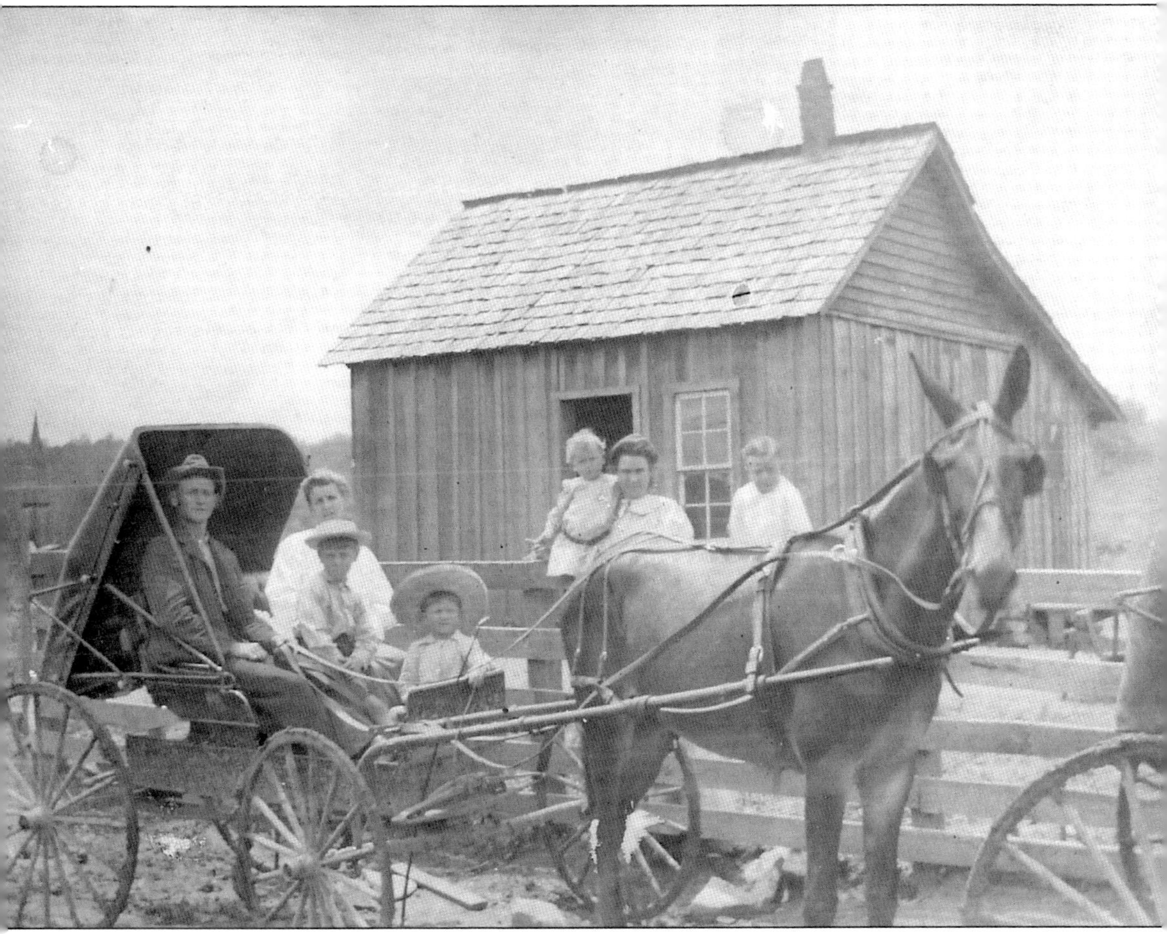

George Parker Newman and his wife, Amanda Triplett, are shown about 1905 in their carriage with their sons, Raleigh (left) and Willis. Carolyn "Kerry" Newman is shown holding her baby, Harlie, with her other son, Pryor.

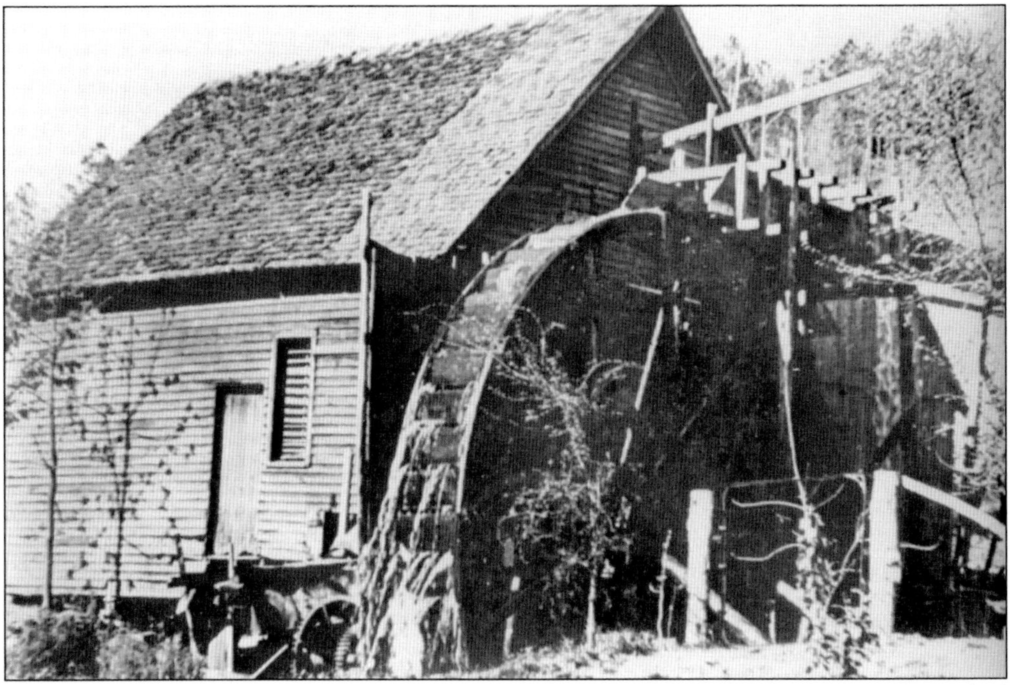

The old mill at Black Fox was built in 1847 for James Miller Johnston. Drumgoole Creek supplied the water that powered this mill. It was well known for its whole-wheat flour.

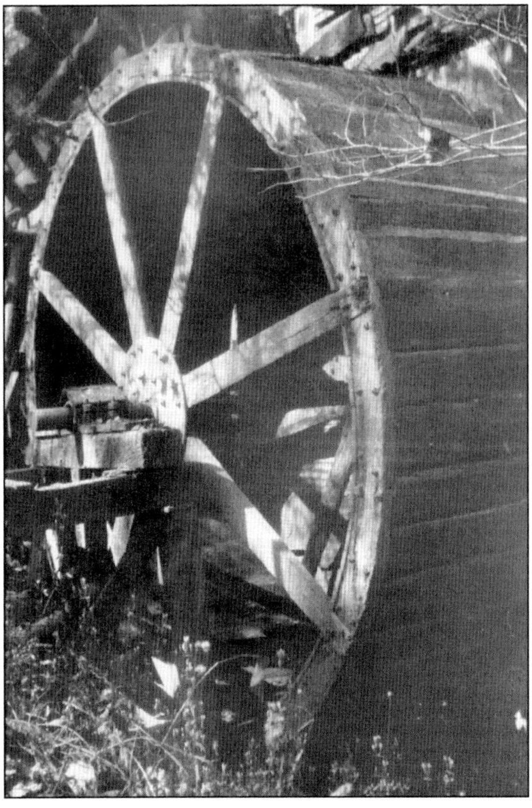

The mill was crucial to the success of a community as it was where agricultural products, such as wheat or corn, were ground into meal suitable for cooking. McCulley's Mill was one of the oldest mills in Bradley County and was located on Tunnel Hill Road. It continued to grind meal until about 1937.

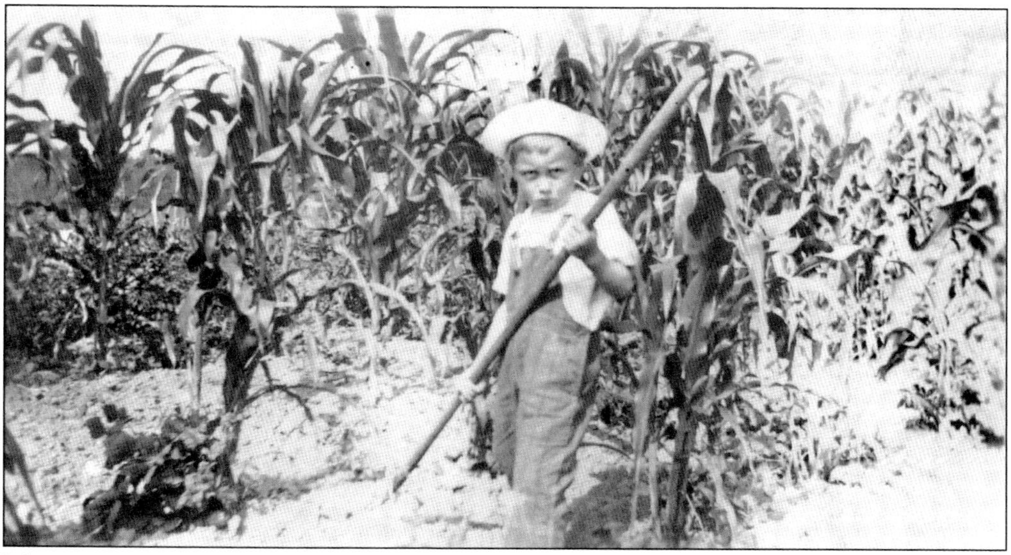

John Henry Kinder Sr. owned a farm on Old Chattanooga Pike. As shown in the cornfield above in the 1920s, he started farming at an early age.

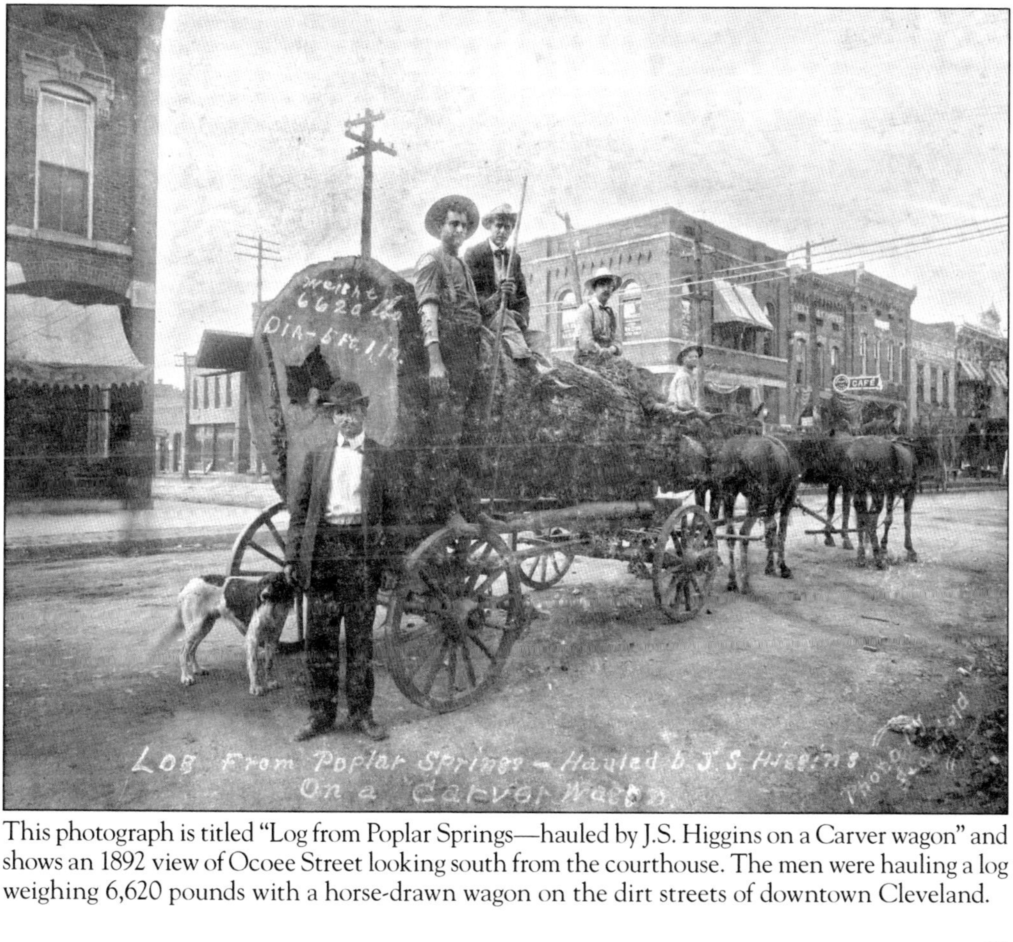

This photograph is titled "Log from Poplar Springs—hauled by J.S. Higgins on a Carver wagon" and shows an 1892 view of Ocoee Street looking south from the courthouse. The men were hauling a log weighing 6,620 pounds with a horse-drawn wagon on the dirt streets of downtown Cleveland.

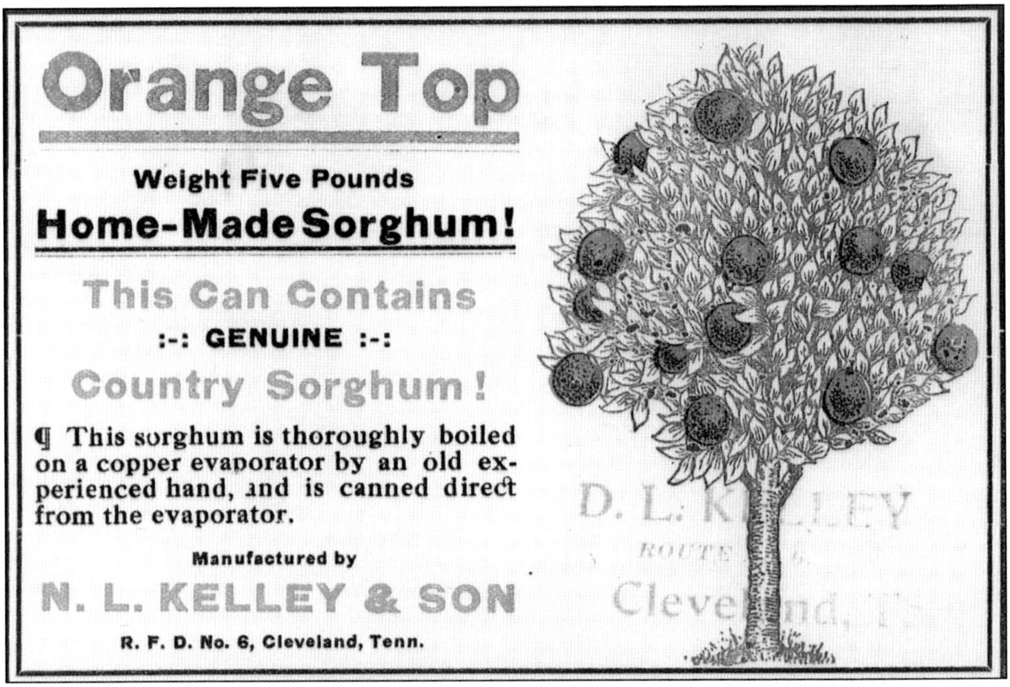

This label from about 1910 was for cans containing homemade sorghum, which was shipped to various parts of the South.

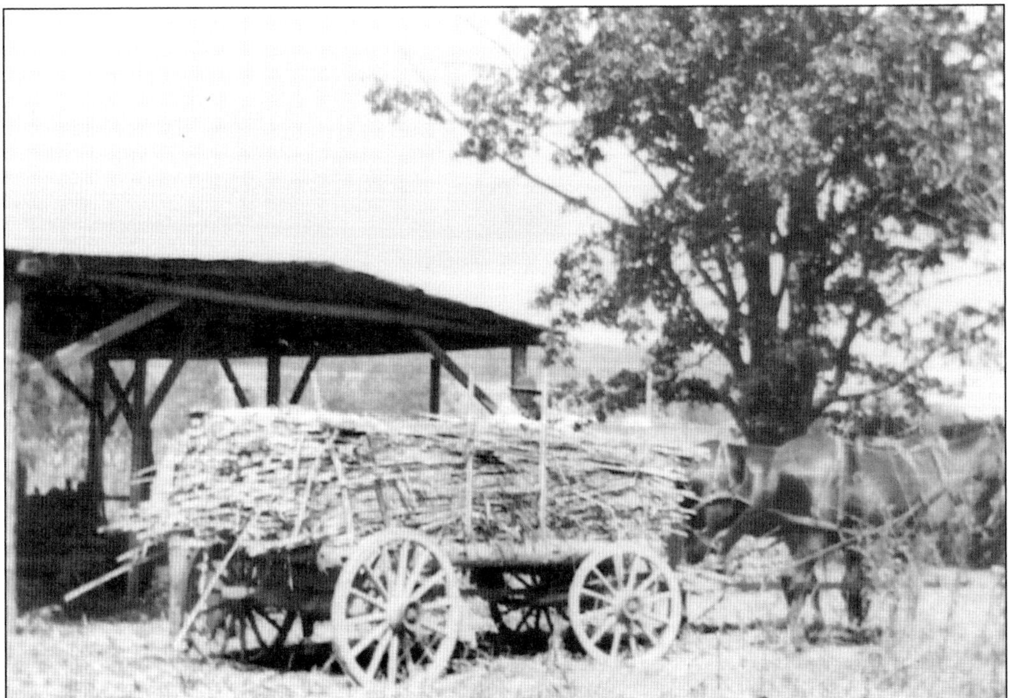

A wagonload of cane hauled by horses is awaiting pressing. The pressed juice from the cane would then be boiled and canned to make a delicious sorghum molasses.

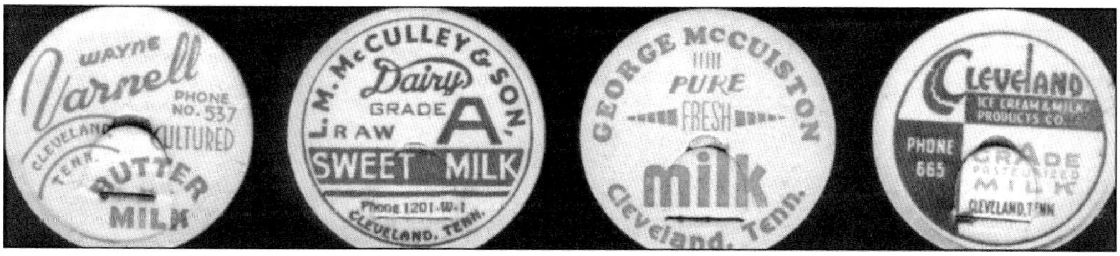

These milk caps were used on glass bottles from various Bradley County dairies. The term "sweet milk" was used to differentiate it from buttermilk.

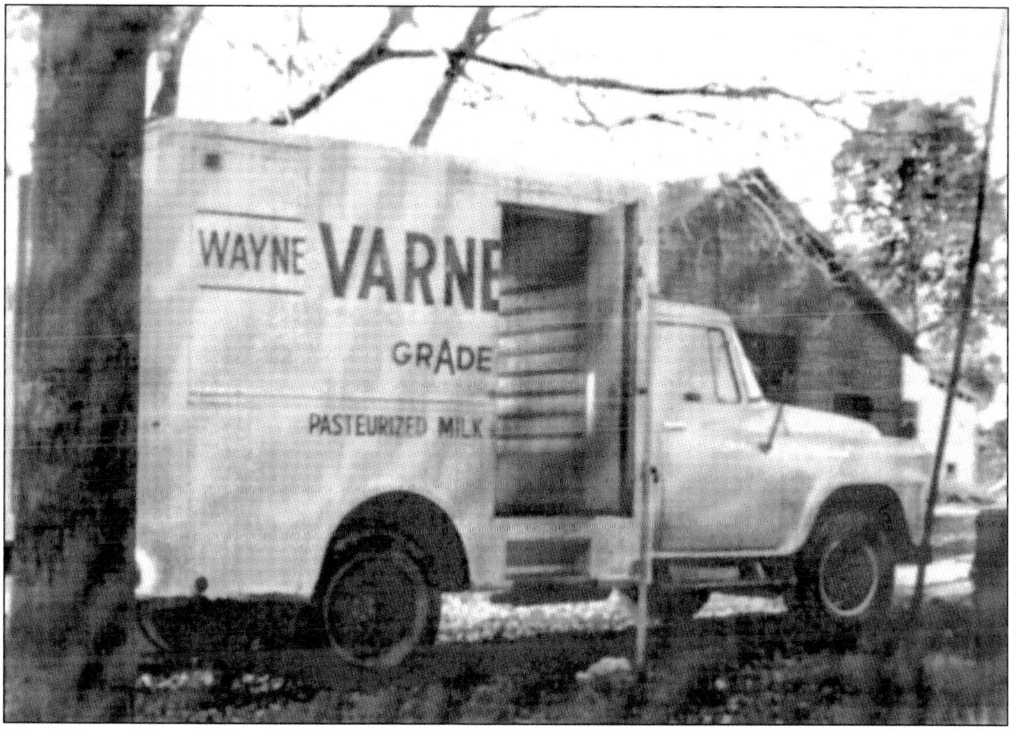

The Wayne Varnell Dairy was located on Old Chattanooga Pike. The truck shown was used to deliver milk to homes in the 1950s.

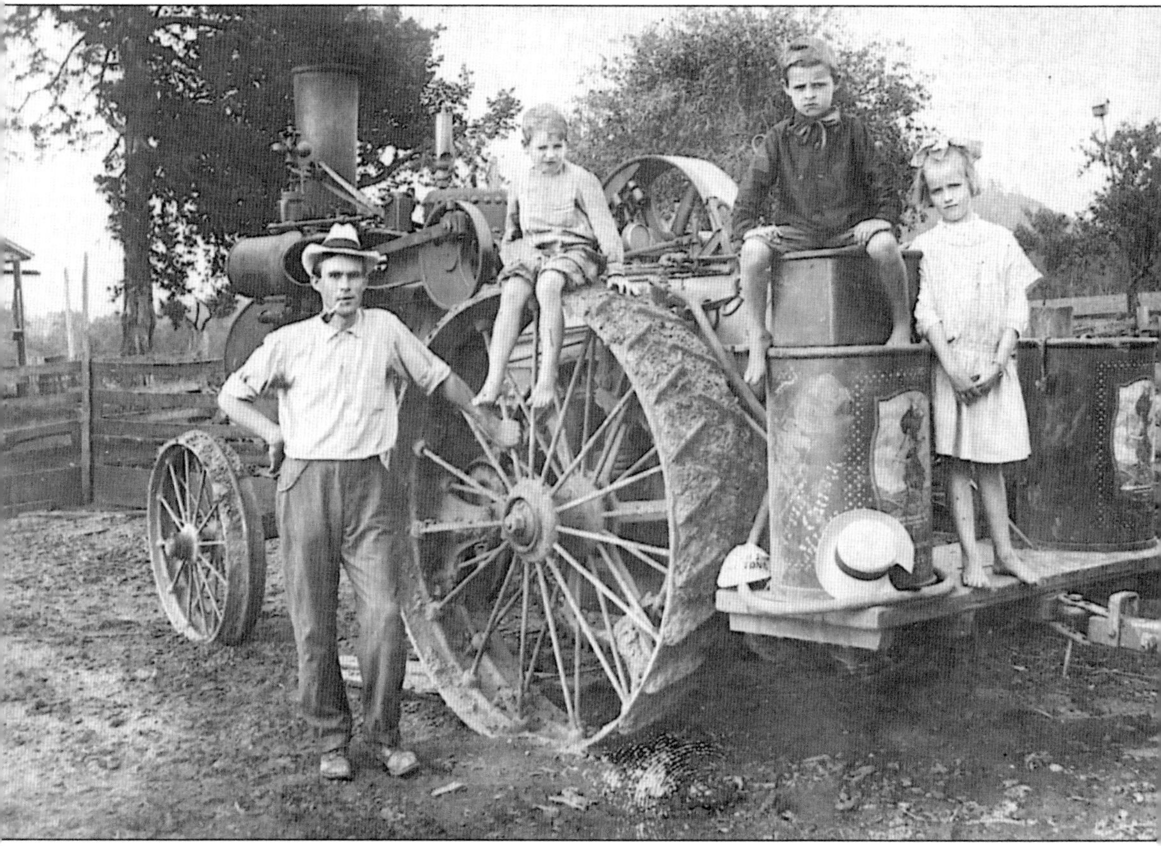

A man and a mule was the way farms were worked for many years. The introduction of the steam engine tractor was a giant leap forward in agricultural productivity. About 1922, Dailey Kelley and his children were very proud of their marvelous tractor. The Kelley Farm is southwest of Cleveland off Tunnel Hill Road. This farm, originally a land grant of 40 acres issued to Richard Kelley in 1840, has remained in the Kelley family and has increased to 250 acres. In the early 1900s, Dailey Kelley had one of the first mechanized farm operations in Bradley County, owning two steam engines, two wheat thrashers, two saw mills, and a well drilling operation. He thrashed wheat and drilled wells all over Bradley and surrounding counties. Kelley raised peanuts and corn for popping, which were sold to movie theatres; tobacco; wheat; vegetables; cattle; hogs; and sheep. Today it is still a working farm with beef cattle and owned by Harold W. Kelley. In 1978, the farm was recognized by the State of Tennessee with a sign reading, "This is a Century Farm With 100 years of Continuous Agricultural Production."

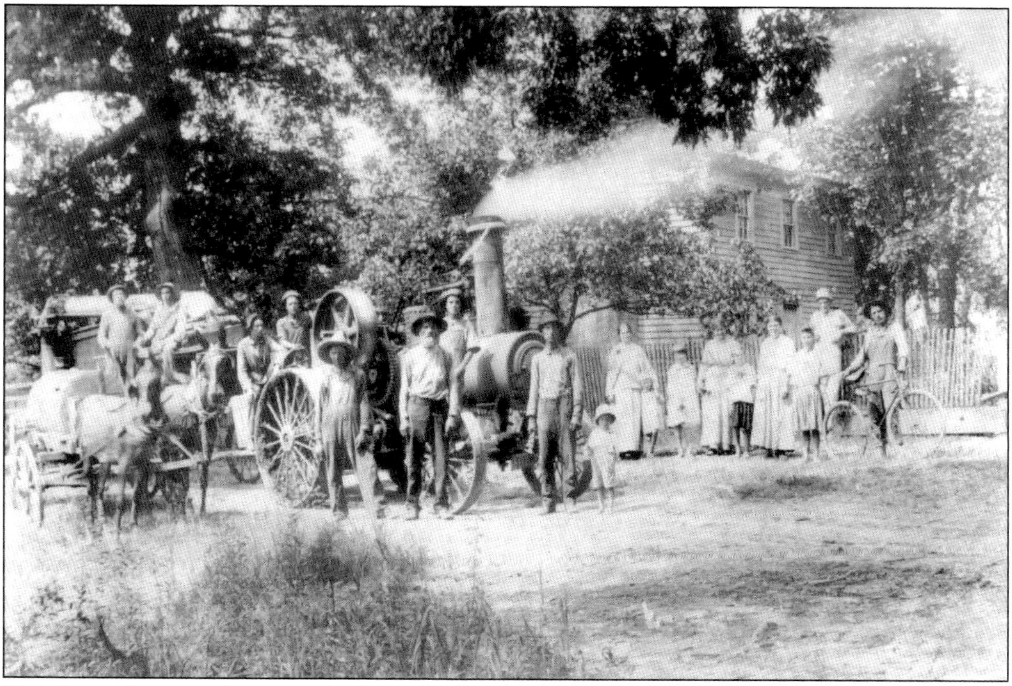

This farm photograph was made about 1915 at the McCulley home on Tunnel Hill Road. G. W. Watson owned the thrasher and water wagon.

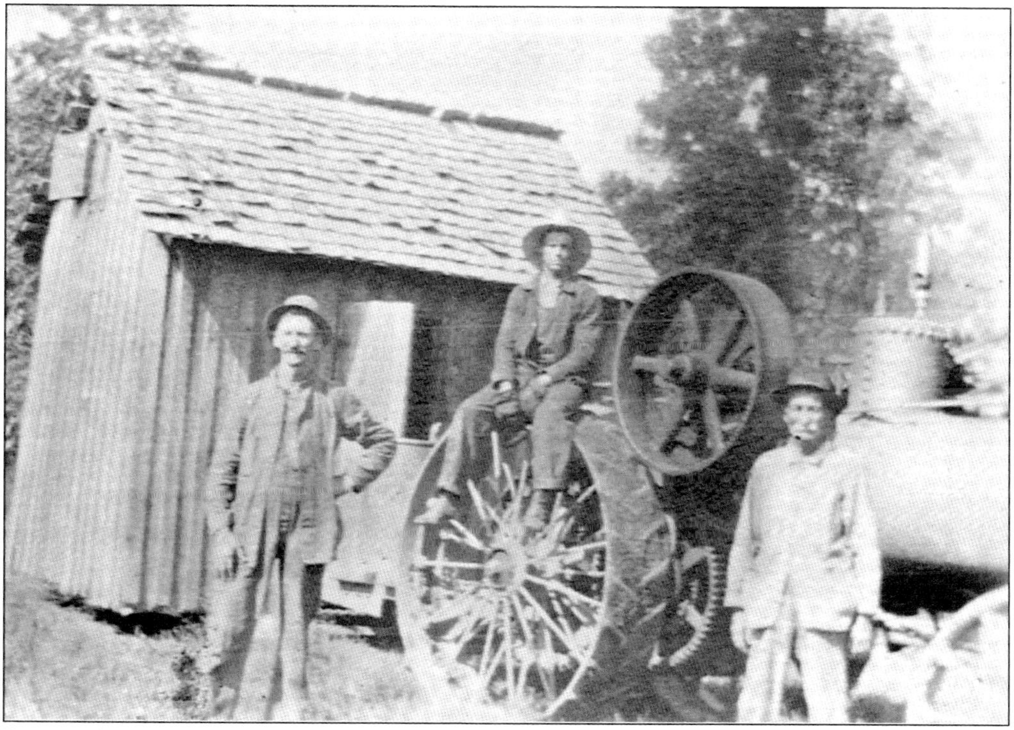

Even with a powerful metal-spoked cleated wheel tractor, workers got tired and needed a break, as seen in this scene about 1910.

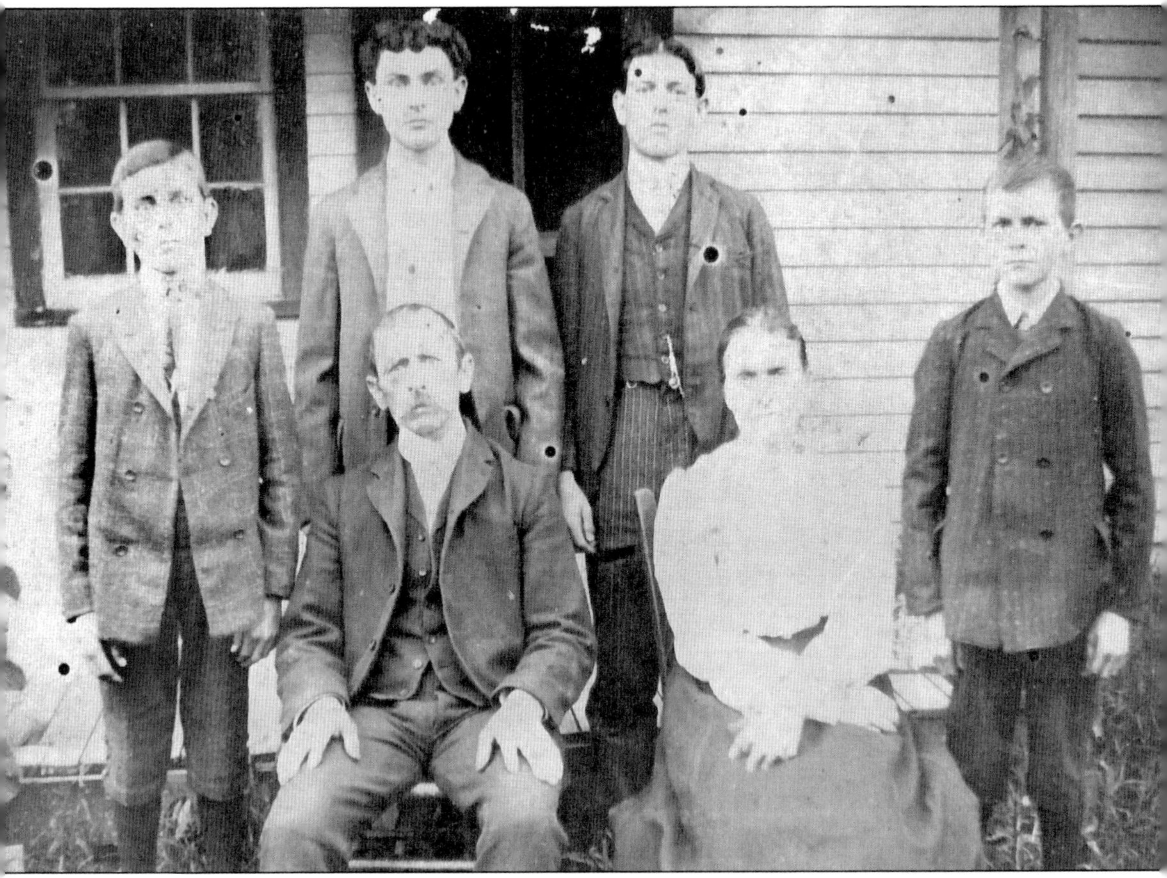

The John David Cook (1858–1934) farm was in the Lead Mine Valley. In 1882, John David Cook (seated) married Margaret Ann Davis (seated). Their four sons are, from left to right, James Burton (Hardwick Stove and Cooke's Furniture Store), William Fred (farmer), Robert Lester (schoolteacher and farmer), and James Marion (Cooke's Food Store).

The blacksmith was extremely important to the smooth running of a farm. He not only kept the animals shod but also fabricated working implements and architectural pieces. Hayes Coe is shown plying his trade.

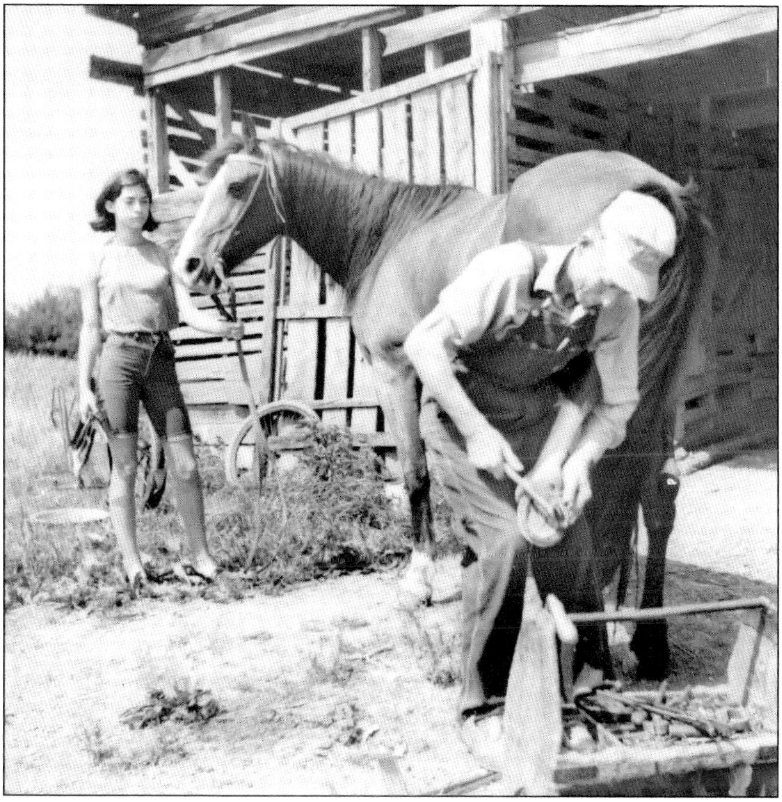

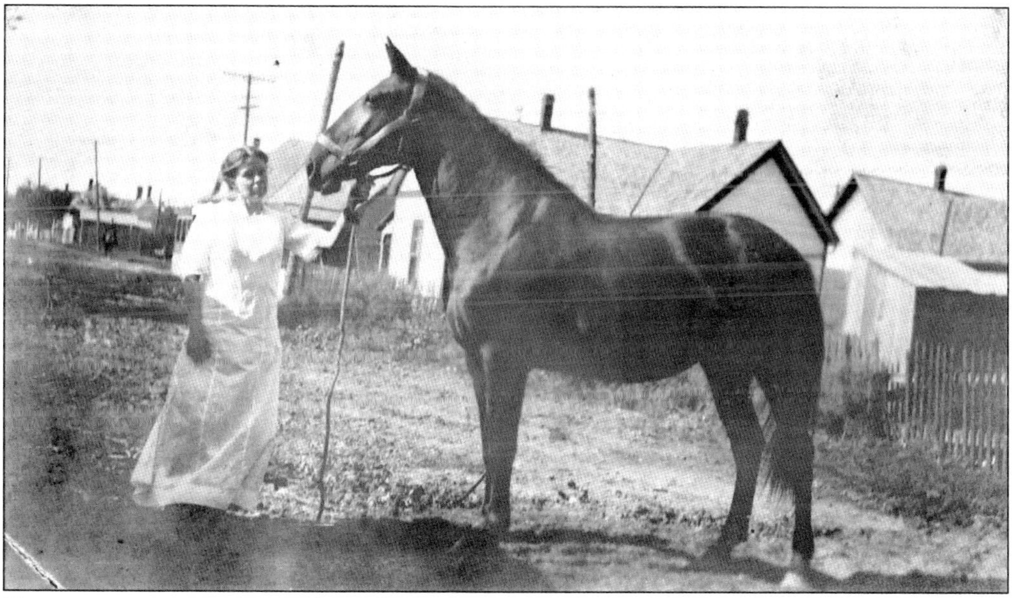

Horses were not only used on farms but in town as well. This lady exhibits a fine-looking horse.

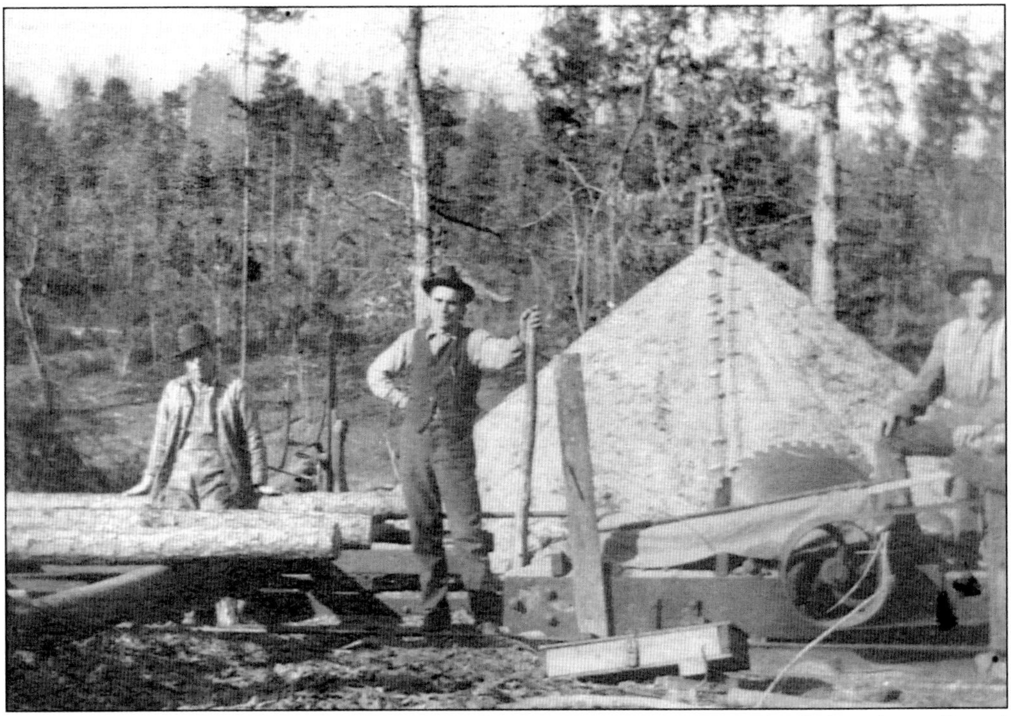

The sawmill was a vital component of a rural economy. Logs were cut, hauled to the mill, and cut into lumber to be used for fencing or farm buildings.

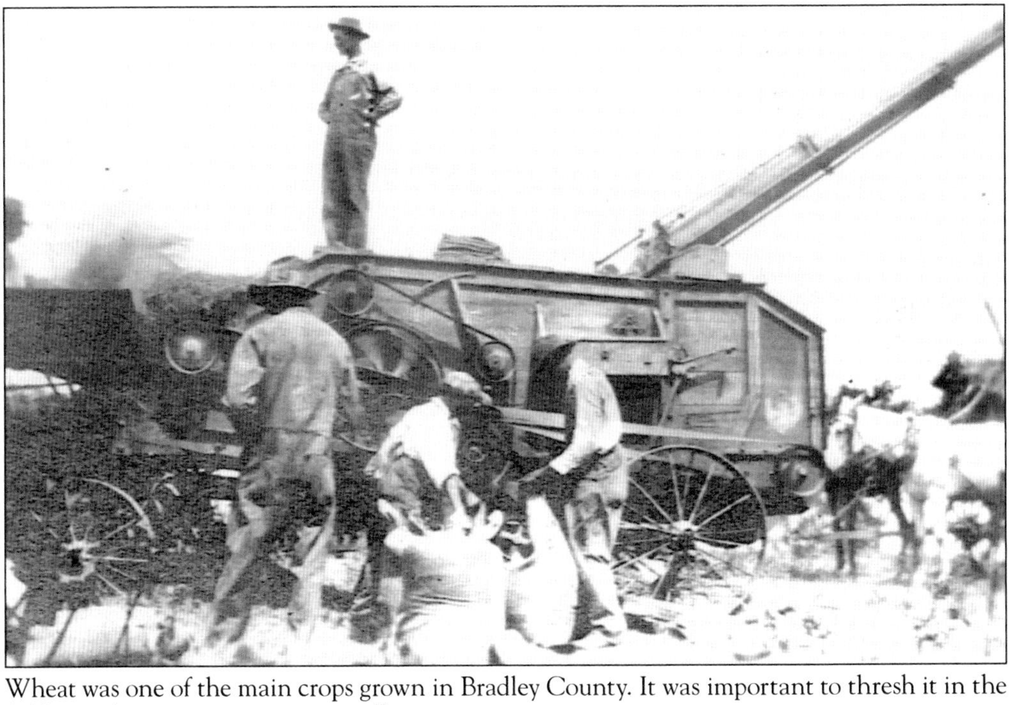

Wheat was one of the main crops grown in Bradley County. It was important to thresh it in the field in order to transport it to a mill.

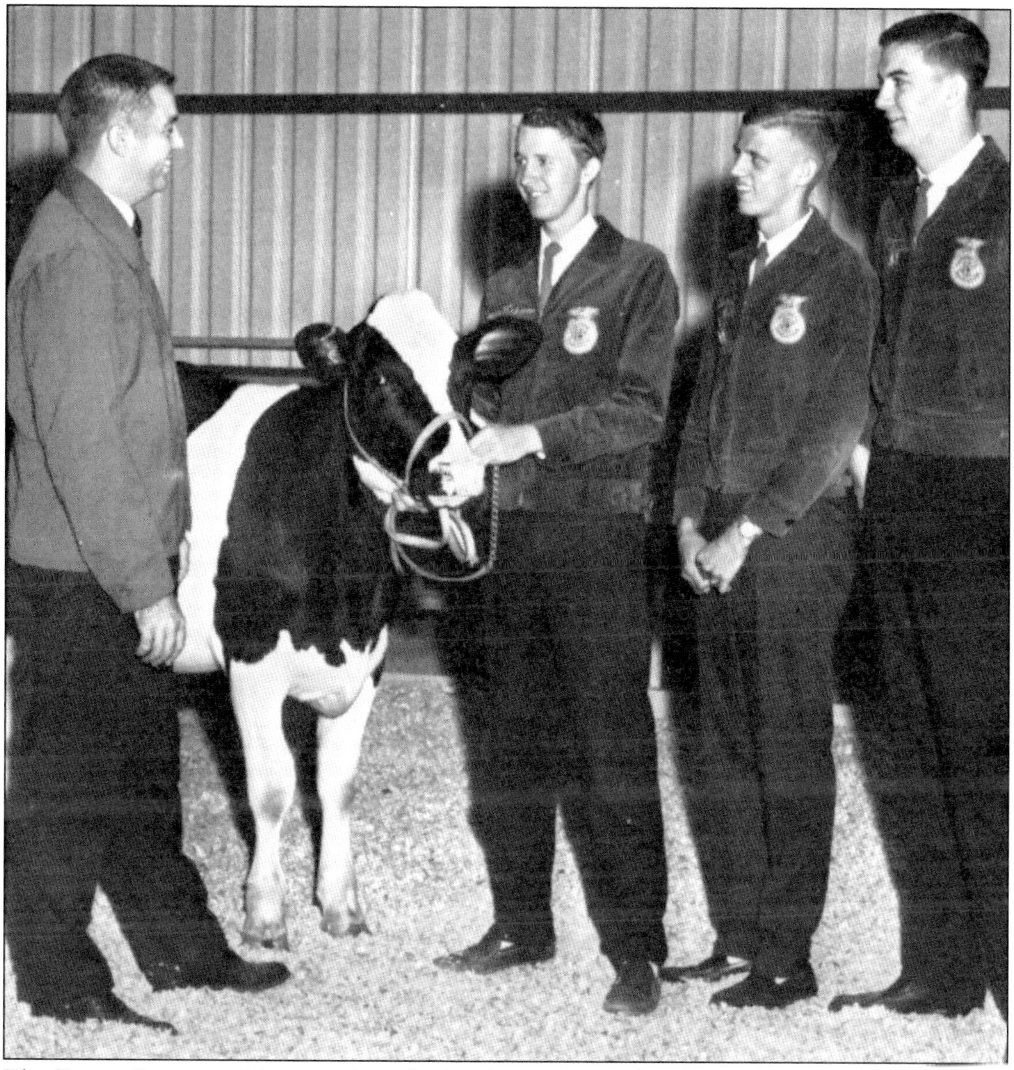

The Future Farmers of America have had a chapter at Bradley Central High School for many years. In 1965, Herbert Lackey, sponsor (left), is shown from left to right with Wayne Hickman, Julius Beaty, and Raymond Brackin, with the chapter winning first place in state and Gold Emblem in national.

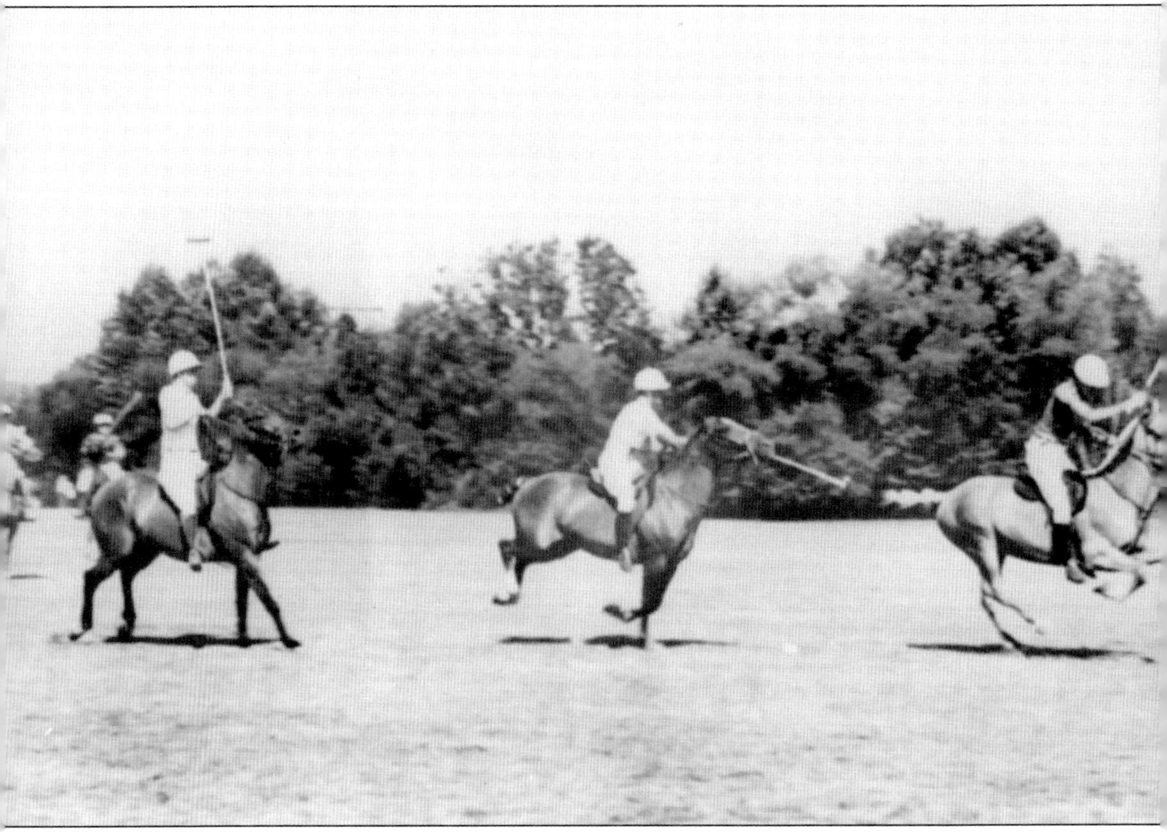

This photograph is of a polo match at Bendabout Farm, owned by Summerfield Johnston, on South Lee Highway. The local team competes in international competition and is the only local team to defeat the Fort Oglethorpe cavalry base team.

Three

CIVIC LIFE

Without popular education no government which rests on popular action can long endure; the people must be schooled in the knowledge and if possible in the virtues upon which the maintenance and success of free institutions depend.

—Woodrow Wilson
1856–1924

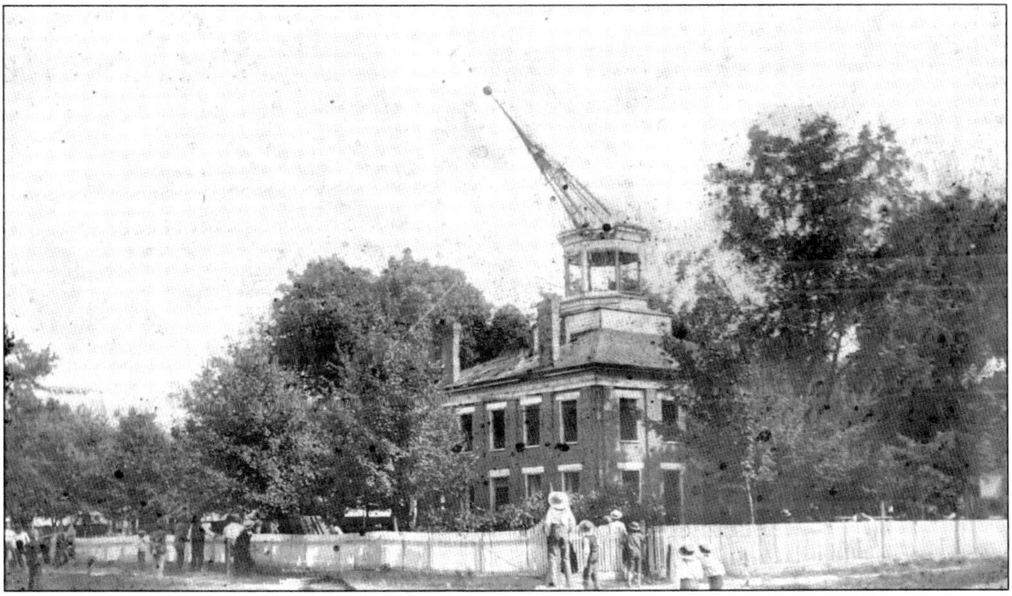

To replace the original log courthouse, Bradley County built a second courthouse in 1840 at a cost of $8,000. It was razed in 1892 with many watching its tower fall.

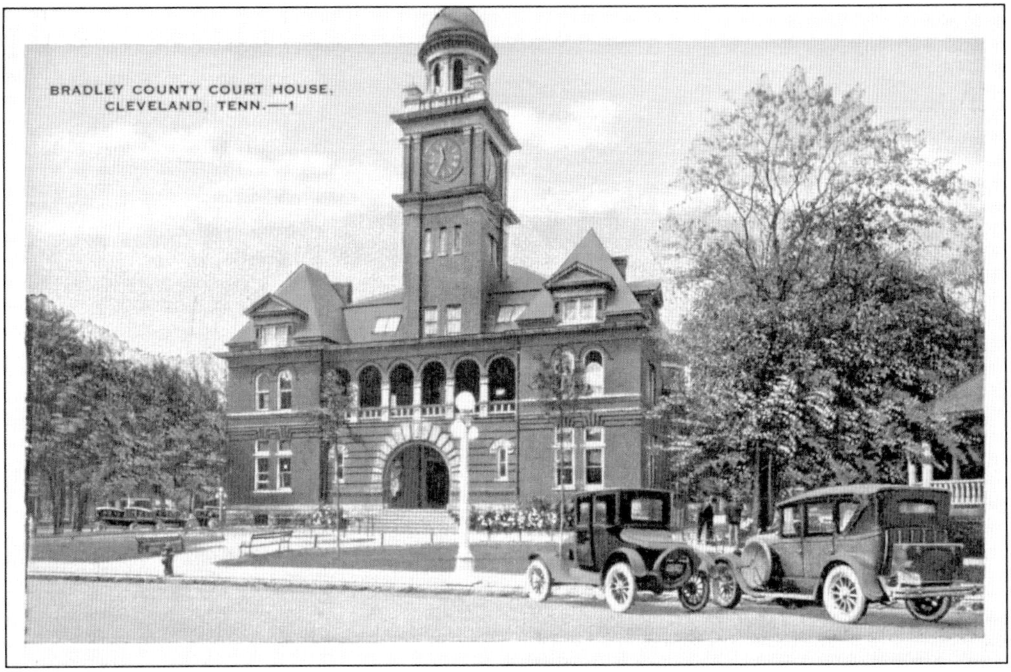

The third Bradley County Courthouse was built in 1892 at a cost of $75,000. This majestic building was revered by all. It was torn down in 1963. A replica of this courthouse by the same architect still stands in Paris, Tennessee.

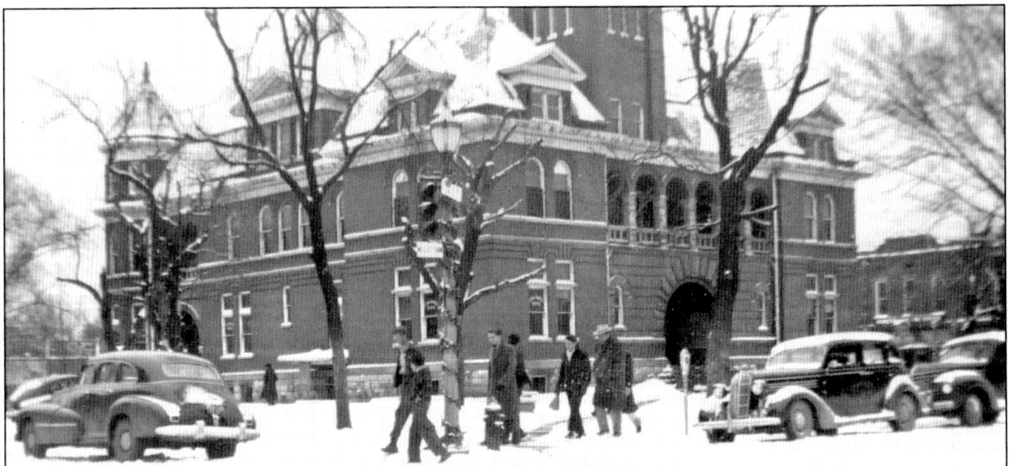

The Bradley County Courthouse got a trimming of white snow on January 24, 1948.

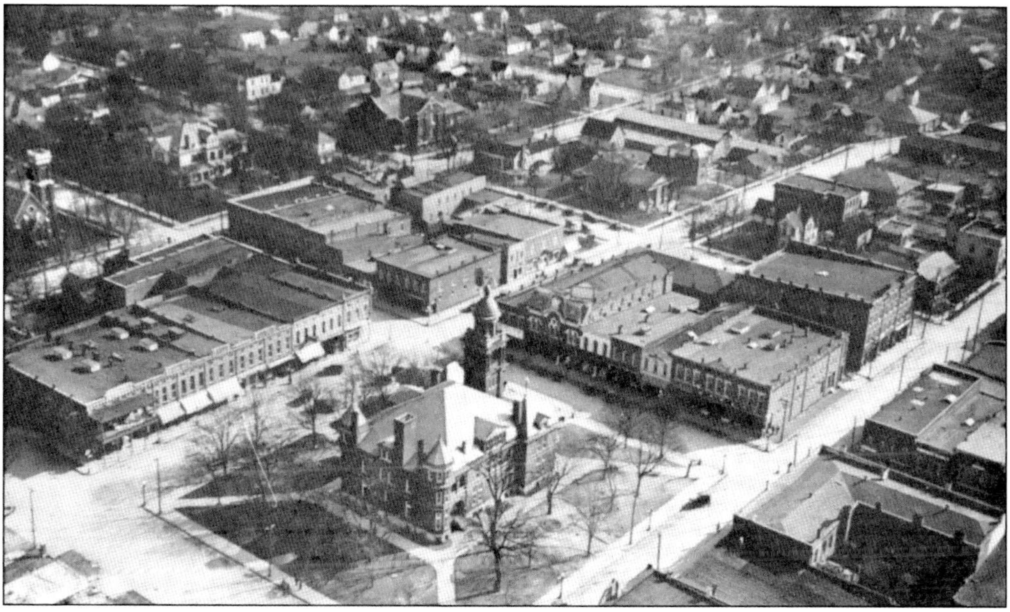

This 1920s view of the central business section of Cleveland reflects the dominance of the courthouse square.

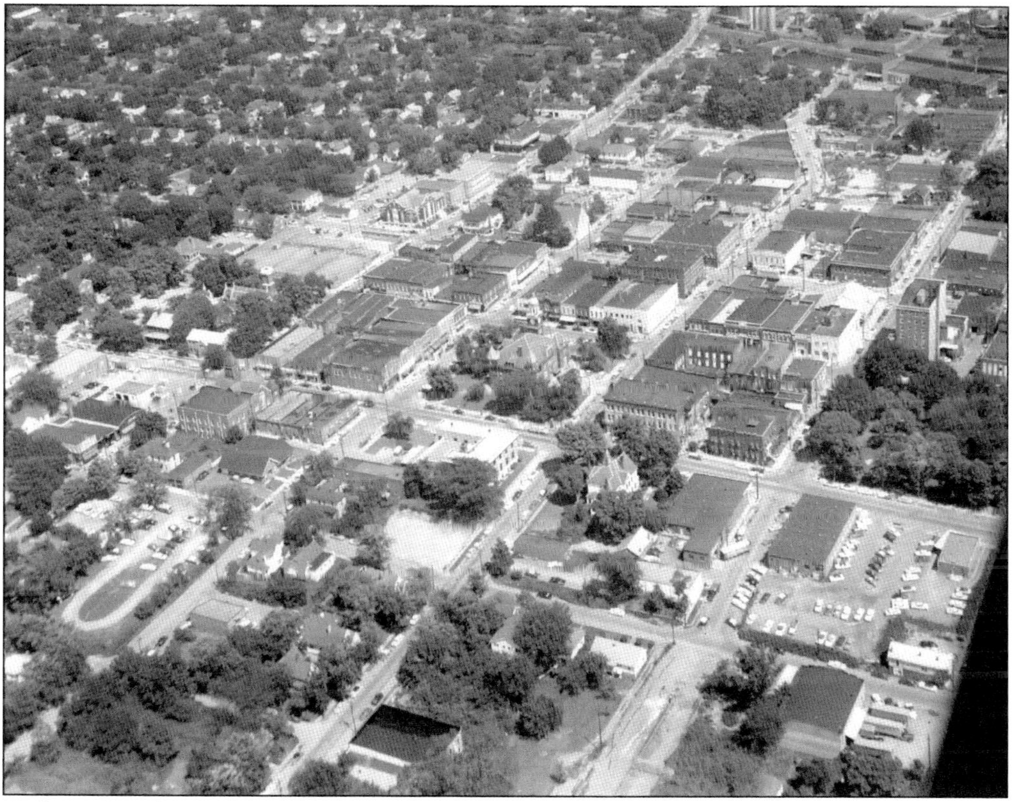

In the 1950s, the courthouse square was still the focal point of downtown Cleveland.

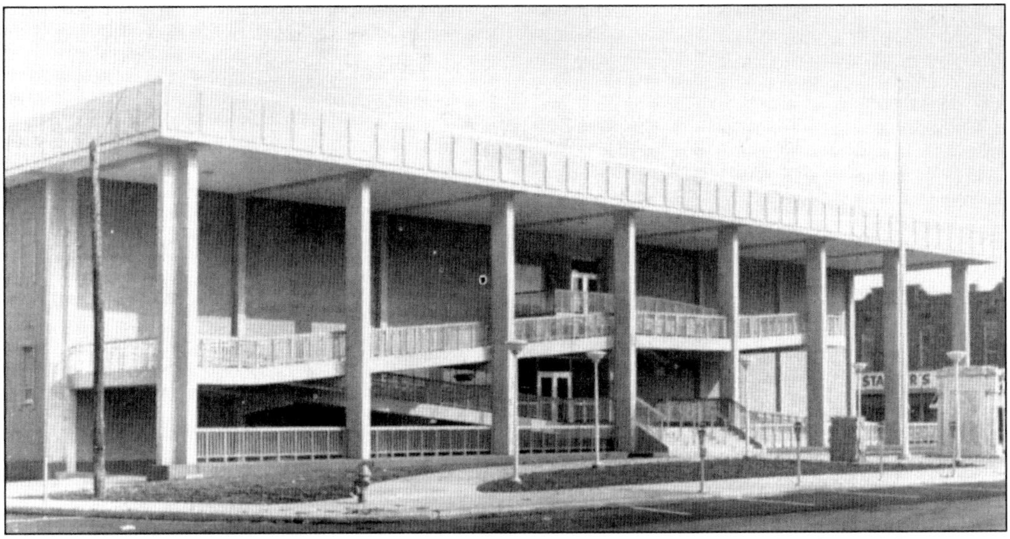

The current Bradley County Courthouse was built in 1964. Judge H. M. Fulbright and the County Commission felt it expressed the progressive spirit of the community.

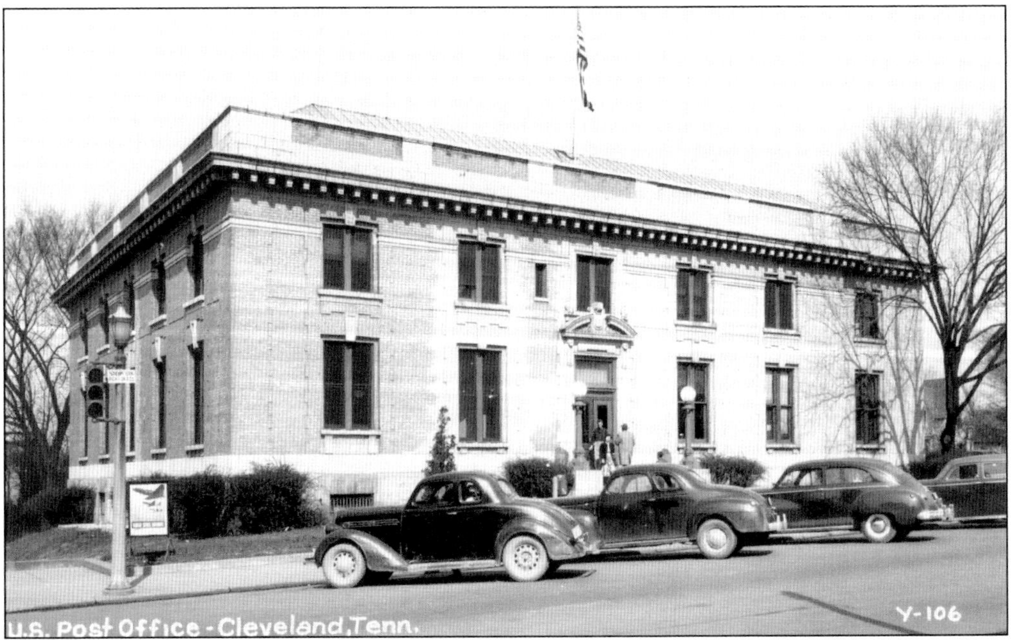

The U.S. Post Office building on Broad Street was completed in 1911. It was the main post office until a new facility was erected on Keith Street in 1981.

The Cleveland Public Library was housed in the Craigmiles Home for 64 years. The beautiful Italianate building was built in 1866 and given to the City of Cleveland in 1923 by John, James, Josiah, Samuel, and William Johnston in honor of their mother, Sarah Tucker Johnston.

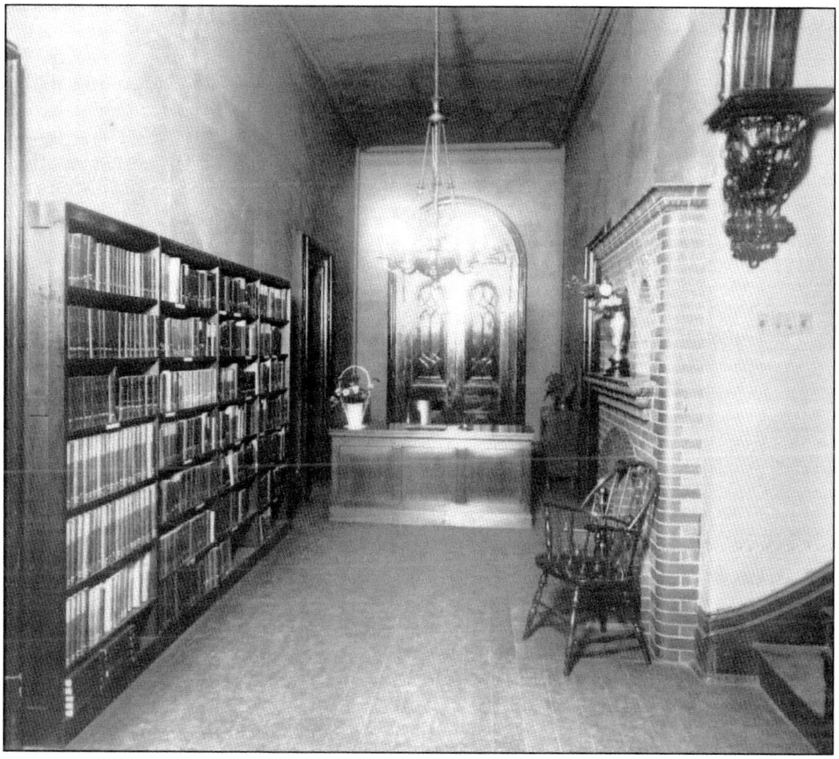

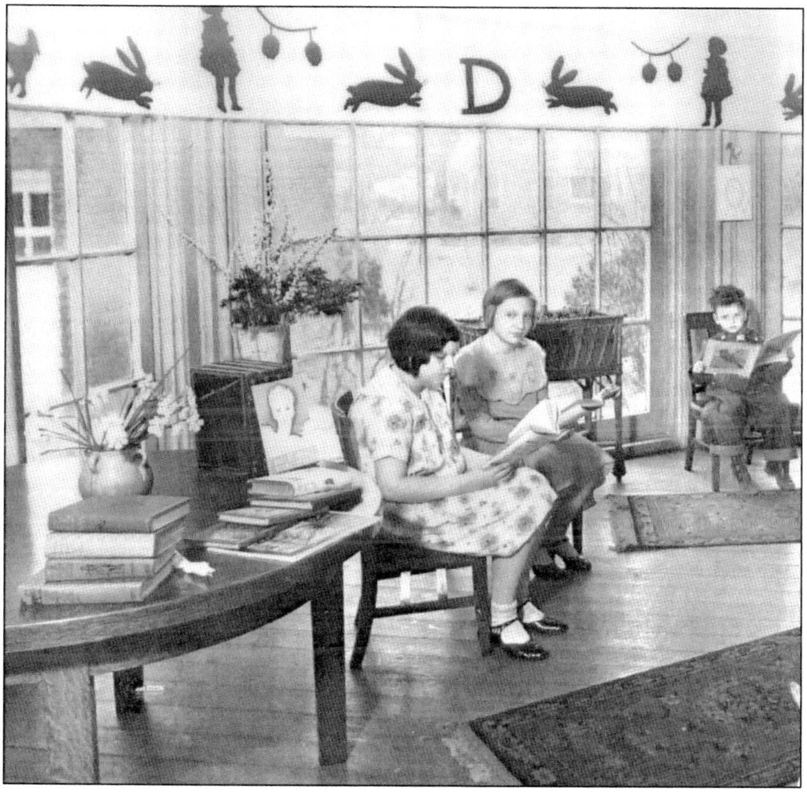

Bess Mayfield (left), Mary Hoyle (middle), and Jimmie Johnston are reading in the children's room of the Cleveland Public Library about 1930.

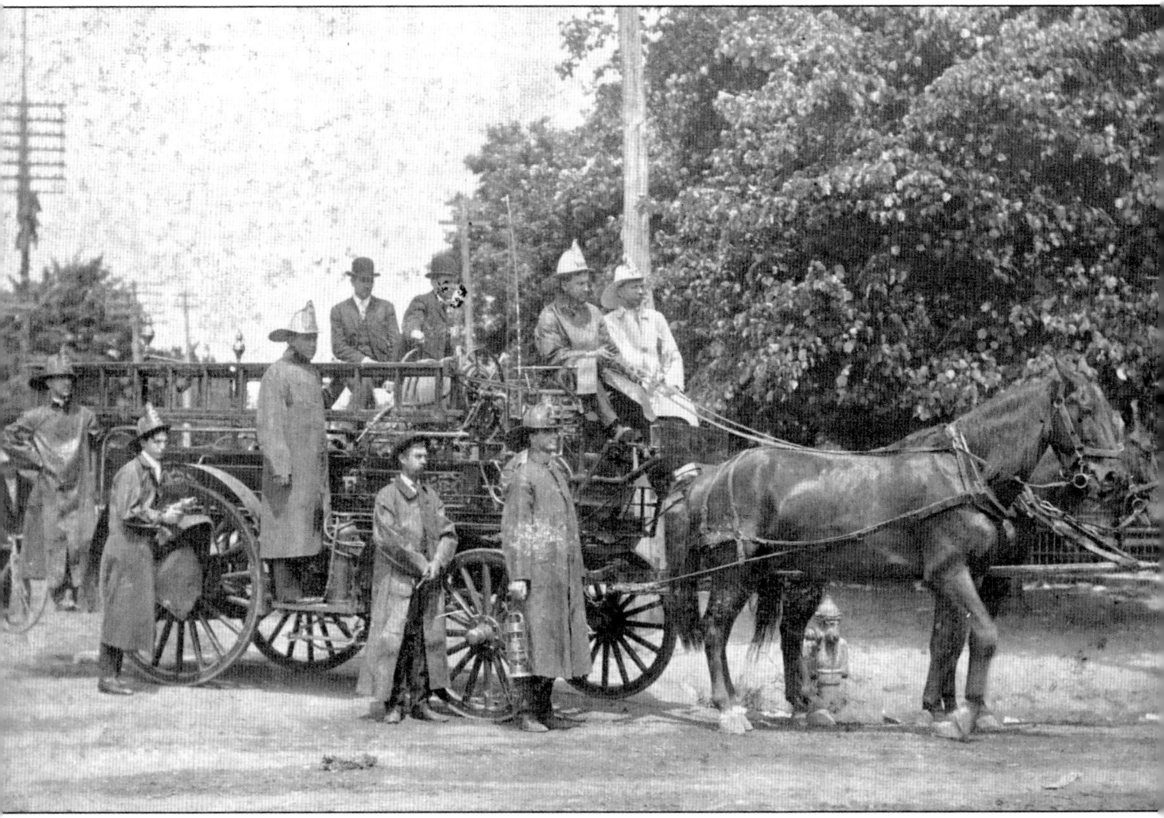

W. O. Horner was the first chief of the Cleveland Fire Department and served from 1898 to 1910. Pictured in 1906 are, from left to right, Alva Frazier, Lawrence F. "Scrubby" McDaris, John H. Smith, Tom McKamy, Sam Paul, Walter Rodgers, John Pierce, Campbell Jones (seated, driver), and W. O. Horner (seated, chief).

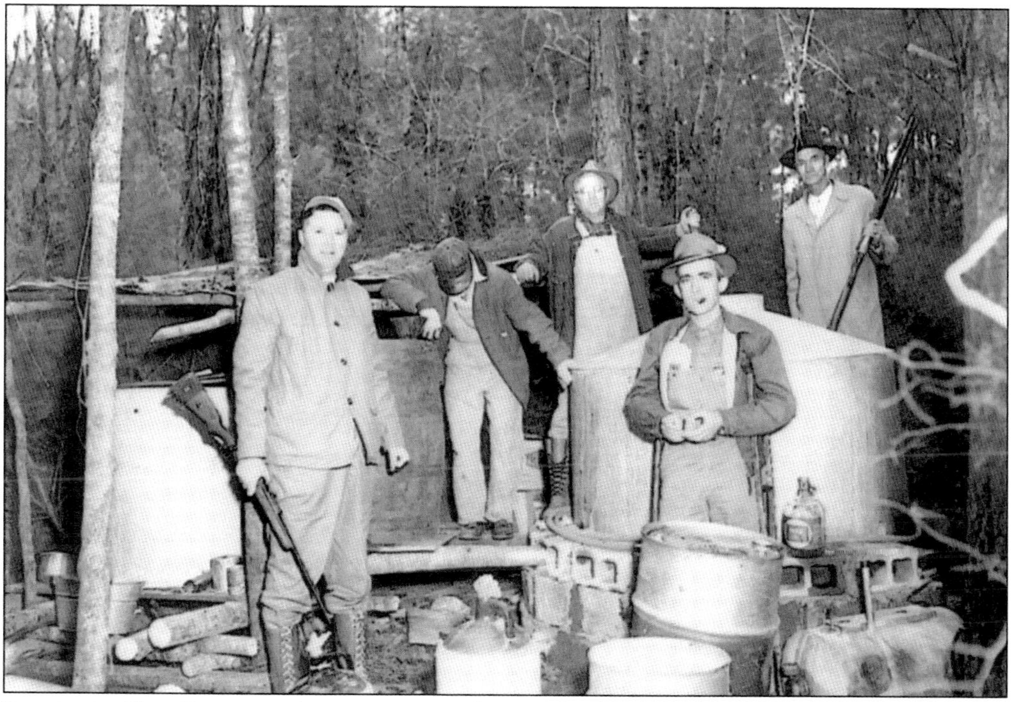

Despite its illegality, moonshine was a popular commodity in rural Tennessee counties. Some of the stills were quite large and sophisticated. Deputies shown are, from left to right, Arthur Howard, Paul Davis, Arthel Davis, J. R. Barger, and unidentified.

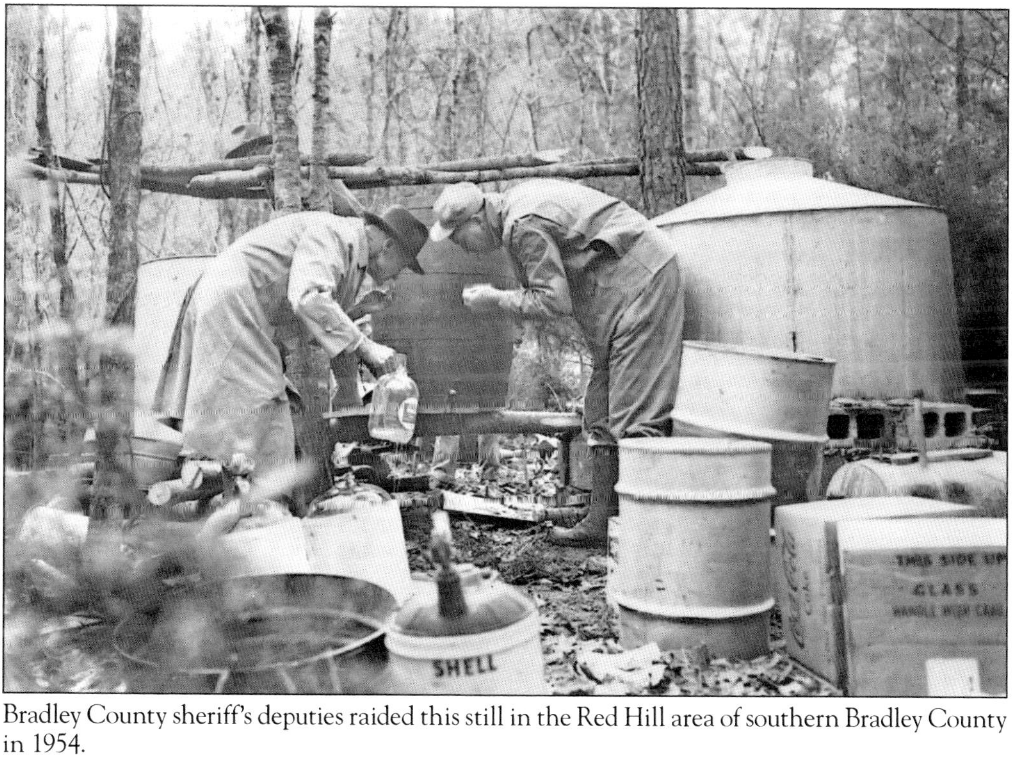

Bradley County sheriff's deputies raided this still in the Red Hill area of southern Bradley County in 1954.

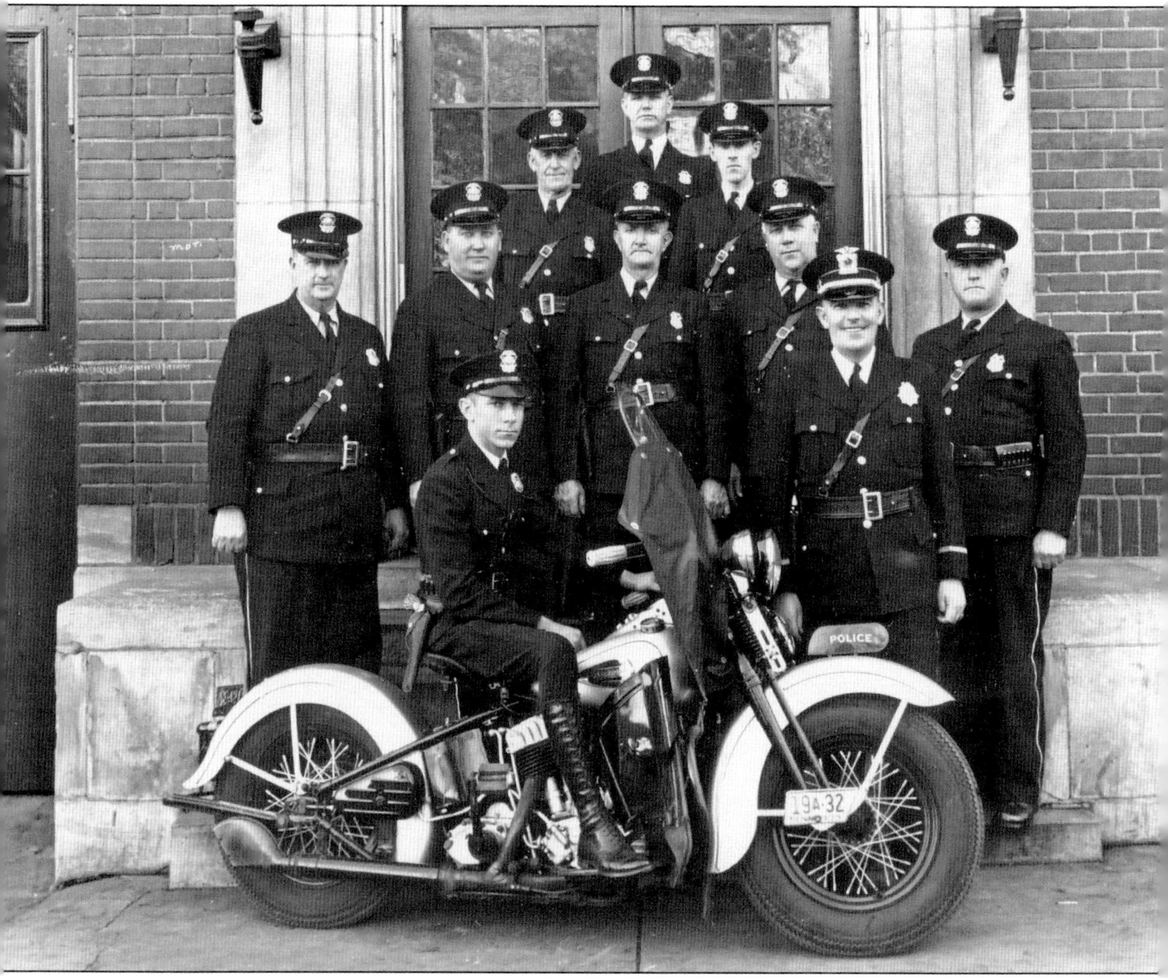

Ten of Cleveland's finest admire the department's new motorcycle in the 1930s. Pictured are Ed Hitt (on the motorcycle), Charlie Geren, Henderson "Cap" Giles, Sim Davis, Arthur Trotter (chief), Bill Arthur, Clarence Cawood, Odell Howard, Rae Crye, and Sim Goodwin. Notice the state-shaped license plate.

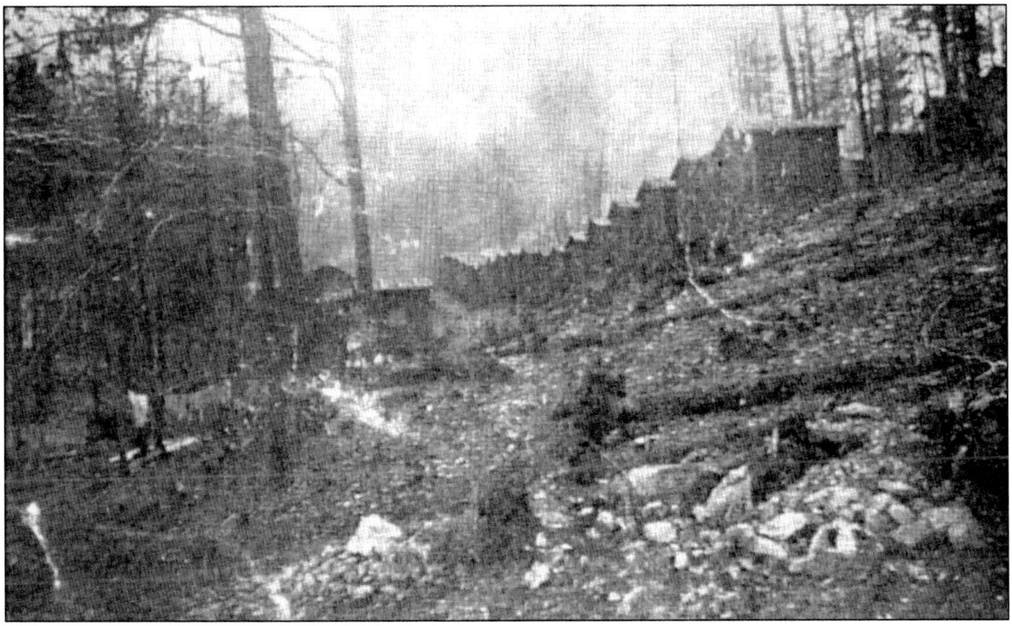

Long before the Tennessee Valley Authority (TVA), the Tennessee Electric Power Company built several dams to generate power in the Tennessee River valley. To build Dam No. 1 at Parksville, segregated living quarters, as shown, were built to house the construction workers.

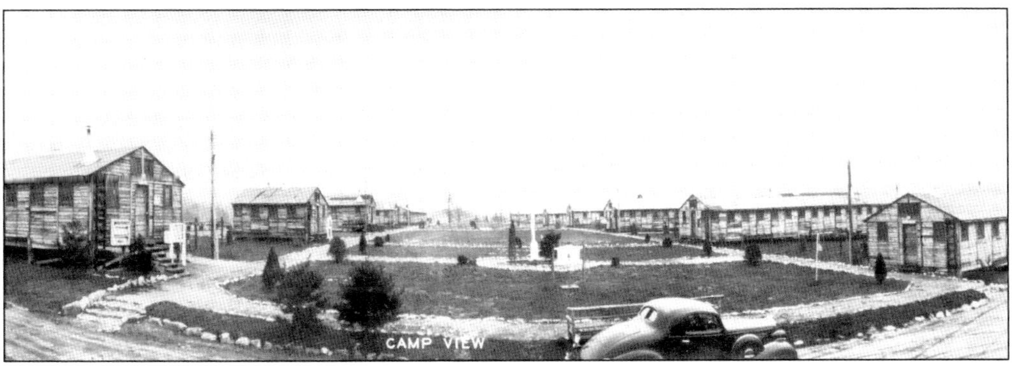

Camp No. 3466-TVA35 was located on 19 acres in Bradley County. This photograph shows a view of the camp. The M&M Mars factory is now located on this site.

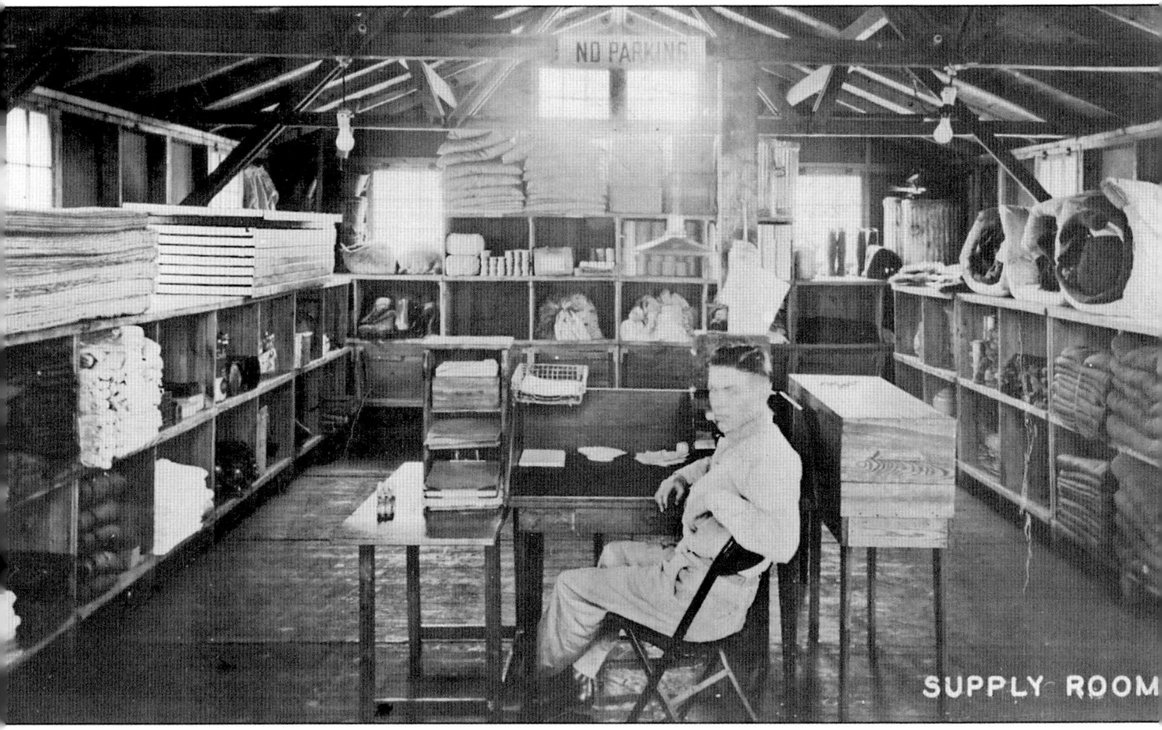

The Civilian Conservation Corps, or CCC, was a New Deal program for unmarried men 18 to 25 years of age. This photograph shows the supply room in one of the barracks in Cleveland in the 1930s.

Four

School Days

When I was a boy of fourteen, my father was so ignorant I could hardly stand to have the old man around. But when I got to be twenty-one, I was astonished at how much he had learned in seven years.

—Mark Twain

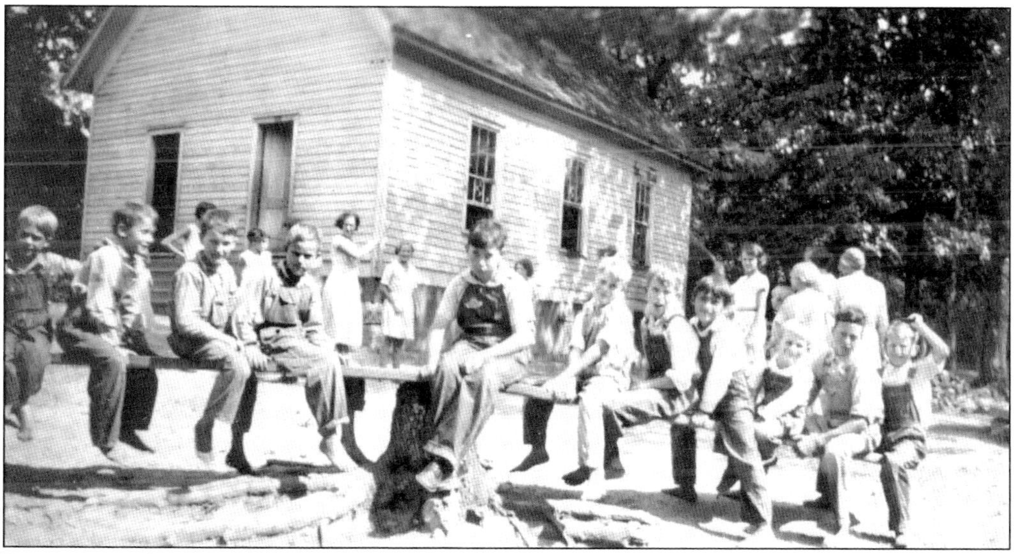

Recess was a favorite subject, as seen in this photograph of students in the 1920s playing on the seesaw at Johnston School, which was closed in the 1950s.

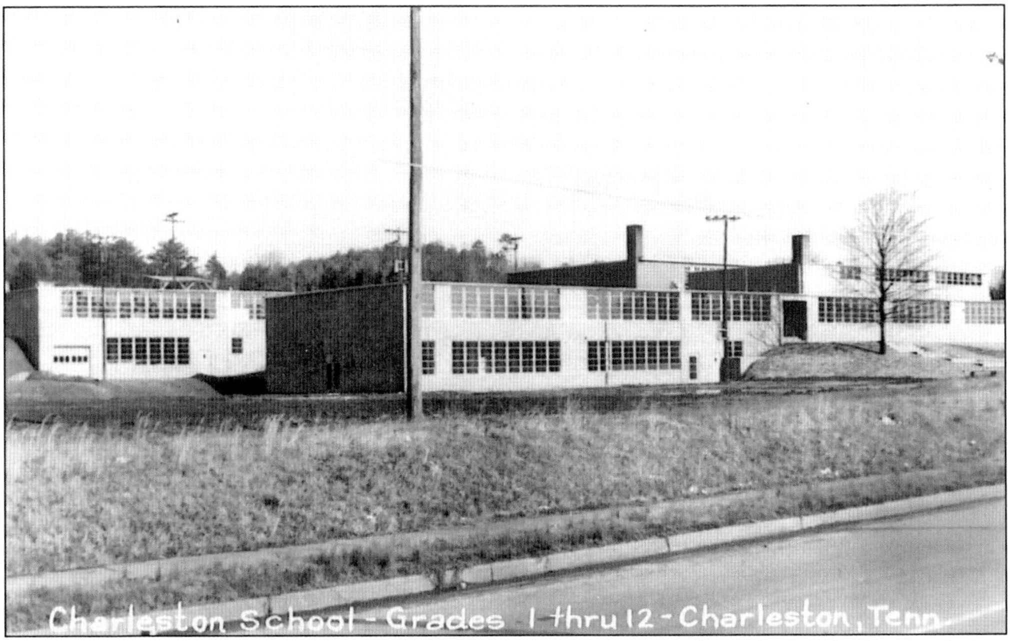

The school at Charleston served grades 1 through 12 until 2001, when the last high school class was graduated. The building now is an elementary school with the high school students attending the new Walker Valley High School.

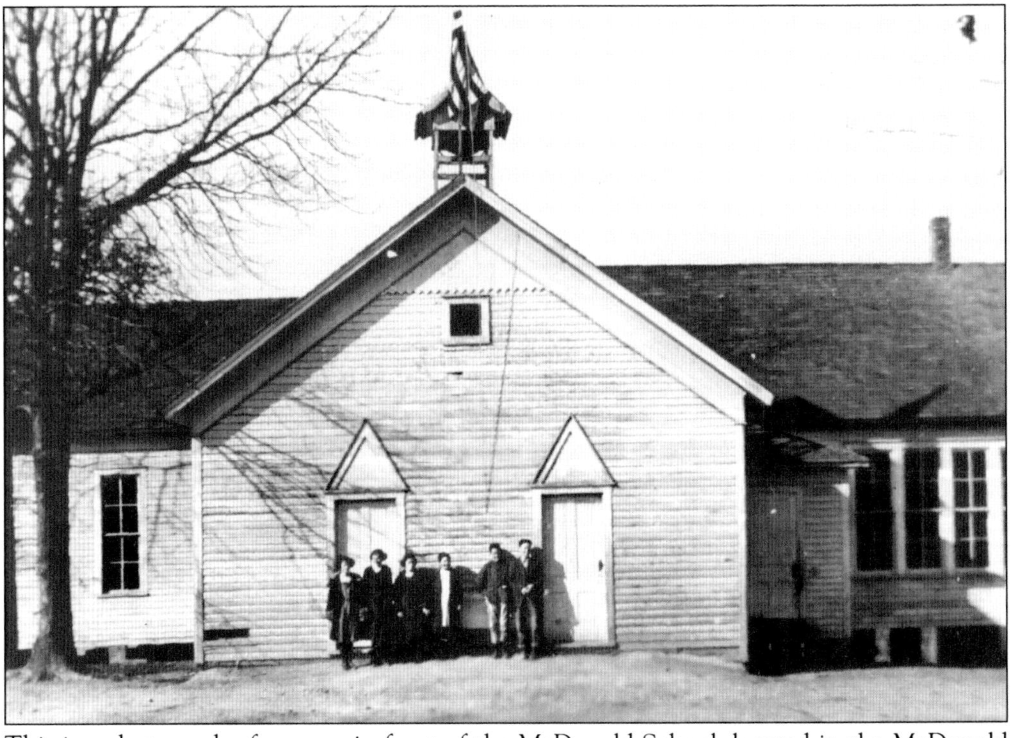

This is a photograph of a group in front of the McDonald School, located in the McDonald community in southwest Bradley County. This building was later replaced by a brick structure, which was used until 1995.

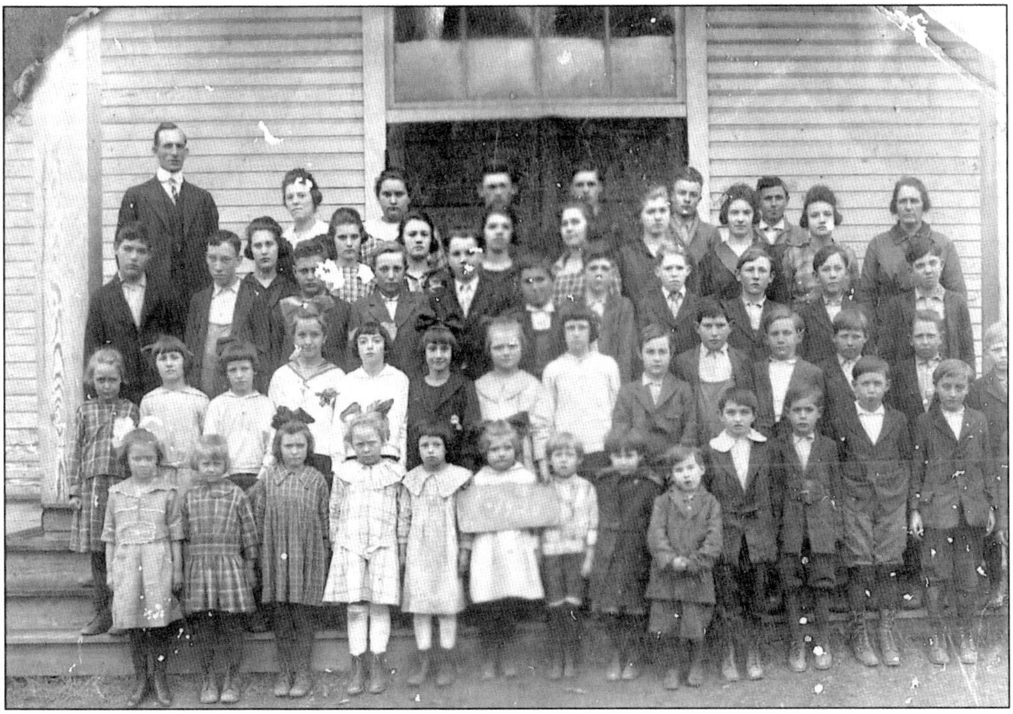

Philippi School began in 1866, its name being changed to Prospect School in 1884. In 1920, a group of students were photographed. The only identified student is Sue LeGarde, fourth from the left on the second row.

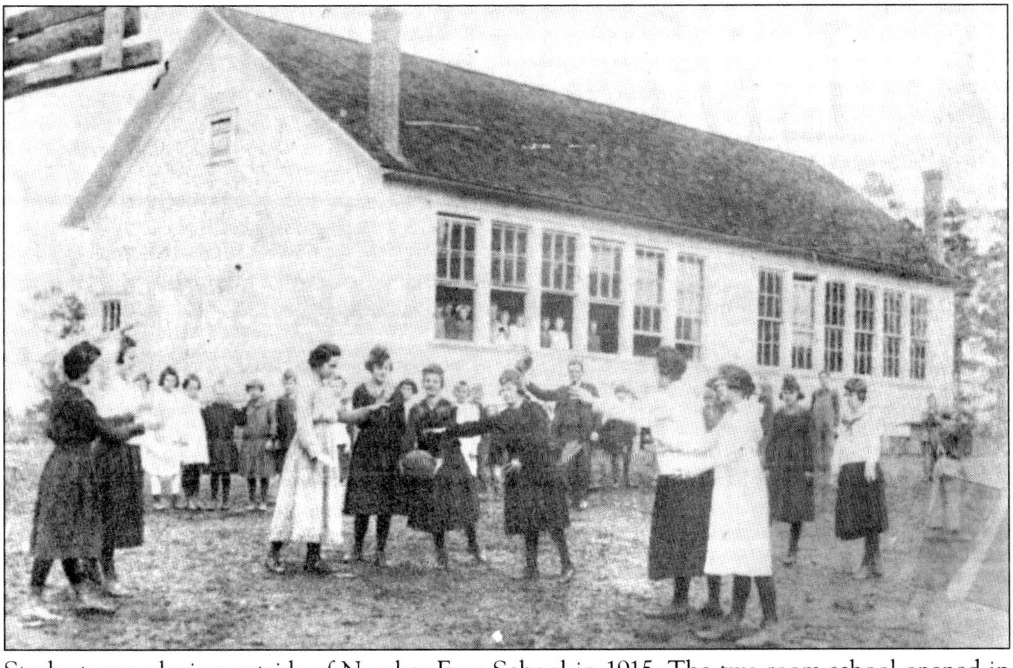

Students are playing outside of Number Four School in 1915. The two-room school opened in 1911 and was consolidated with Valley View School in 1952.

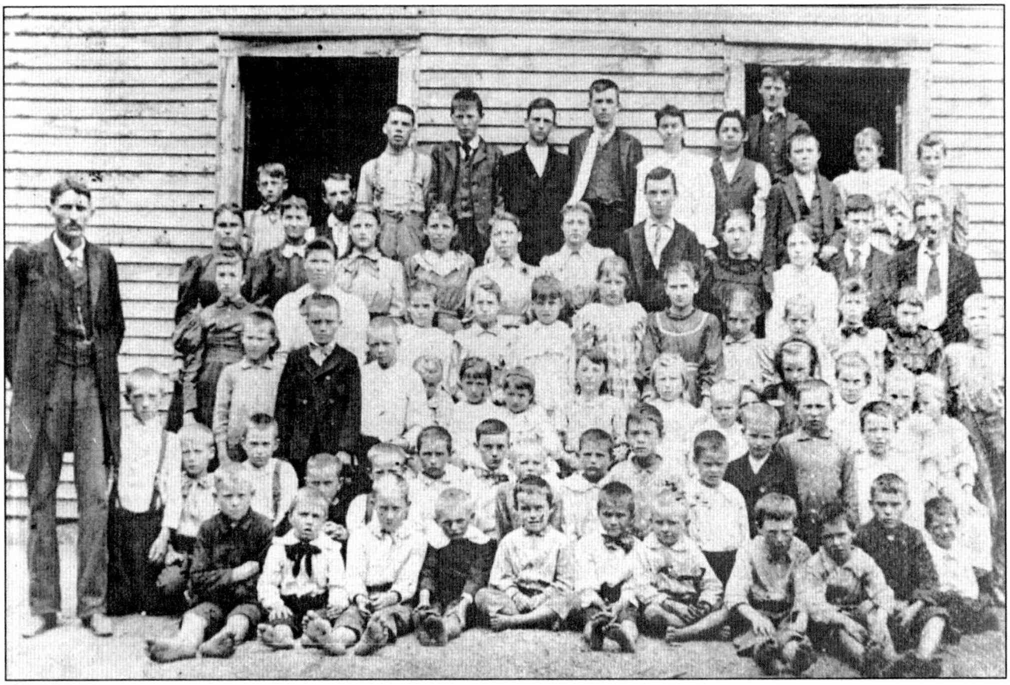

Pine Hill School was located on Old Alabama Road near the Pine Hill Cumberland Presbyterian Church. The well pump located in the front yard is the only landmark left of the school. This school picture was made about 1898.

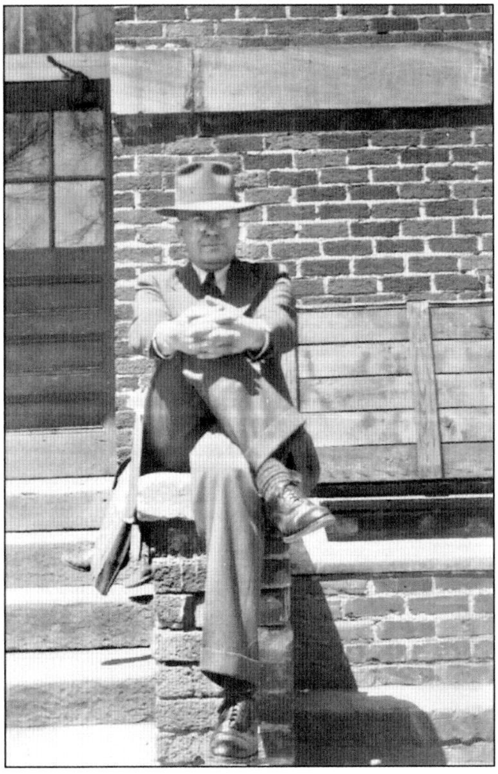

This is a 1947 photograph of Ernest L. Ross taken at Allen School. In addition to his being a noted educator, he is acclaimed for his research on Bradley County education and his census of cemeteries in Bradley County. E. L. Ross Elementary School is named for him.

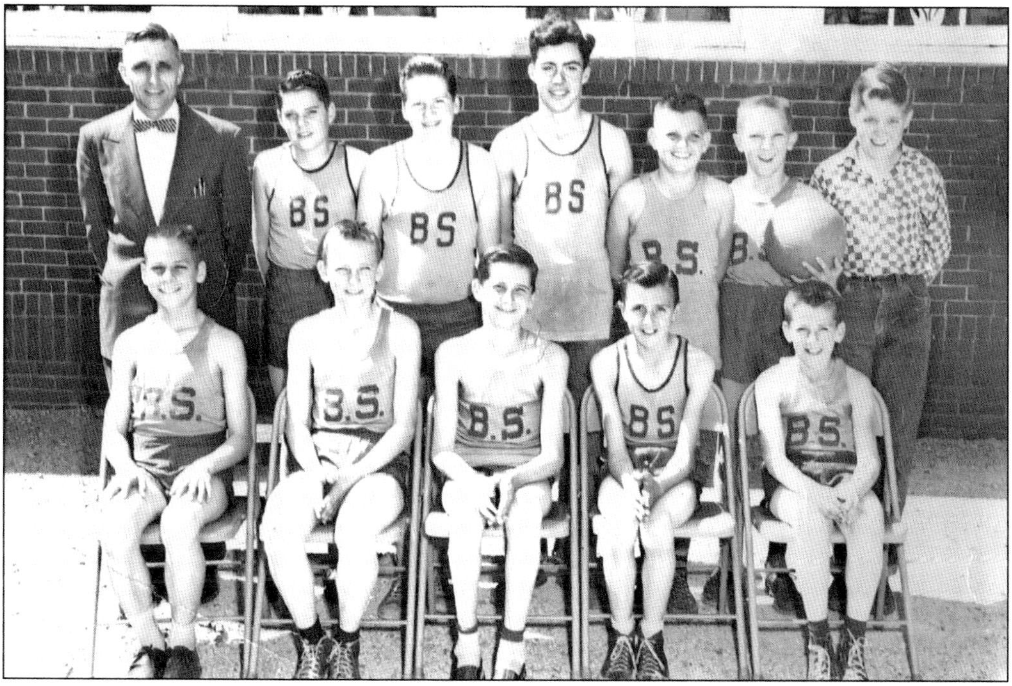

Big Springs Elementary School had a powerhouse team in 1956. Notice the footgear on these stars. Members from left to right are (first row) Eddie Botts, Harold Gibson, Jimmy Cissom, Billy Miller, and Larry Bird; (second row) principal/coach J. W. Rymer, Adrian Ownby, Dudley Nichols, J. D. Pullen, Kenneth Emerson, Sammy Elliott, and Jenson Oxford.

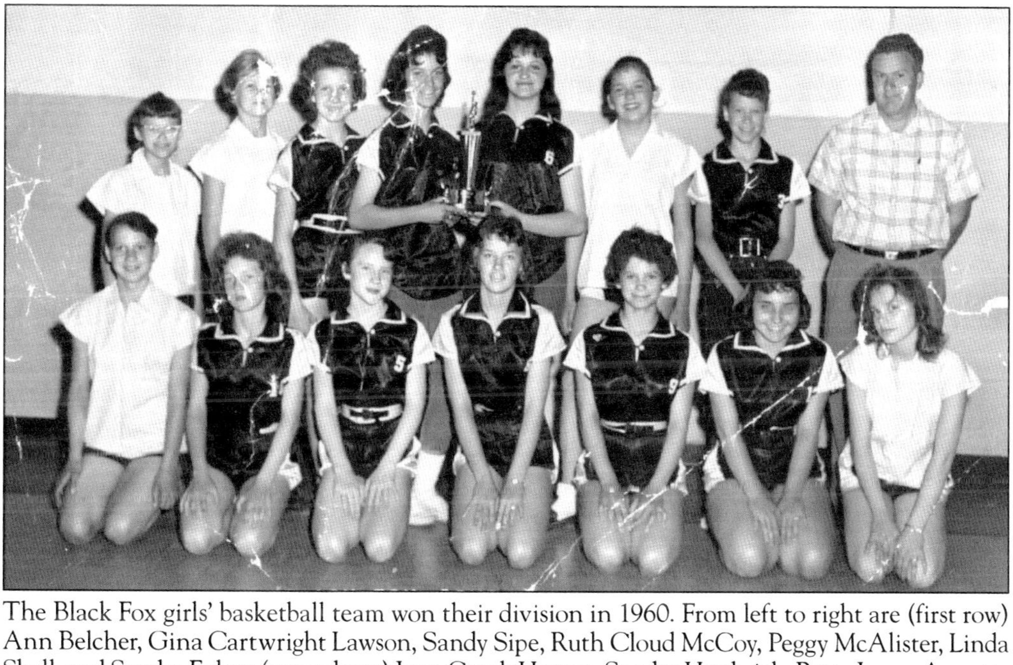

The Black Fox girls' basketball team won their division in 1960. From left to right are (first row) Ann Belcher, Gina Cartwright Lawson, Sandy Sipe, Ruth Cloud McCoy, Peggy McAlister, Linda Shell, and Sandra Eaker; (second row) Joan Crook Hatton, Sandra Hardwick, Betty Jones, Annette Johns Smith, Shirley Green, Marilyn Stansberry, Jean Crook Malone, and Johnny Cartwright, coach and teacher.

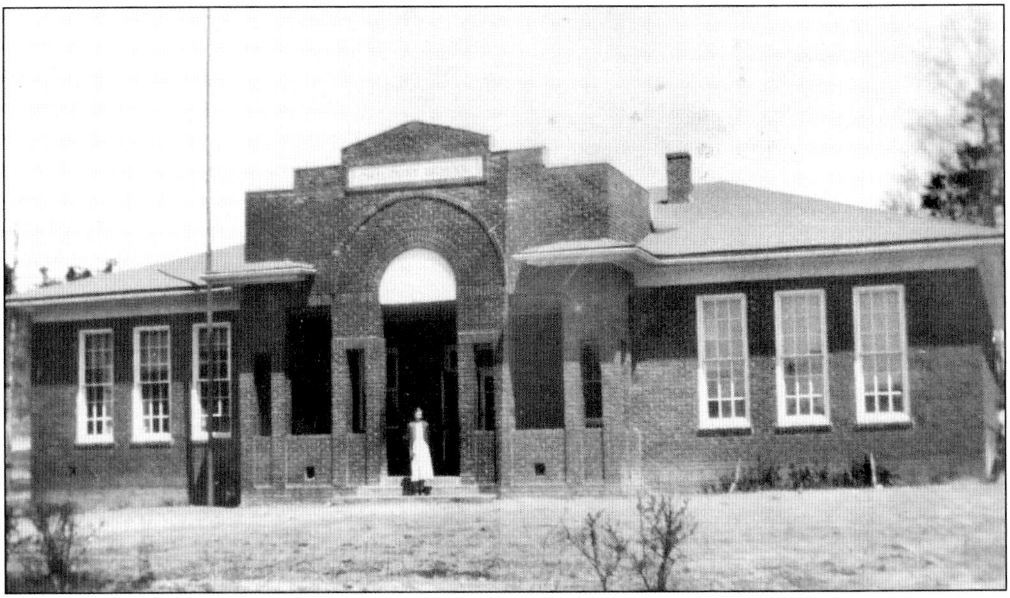

Virginia Kirkpatrick was photographed in front of Chilcutt School about 1936. The school was located eight and a half miles east of Cleveland on Chilcutt Road next to Chilcutt Methodist Church and cemetery.

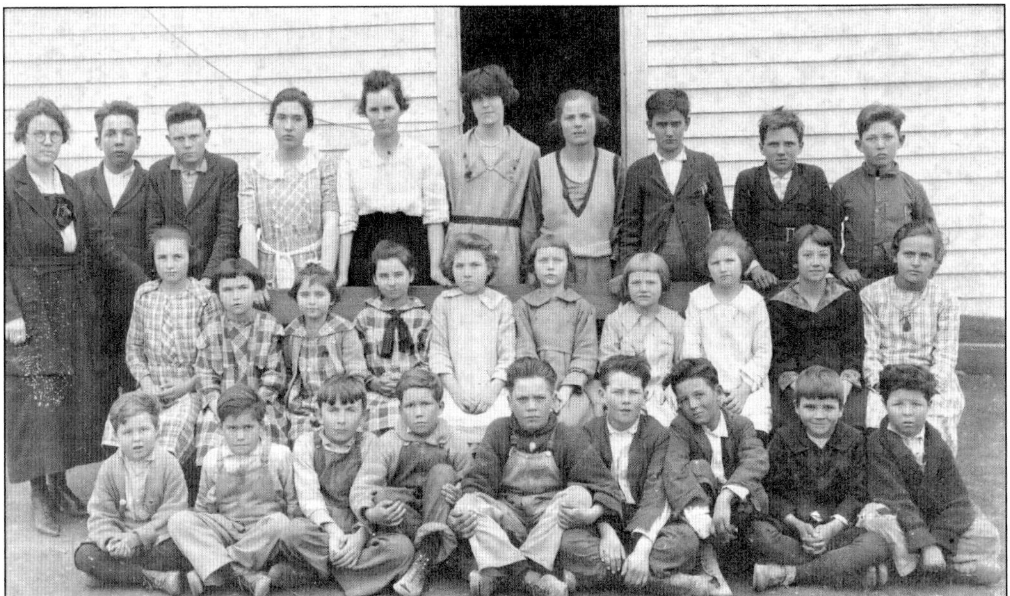

The Rogers School was located off Chestuee Road on the old Bascom Rogers farm. When the Fred Cooke family bought the farm, three of their daughters attended the school. This 1920 photograph shows, from left to right, (first row) Arvil Wilson, Lester Ash, Howard Broomfield, Austin Ash, Hamilton Goins, Mac Moore, Lester Moore, Ronald Milsap, and Robert Wilson; (second row) Naomi Gatlin, Thelma Cooke, Margaret Cooke, Christine Cooke, Mary Gatlin, Edna York, Ottie Goins, Irene Gatlin, Nona Dunn, and Mary Lou Broomfield; (third row) Anna Mae Officer (teacher), J. T. Gatlin, Arthur Wilson, Emily Gatlin, Grace Moore, Icye Broomfield, Ora Goins, Luke Ash, Alden Milsap, and Kenneth Gatlin.

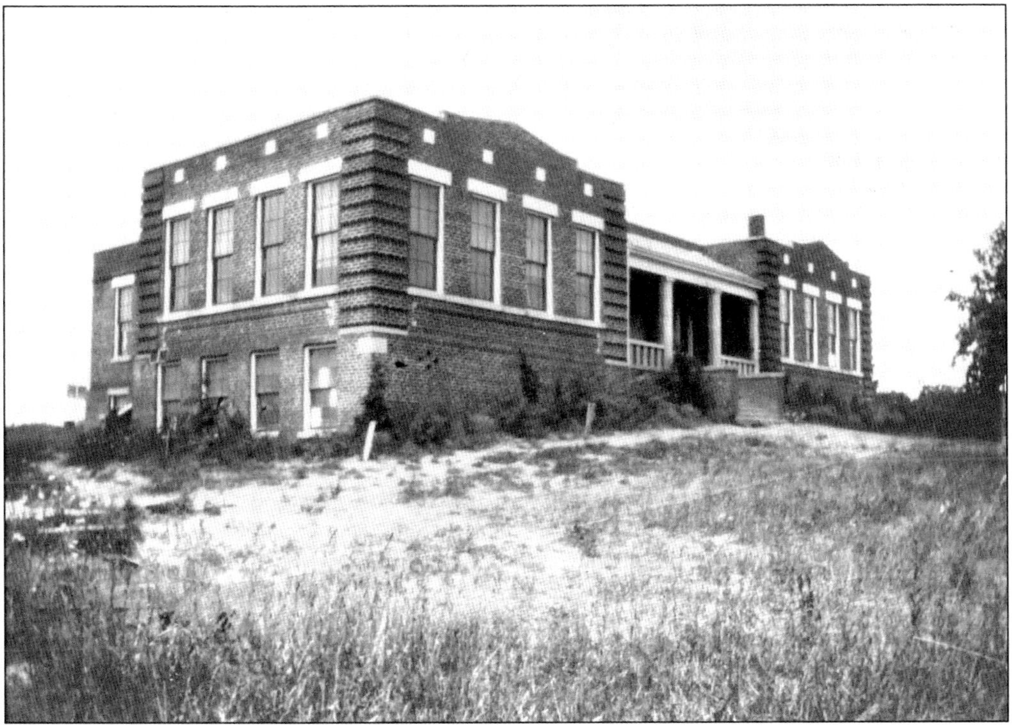

The Hopewell community was extremely proud of its high school, which opened in 1922 and closed in 1938.

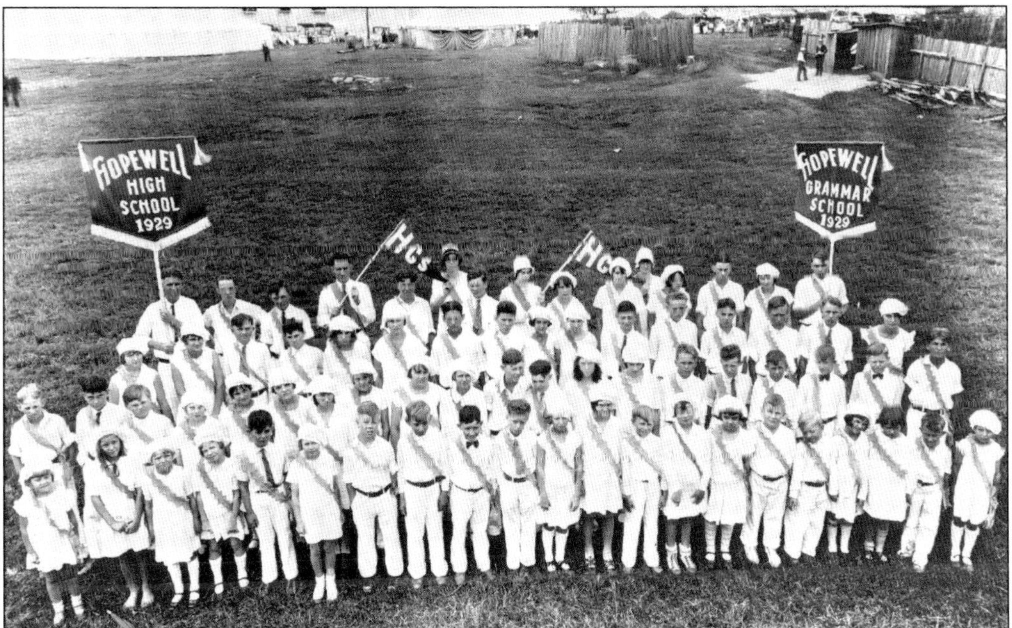

Hopewell High School and Grammar School were participants in the Bradley County Fair in 1929.

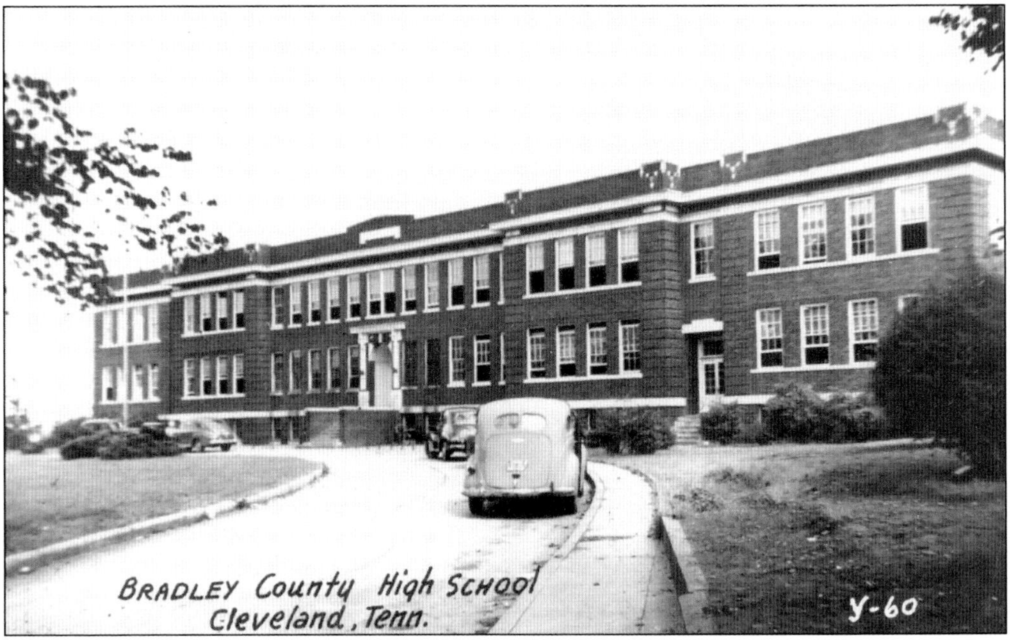

Bradley Central High School was formed by the merger of Bradley County High School of Charleston and Central High School of Cleveland. The new high school was built in 1916 on Ocoee Street at the northern edge of the city of Cleveland. It grew to be one of the largest high schools in the state of Tennessee.

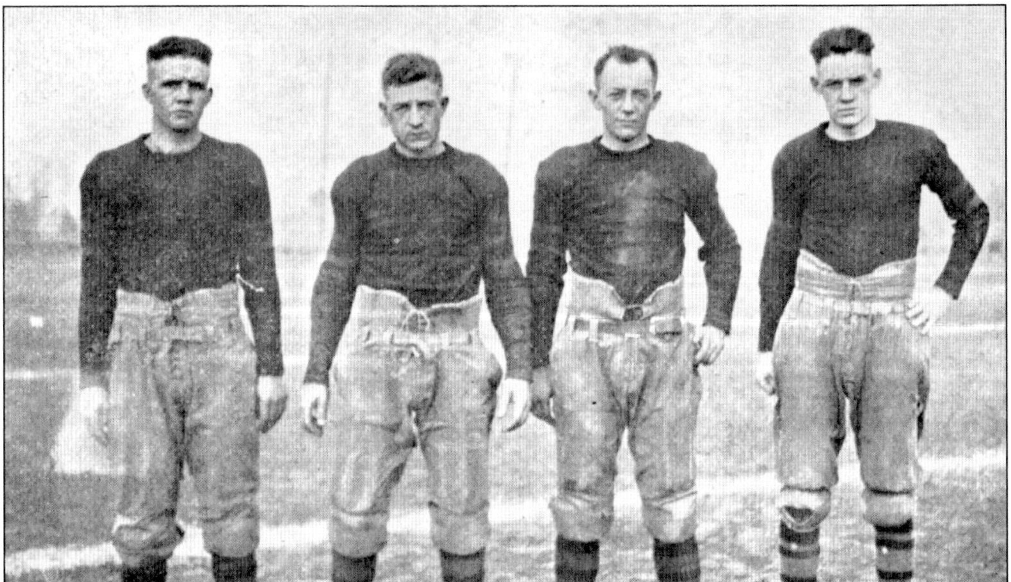
These are the tackles on Coach James T. Lovell's Bradley Central High School football team in 1922.

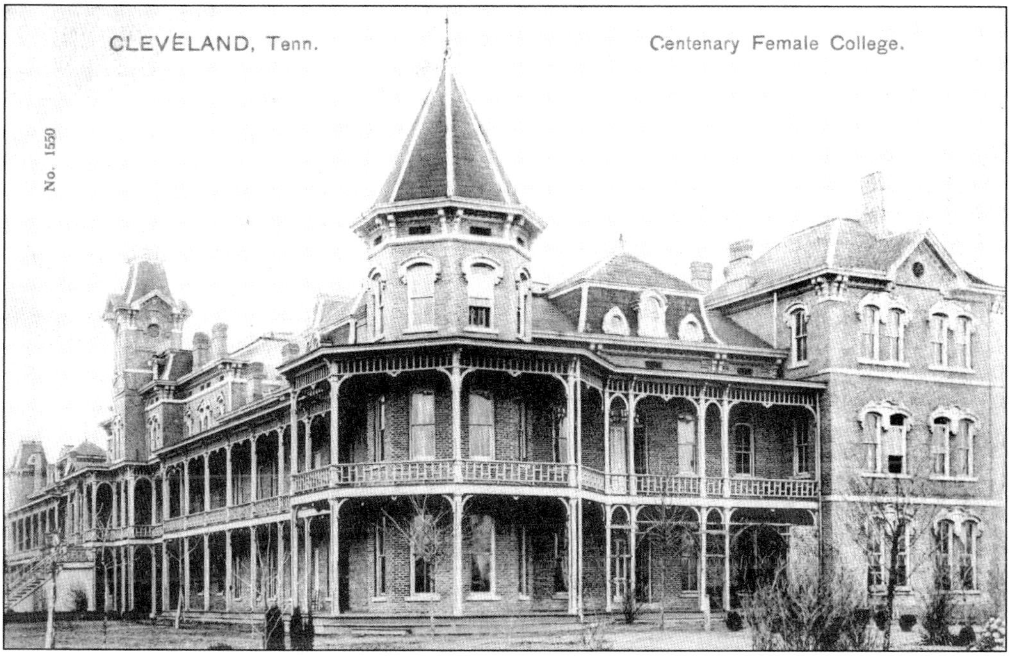

Centenary Female College was founded in 1884 to commemorate the centenary of Methodism in America. It was sponsored by the Holston Conference of the Methodist Episcopal Church, South. The school closed in 1929.

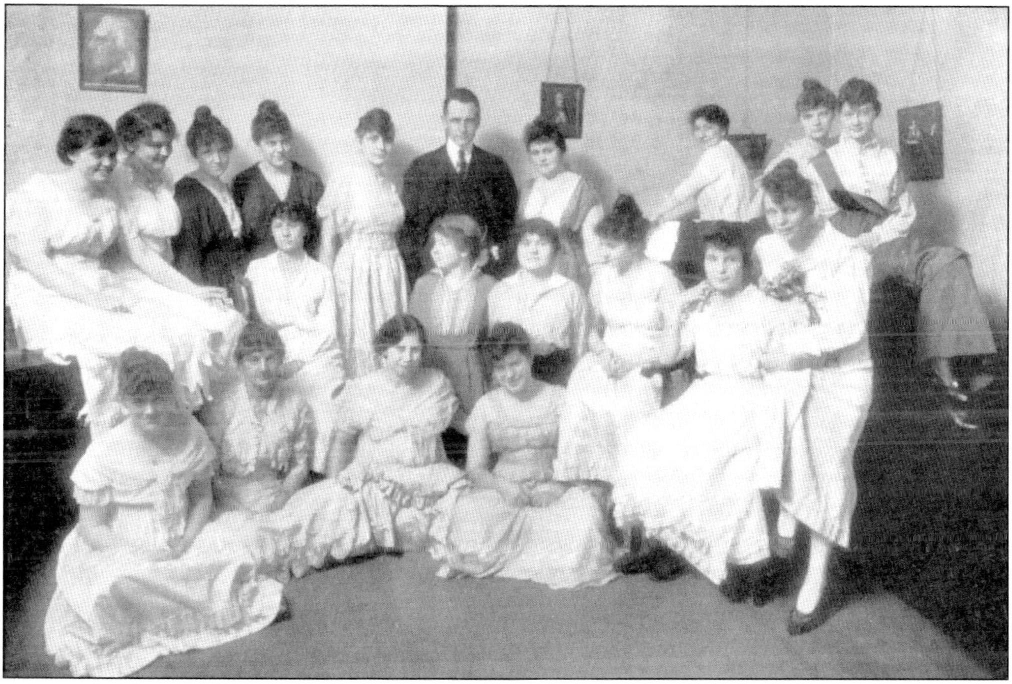

Carl and Gunhild Fallberg were on the faculty of Centenary College and Conservatory of Music from 1910 to 1917. Carl Fallberg was the director of the music department. The Fallbergs held classes in piano, organ, violin, voice, theory, and harmony. In this 1916 photograph, Professor Fallberg is shown with some of his students.

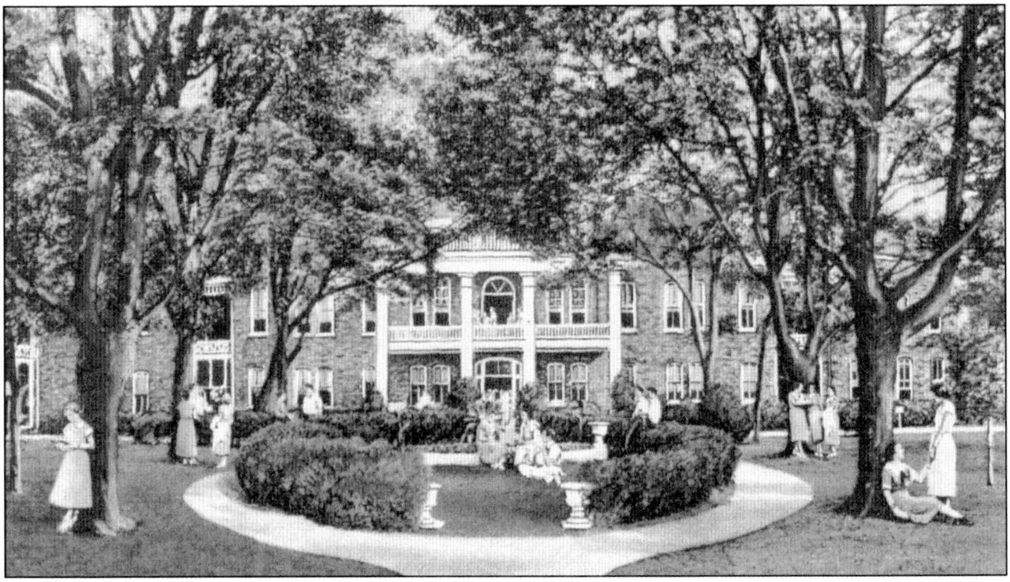

Dr. Bob Jones Sr., a southern Methodist evangelist, relocated his interdenominational school from Florida to Cleveland in 1933. He acquired the campus of the former Centenary Female College. While a strong ministerial program was the main emphasis of the school, cultural programs in drama, art, and music drew international recognition. Bob Jones College grew to be the largest liberal arts college in the state of Tennessee. Although the college flourished in Cleveland, it outgrew the physical campus and moved to South Carolina in 1947.

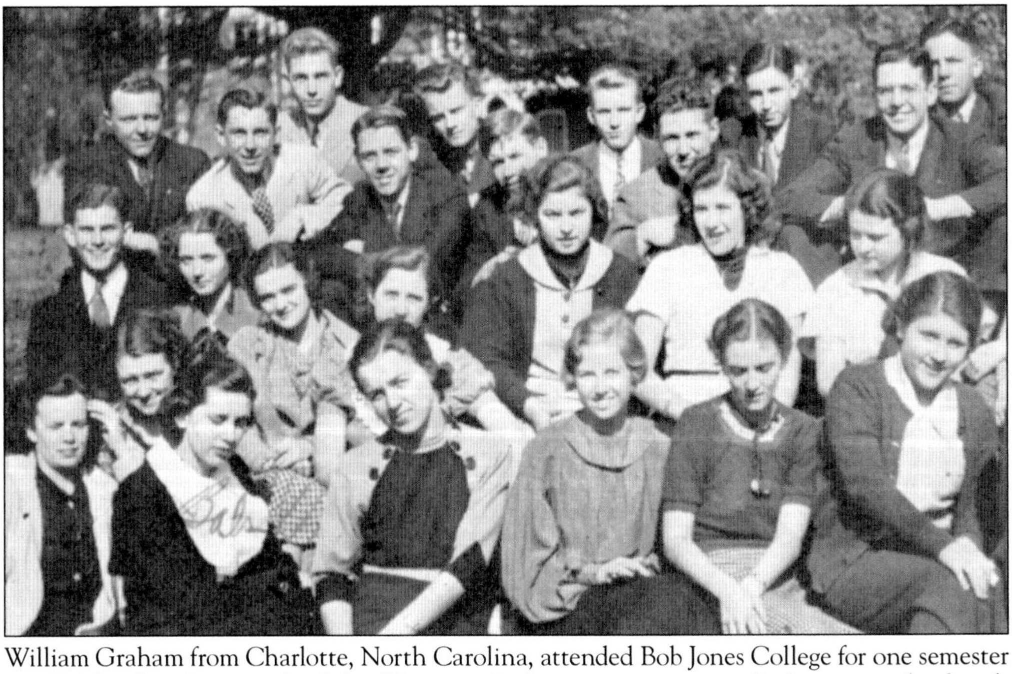

William Graham from Charlotte, North Carolina, attended Bob Jones College for one semester in 1936. In this photograph of the Christian Endeavor organization, Graham is in the fourth row, second from the left. While a student, Billy Graham preached his first sermon at Charleston Methodist Church and his second at Antioch Baptist Church. He later became a world-renowned evangelist.

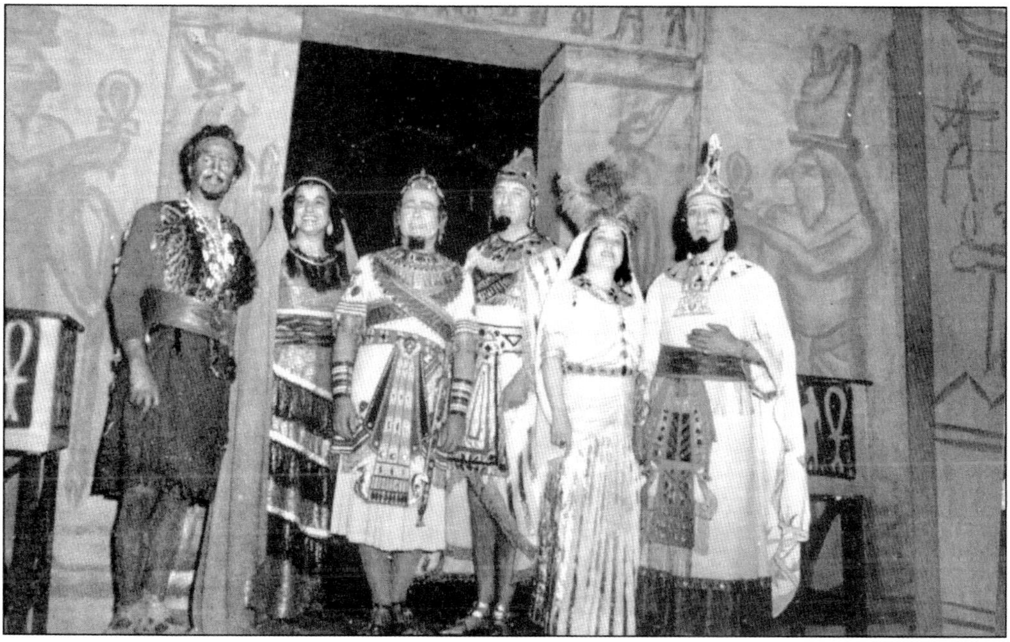

The opera *Aida* was performed at Bob Jones College on December 11, 1943. Mobley Lushanya was Aida; Elizabeth Wysor, Amneris; Frederick Jagel, Rademes; Carlo Morelli, Amonasro; Nino Ruisi, Ramfis; and Burton Cornwall, the King of Egypt. These principals are shown at the entrance of Temple of Phtah.

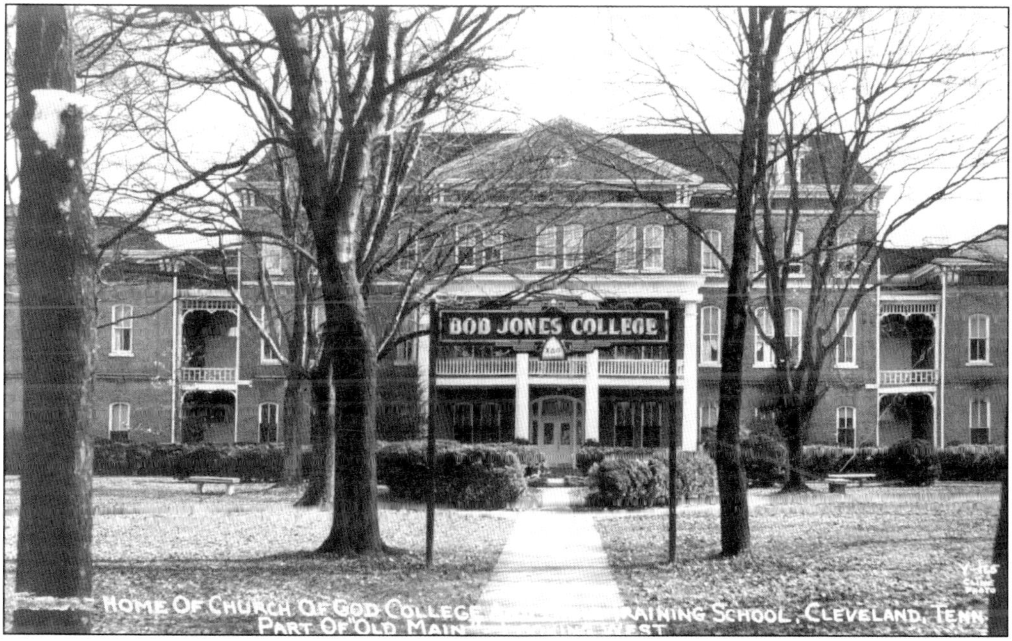

This is a postcard titled "Future Home of the Church of God College and Training School." The Church of God purchased the Bob Jones College property in 1947 and moved its Bible Training School from Sevierville, Tennessee, to Cleveland, where it became a two-year junior college named Lee College in honor of the second Church of God general overseer, Flavius J. Lee.

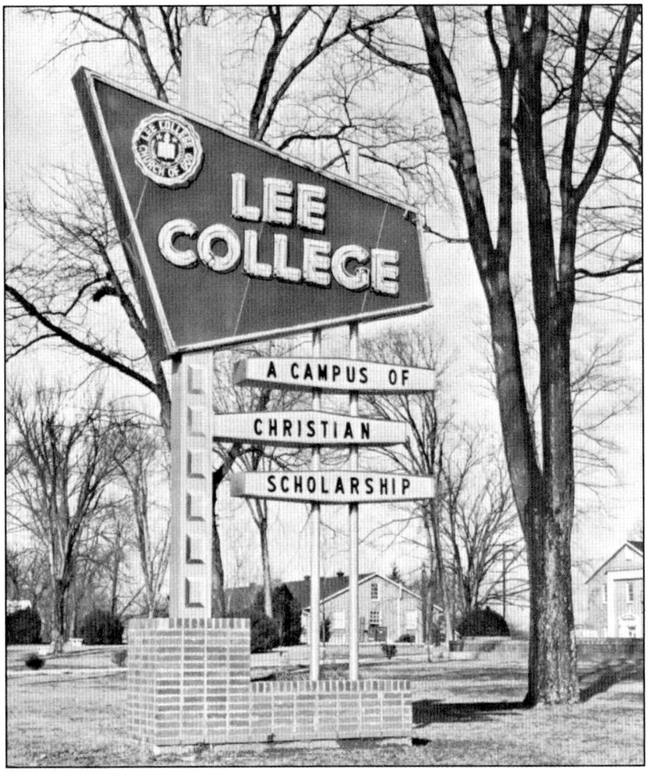

In 1918, the Church of God founded the Bible Training School, which had long been a dream of general overseer A. J. Tomlinson. Having originated in Cleveland, the school later moved to Sevierville and then moved back to Cleveland. Lee College had, as did its predecessors Centenary and Bob Jones, a preparatory school for younger students. Eventually Lee College become a four-year college and has in recent years, since becoming Lee University, experienced a dynamic growth in student population.

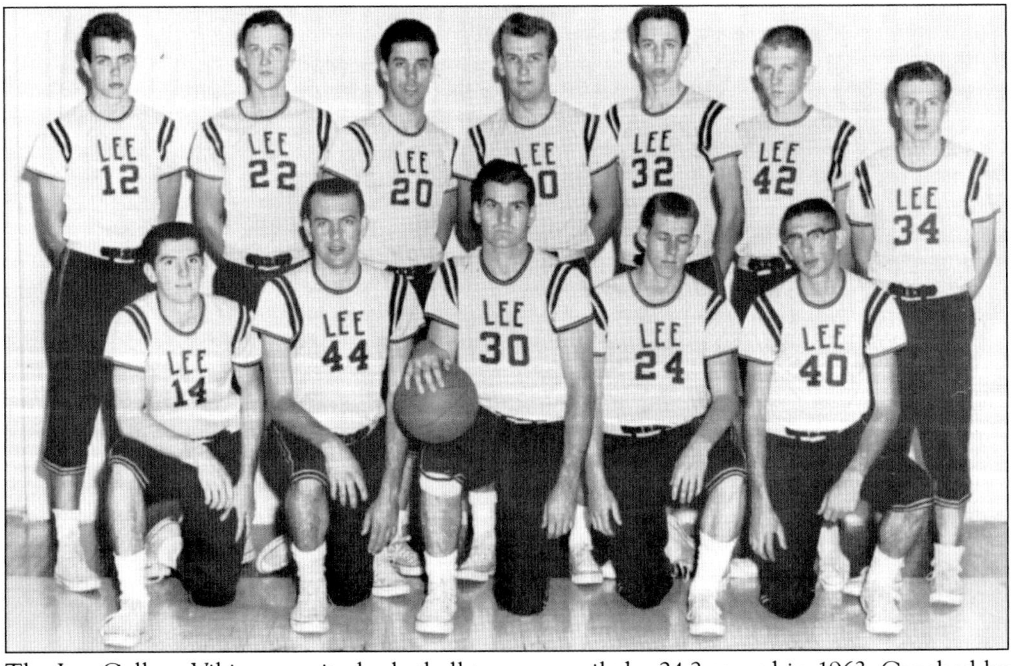

The Lee College Vikings varsity basketball team compiled a 24-2 record in 1963. Coached by Hubert Black, the team members include, from left to right, (first row) Wayne Woodard, Bob Varner, Captain Don Jenkins, Don Gadbury, and Cocaptain John Pigg; (second row) Joel Jinkerson, Bob Llewellen, Archie Miller, Dale Hughes, Ken Hyde, Joe McCoy, and Ted Bowman.

Five

TAKING CARE OF BUSINESS

Business will be better or worse.

—Calvin Coolidge

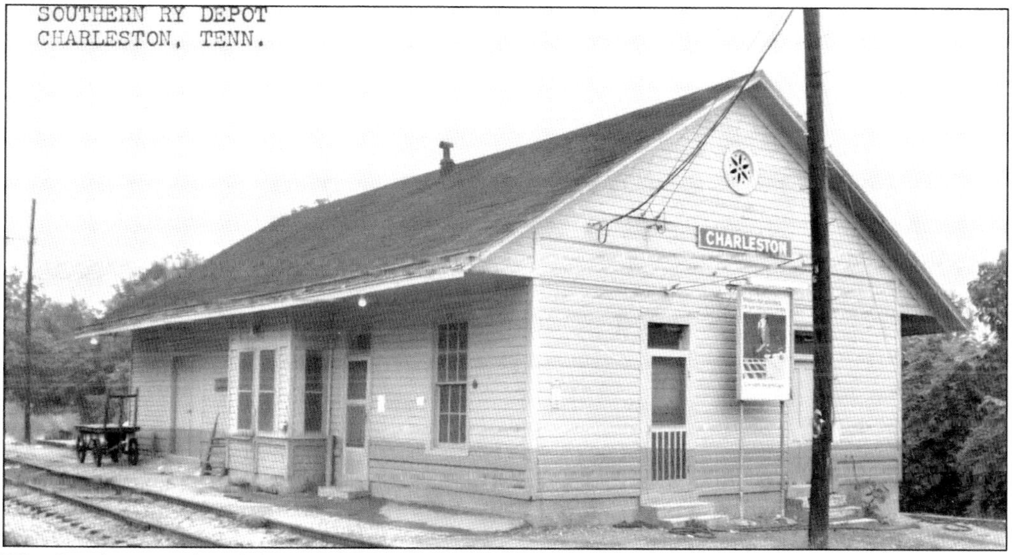

The Southern Railroad depot in Charleston was a very lively depot, especially during the filming of 20th Century Fox's *Wild River*, starring Montgomery Clift and Lee Remick in 1952. Several local residents had roles in this movie: Mark Anthony, Ross Apperson, Mike Dodd, C. C. L. Ray, Edna Snapp, Francis Cheatam, Mary Alice Byrd, Judy Harris, and Jimmy Menard. The business district of Charleston became "Garthville." The movie story line was of an elderly woman who did not want to leave her home on Garth Island to make way for the TVA to flood the island.

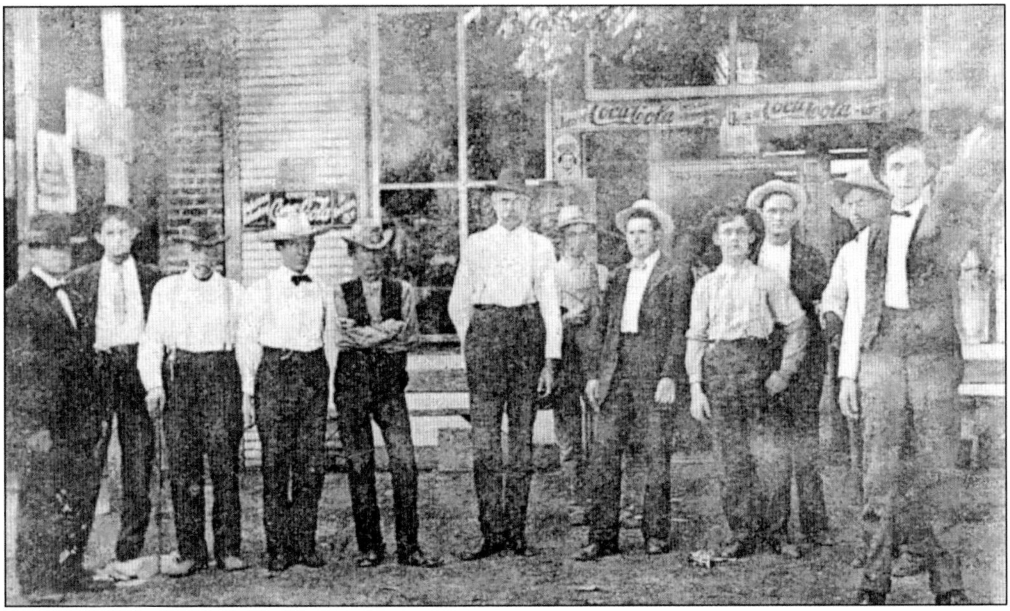

In 1908, several residents of Charleston gathered in front of Hambright Drug Store. From left to right are the Reverend J. H. Clemons (pastor of the Charleston, Calhoun, Henegar's Chapel, and Tasso Methodist Churches), Lloyd Kaylor, Tom Jones, Fate Hambright (drugstore owner), Billy Barrett (sheriff of Bradley County 1888–1890), Joe Cate, Rusty Miller, Dr. T. E. P. Chambers, Ernest Hambright, Reece McKnight, Arnold Henry, and Dr. J. Lake McClary.

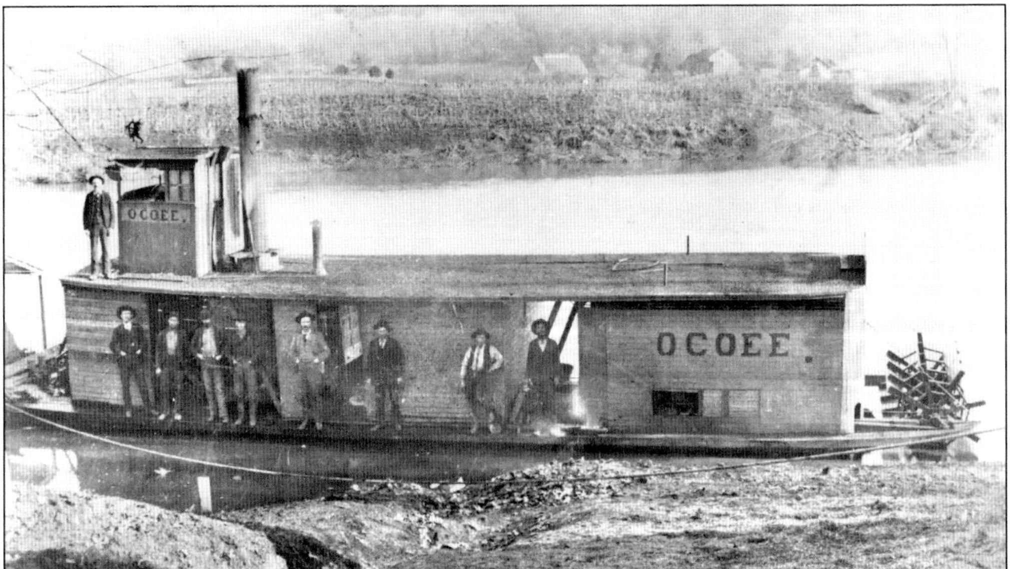

The *Ocoee*, a riverboat, was used to haul produce and logs from the Charleston area to the Tennessee River. Capt. Ben Ferguson is standing by the pilot house on top. The boat had stopped at Raht Landing on the Hiwassee River.

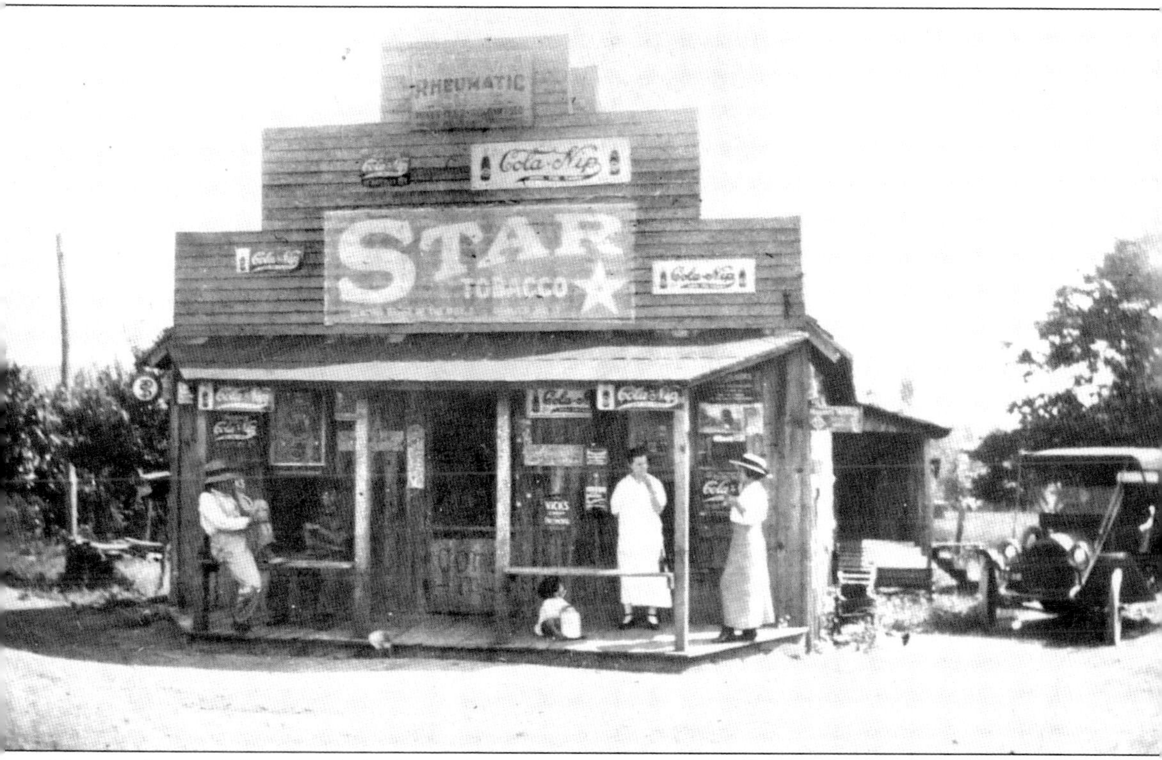

Shown about 1915 is the Parks Store, located on Tunnel Hill Road. M. H. Parks owned and operated this store for 50 years. Note the signs for Cola-Nip, a short-lived competitor of Coca-Cola. General stores thrived in rural areas as residents could not just "run into town" as has become the modern custom.

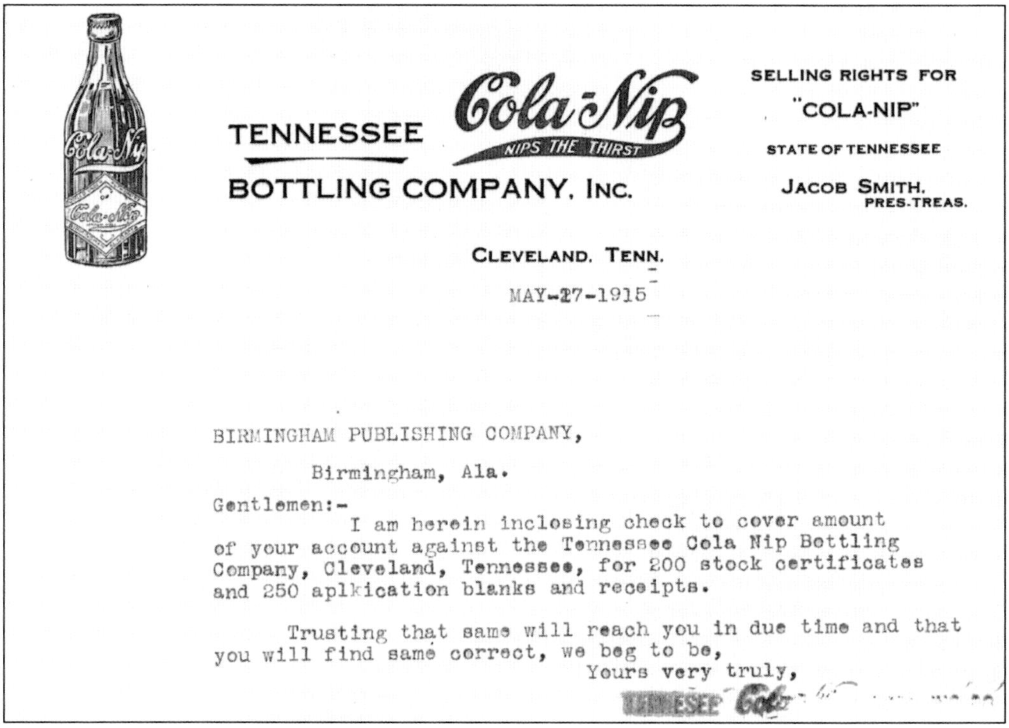

SELLING RIGHTS FOR "COLA-NIP" STATE OF TENNESSEE

JACOB SMITH. PRES.-TREAS.

TENNESSEE Cola-Nip NIPS THE THIRST BOTTLING COMPANY, INC.

CLEVELAND, TENN.

MAY-27-1915

BIRMINGHAM PUBLISHING COMPANY,

Birmingham, Ala.

Gentlemen:-

I am herein inclosing check to cover amount of your account against the Tennessee Cola Nip Bottling Company, Cleveland, Tennessee, for 200 stock certificates and 250 aplkication blanks and receipts.

Trusting that same will reach you in due time and that you will find same correct, we beg to be,

Yours very truly,

This stationery was for the Tennessee Bottling Company, which had the rights for the state of Tennessee to bottle Cola-Nip, an early competitor in the cola wars.

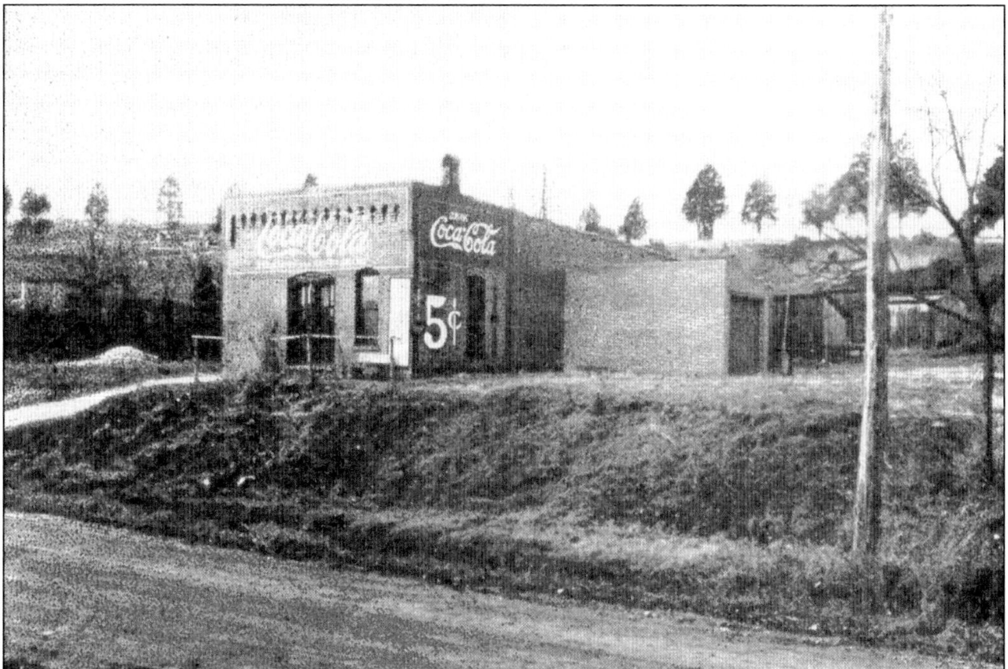

The Cleveland Bottling Works was established in the year 1904 by C. A. Mee and J. Hardie Johnston. The firm bottled Coca-Cola, Nu-Grape, and soda waters.

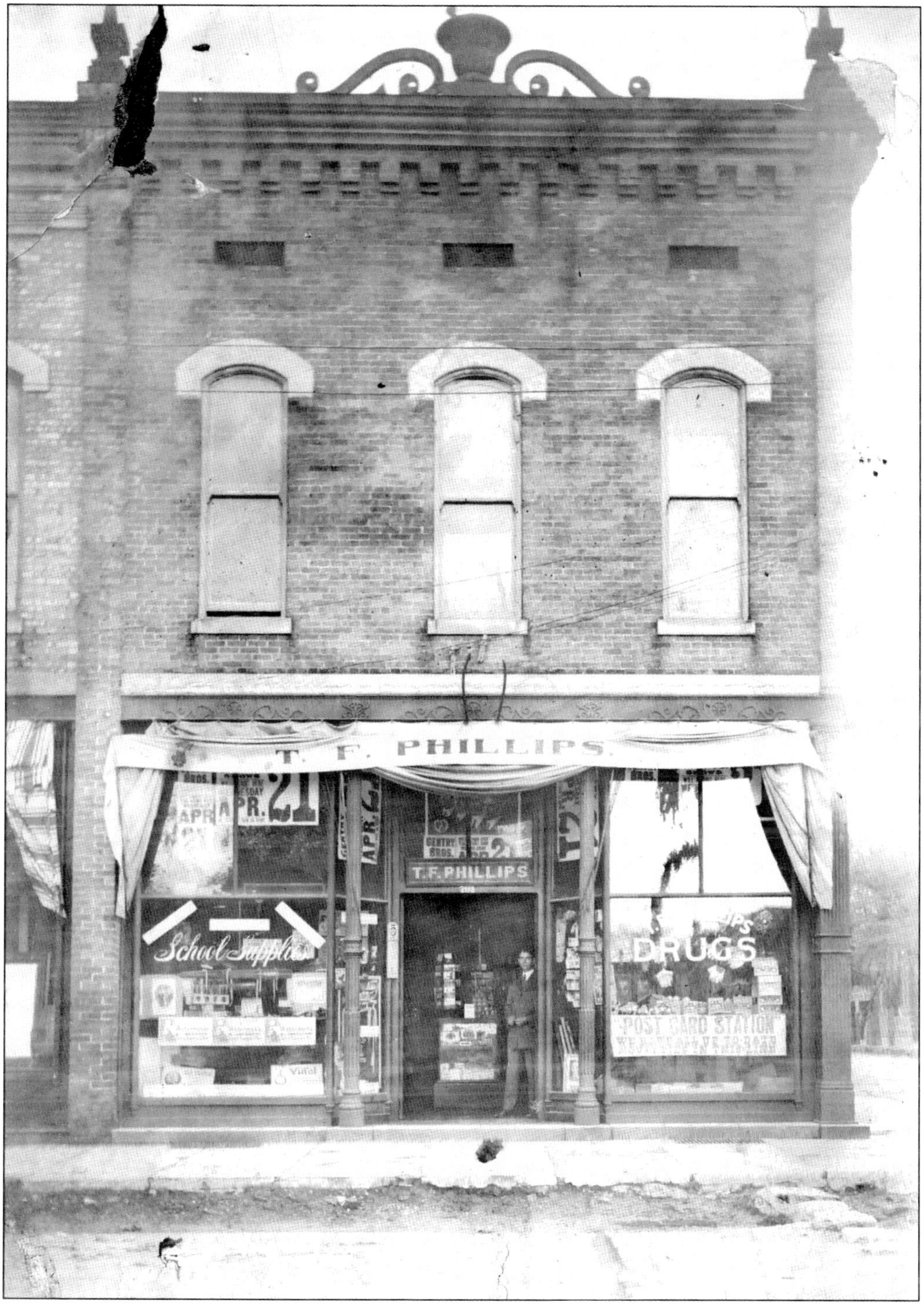

T. F. Phillips was a druggist who also sold postcards and school supplies. After Phillips closed the store, the building was remodeled and used by People's Bank.

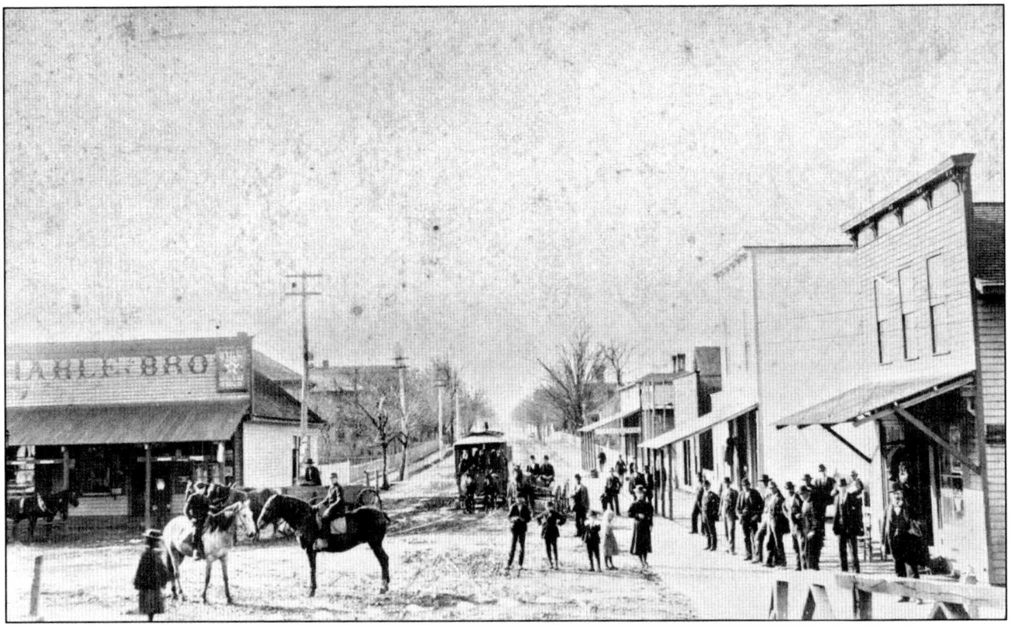

In the 1890s, Five Points was a busy area of Cleveland. Note the J. H. Harle and Brothers store and the horse-drawn streetcar on the dirt street.

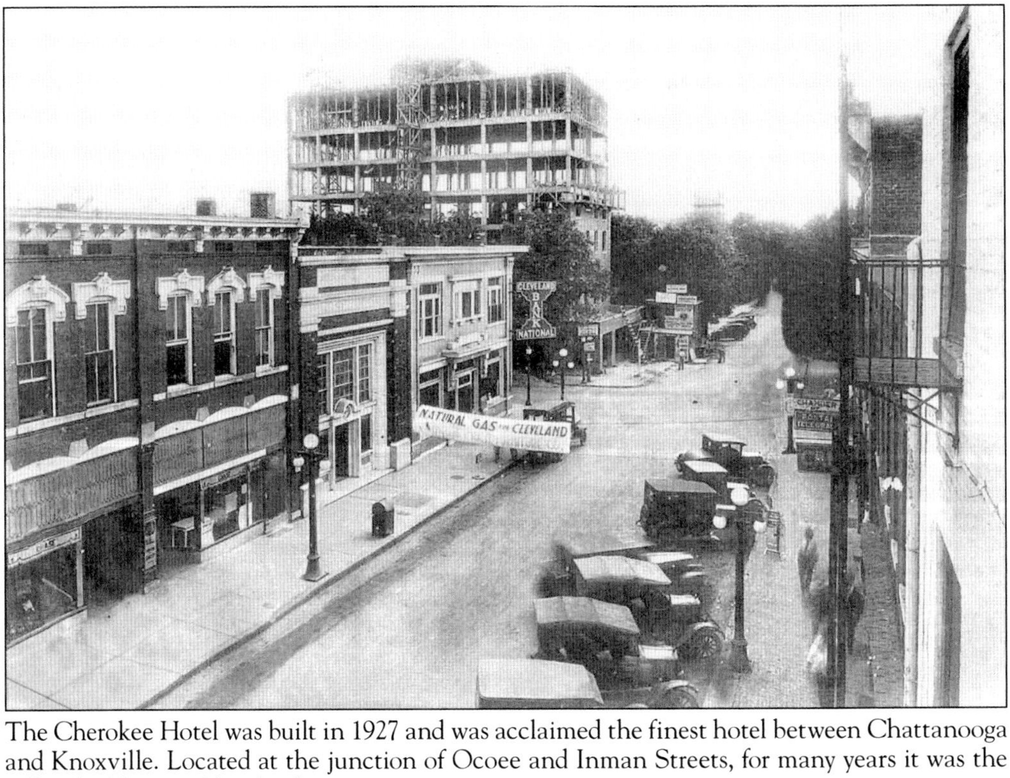

The Cherokee Hotel was built in 1927 and was acclaimed the finest hotel between Chattanooga and Knoxville. Located at the junction of Ocoee and Inman Streets, for many years it was the tallest building in Cleveland.

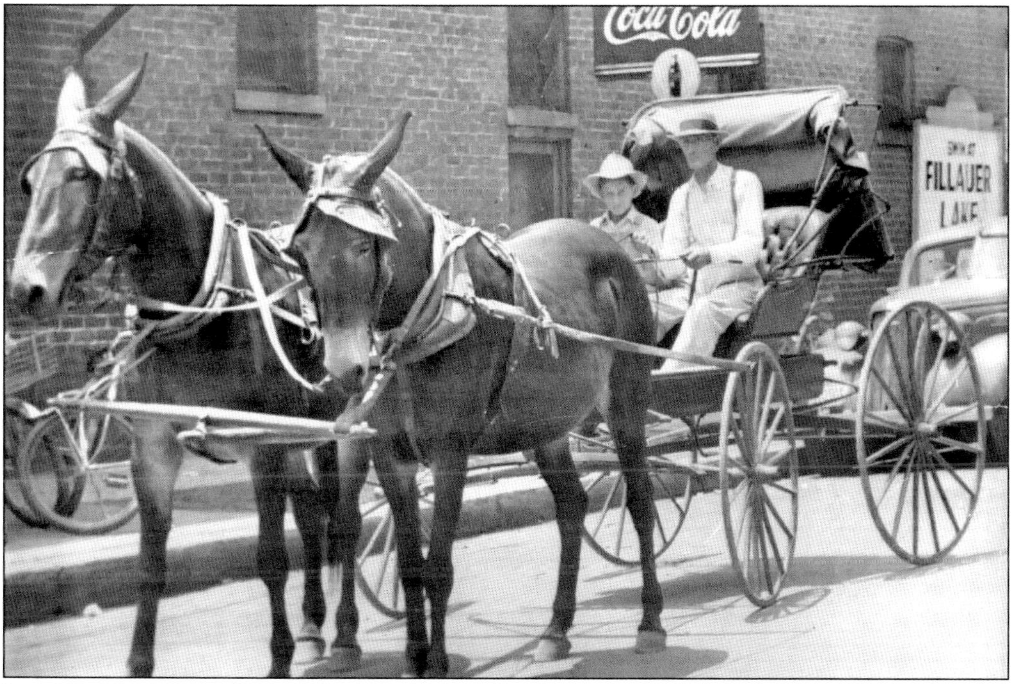

Jess Goins is driving this carriage. Note the sign for Fillauer Lake and the one for Coca-Cola.

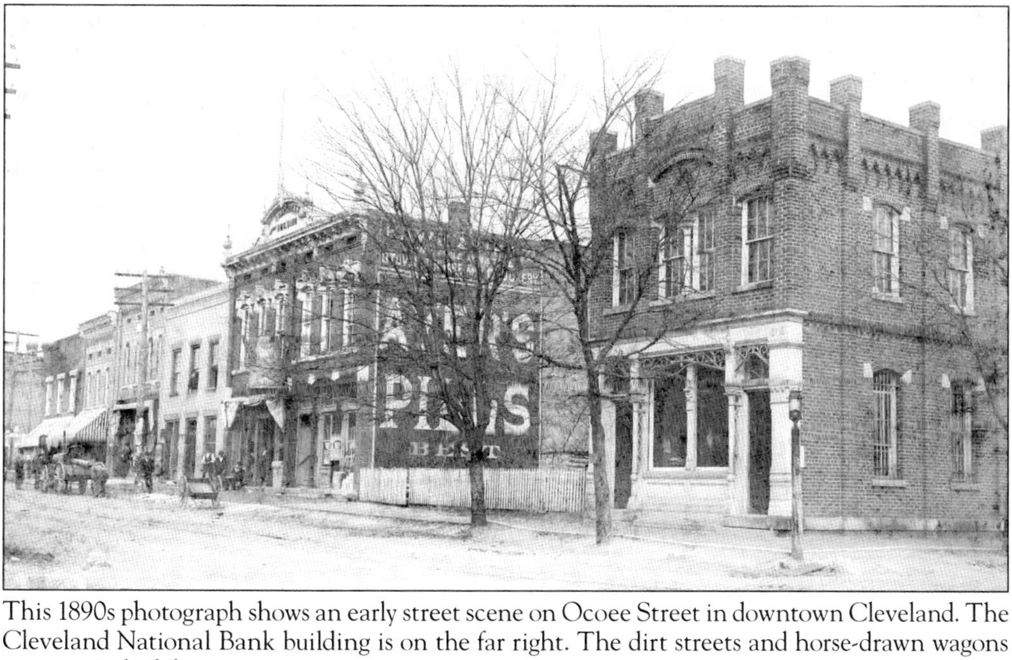

This 1890s photograph shows an early street scene on Ocoee Street in downtown Cleveland. The Cleveland National Bank building is on the far right. The dirt streets and horse-drawn wagons were typical of that era.

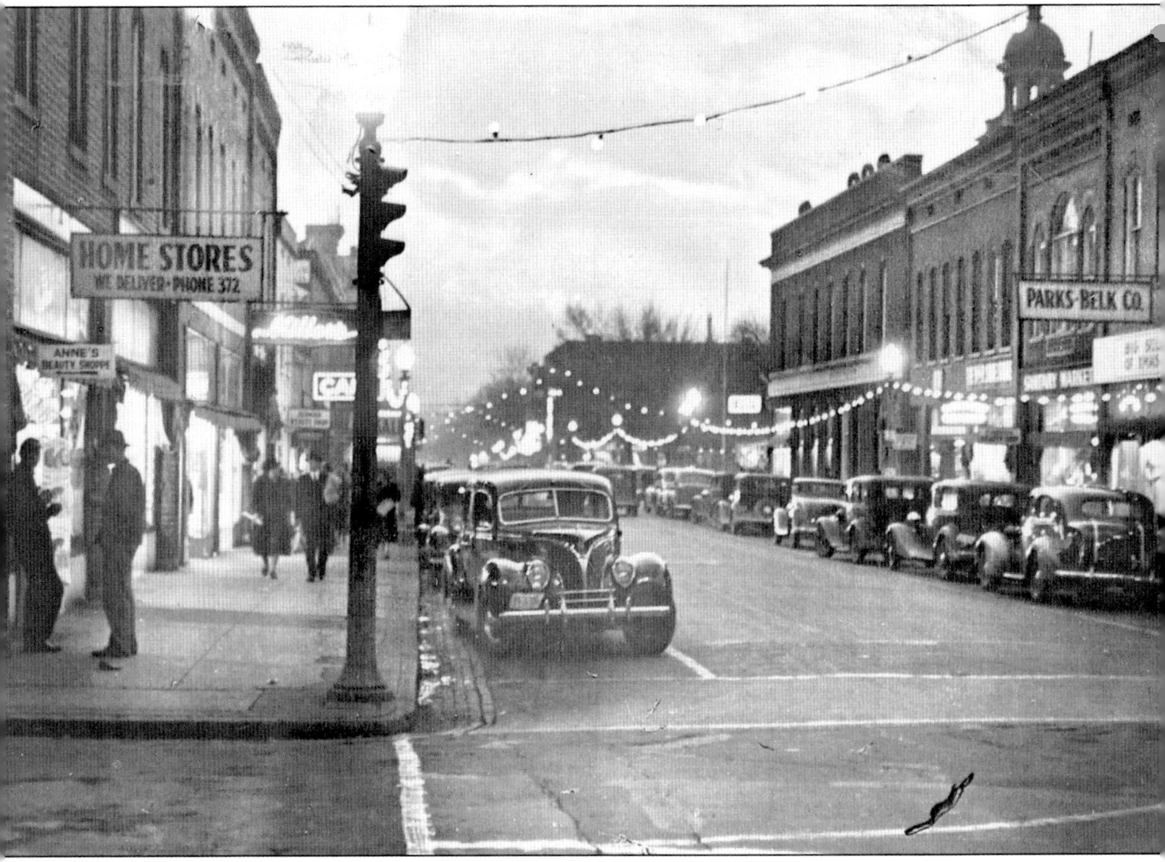

This beautiful scene is of the Christmas lights on Ocoee Street about 1940. The courthouse is seen in the distance. Businesses located on this part of Ocoee were Home Stores, Miller's, Sanitary Market, Parks-Belk Company, and Annie's Beauty Shop.

The Cleveland Bank and Trust Company was located on Ocoee Street next to the Cleveland National Bank. J. E. Johnston was president of both institutions. In this 1922 photograph are, from left to right, William Jackson McReynolds, J. E. Johnston, Sally Hoskins, and Pryor Newman.

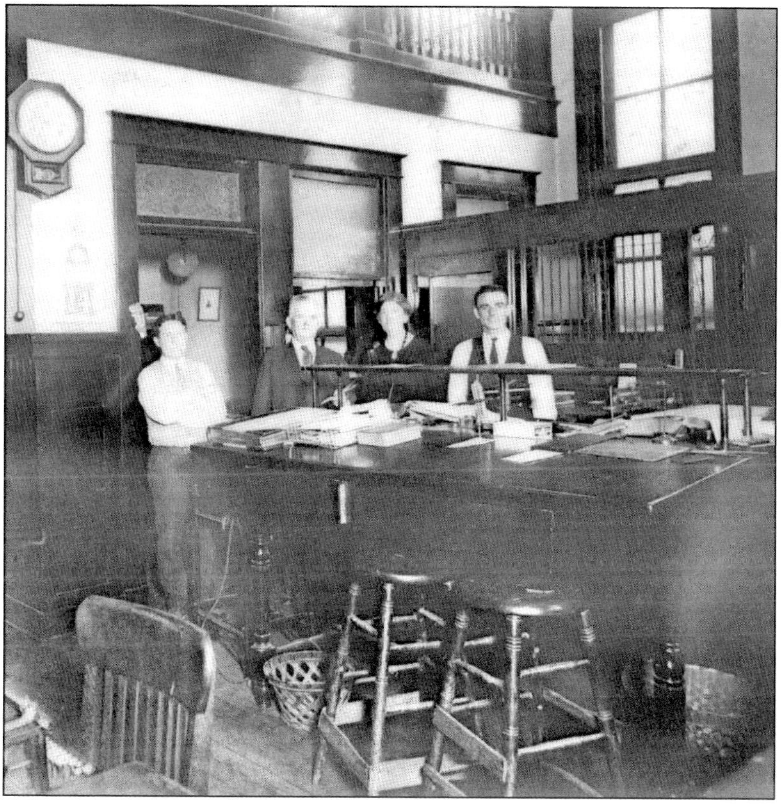

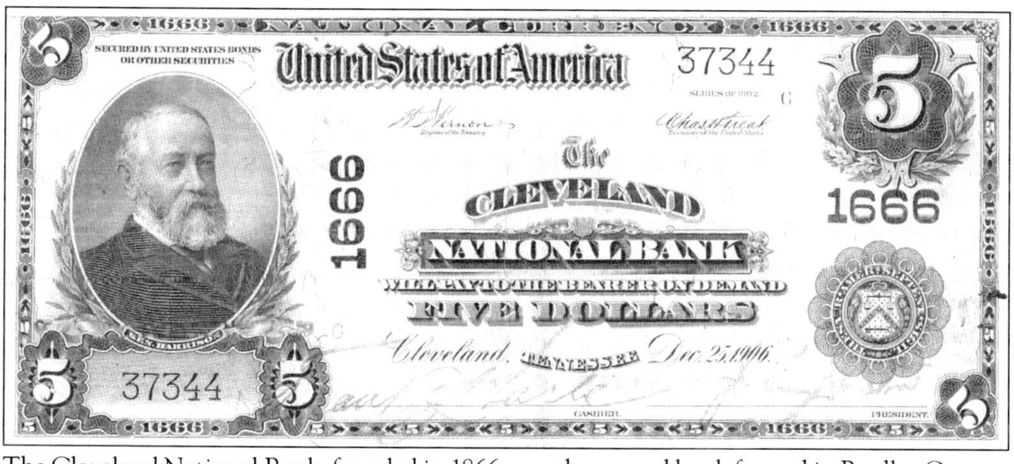

The Cleveland National Bank, founded in 1866, was the second bank formed in Bradley County. It was the only national bank in the county, charter number 1666. This $5 note issued by the Cleveland National Bank on December 25, 1906, was signed by Frank J. Harle, cashier, and J. E. Johnston, president.

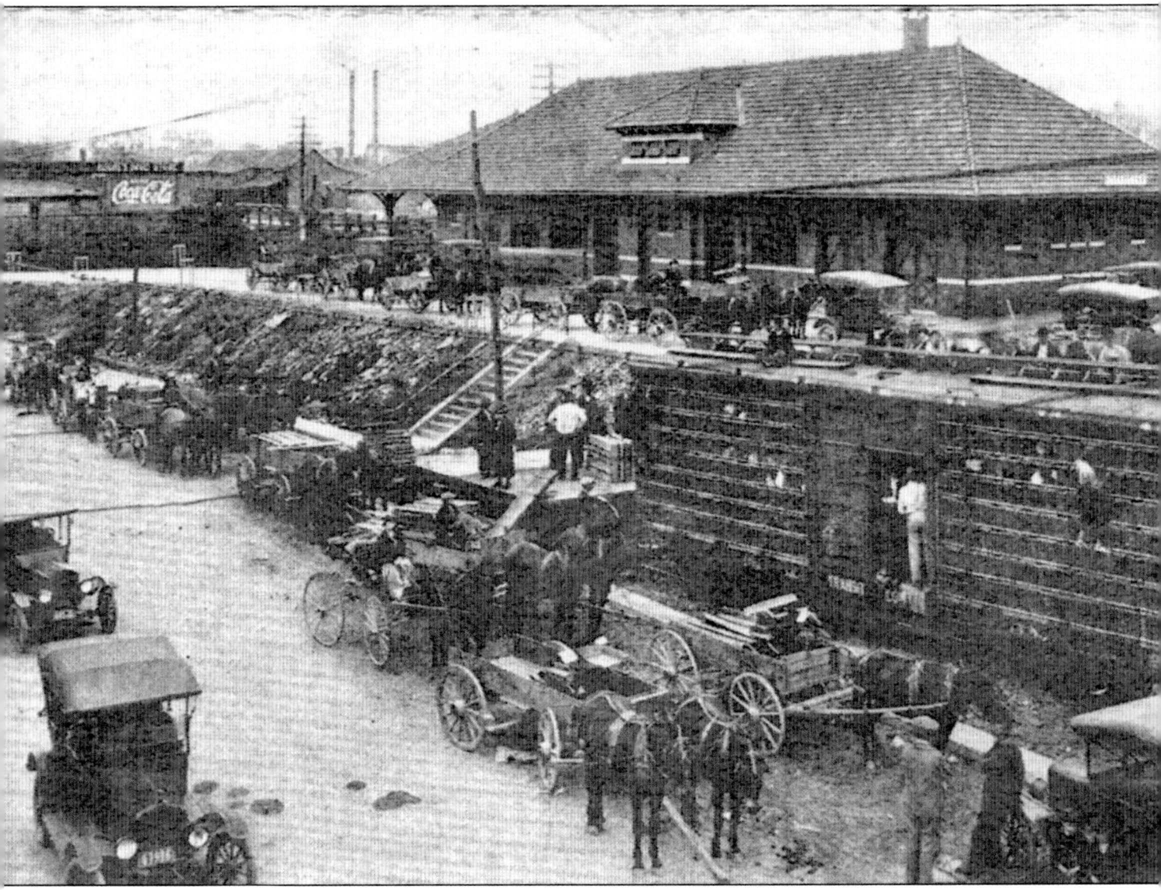

The railroad depot at Cleveland was a busy place in the early 1900s. Notice the horse-drawn wagons as well as automobiles. The chickens and produce were loaded directly from the rail car to the wagons.

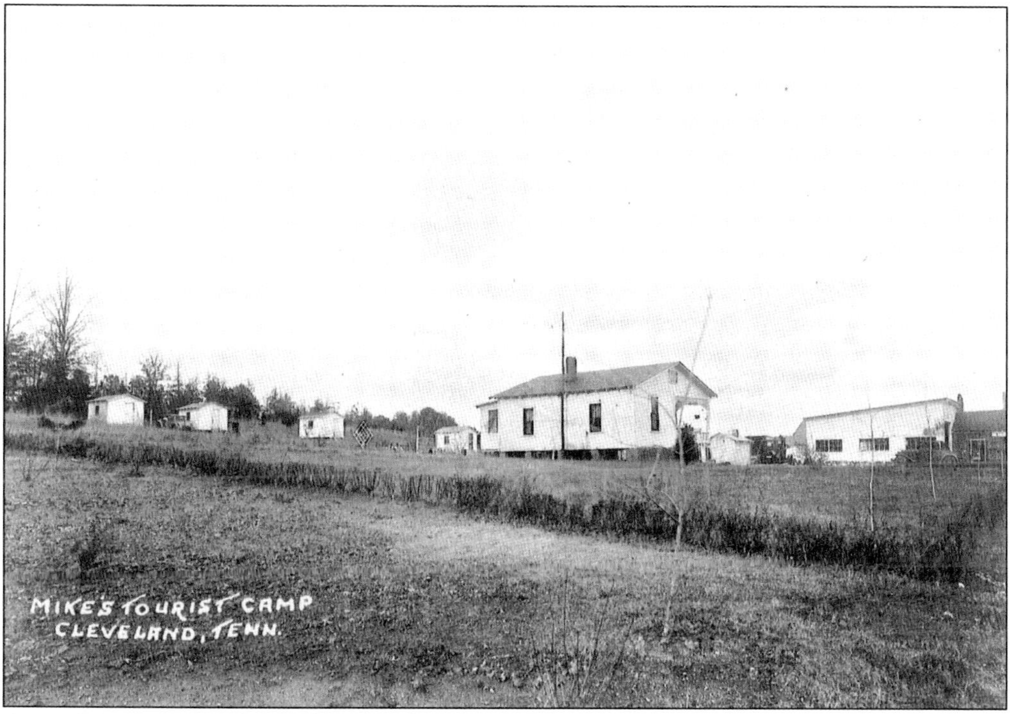

An early tourist camp located on South Lee Highway is shown in this 1920s view.

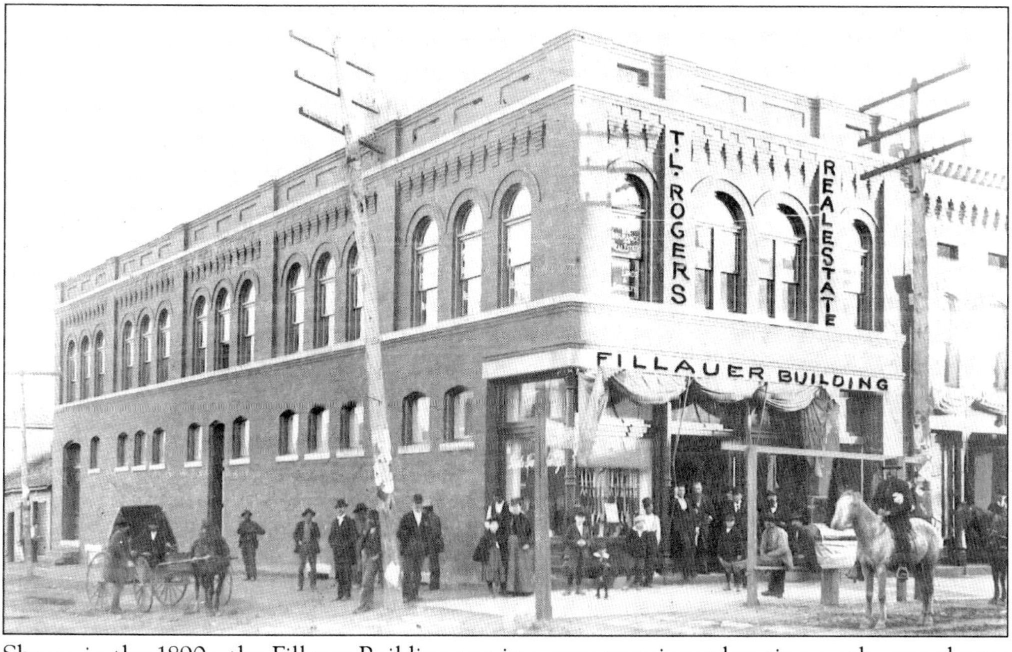

Shown in the 1890s, the Fillauer Building was in a very prominent location on the courthouse square in Cleveland. Notice the dirt streets and the mounted policeman.

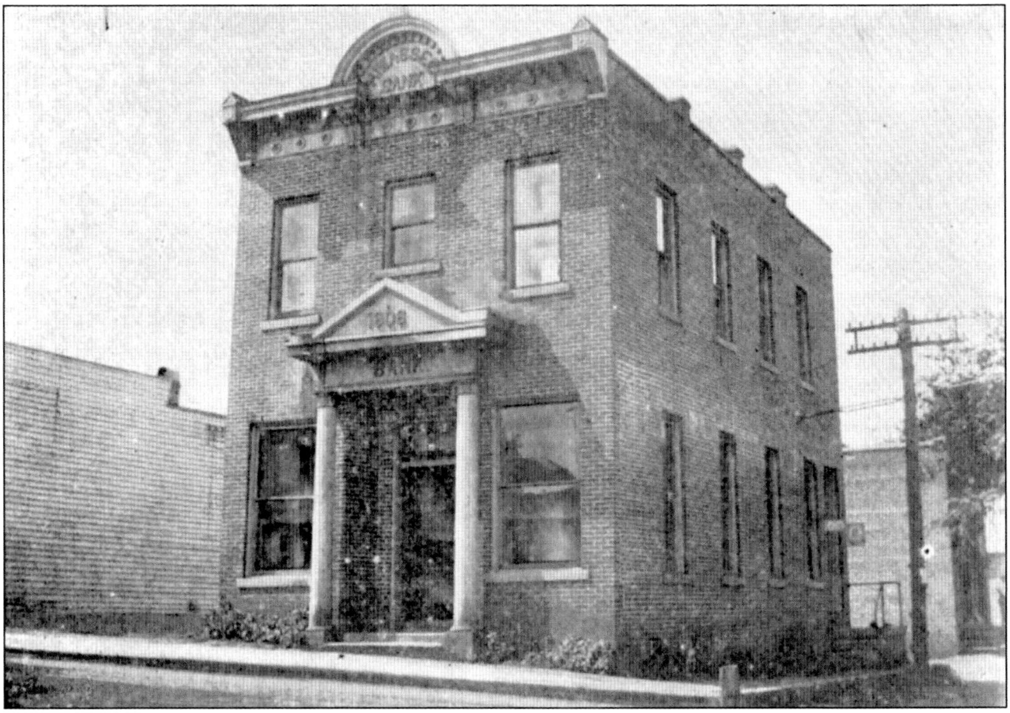

The Hiwassee Bank opened in Charleston in 1907. The president was B. A. Edwards, and the cashier was J. E. Quisenberry. The bank survived the Depression but was later purchased by the Cleveland National Bank in 1954.

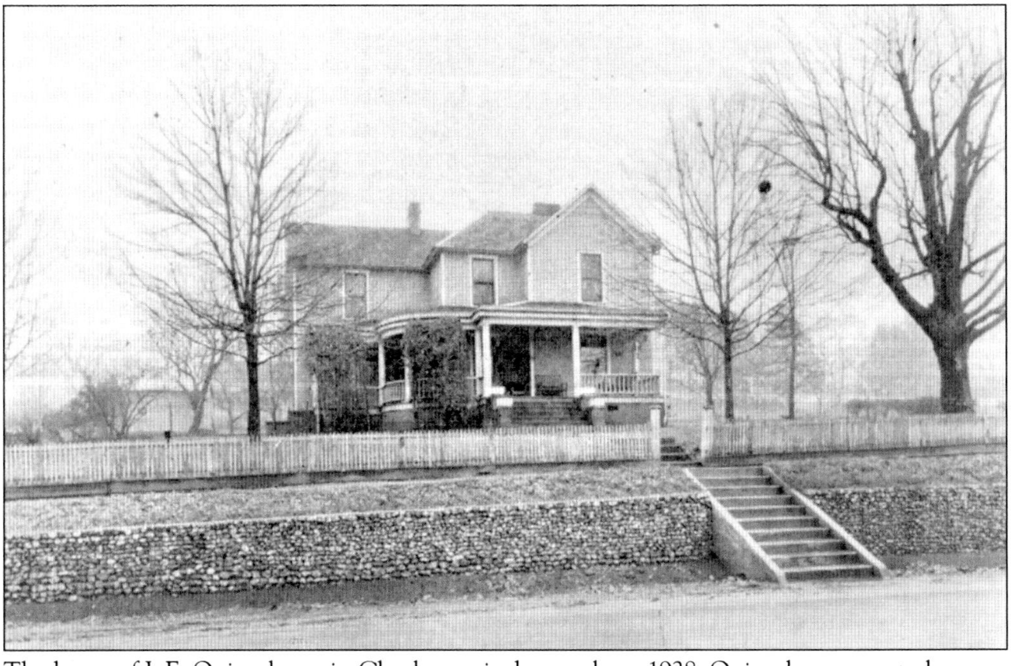

The home of J. E. Quisenberry in Charleston is shown about 1928. Quisenberry rose to become president of the Hiwassee Bank. He was known by adults for his sound bank practices and by young boys and girls for his candy treats when they added money to their savings accounts.

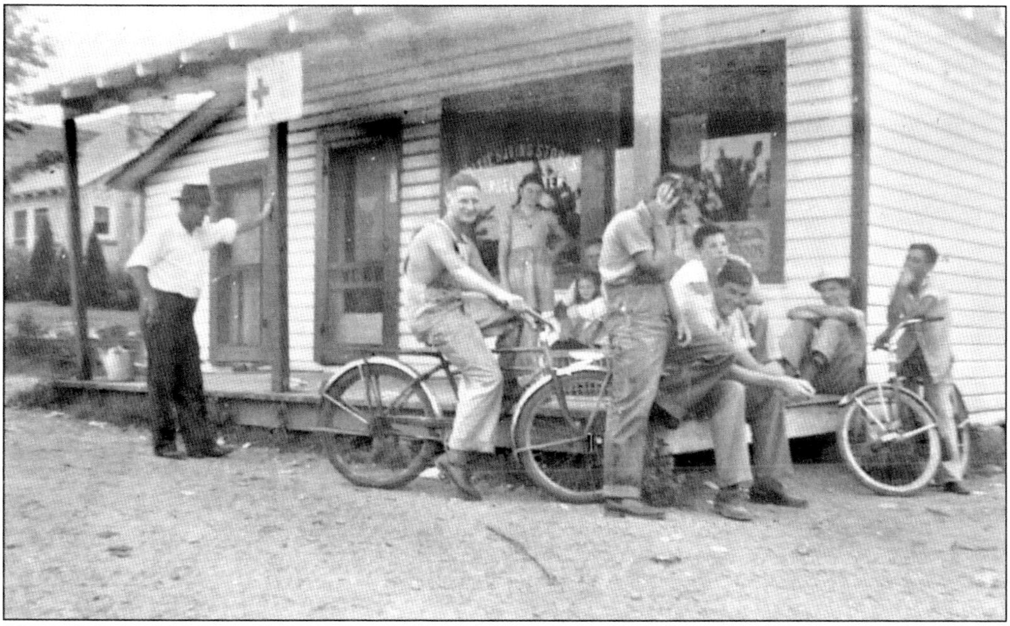

This photograph was taken in front of Virgil Parker's store in McDonald in 1943. From left to right are Walter Cordell, Avery Rainey, Billy Parker, "Spike" Olinger, "Possom" Brock, Ernest Carson, Gail Carson, Mona Dean Parker, Cherry Thomas, and George Rector.

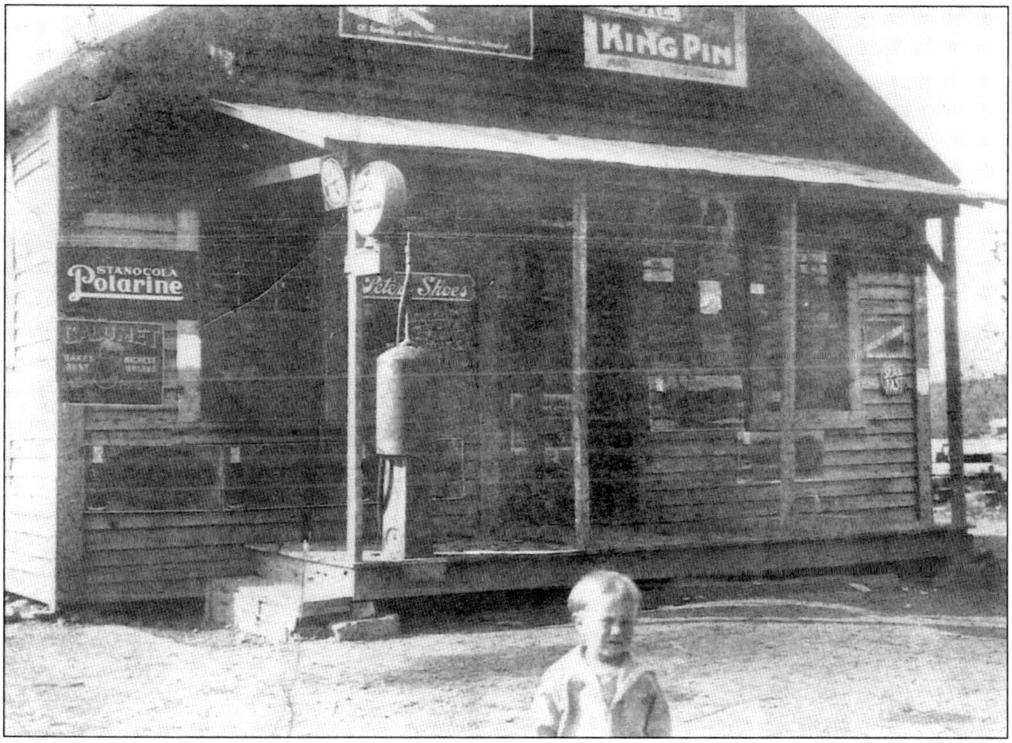

J. M. Cooke opened his first grocery store on Lead Mine Road. His son, Carl, is shown at age four in front of that store. Later Cooke's Food Store moved to Inman Street, the courthouse square, and Broad Street, and it currently has two locations, Keith Street and Springplace Road.

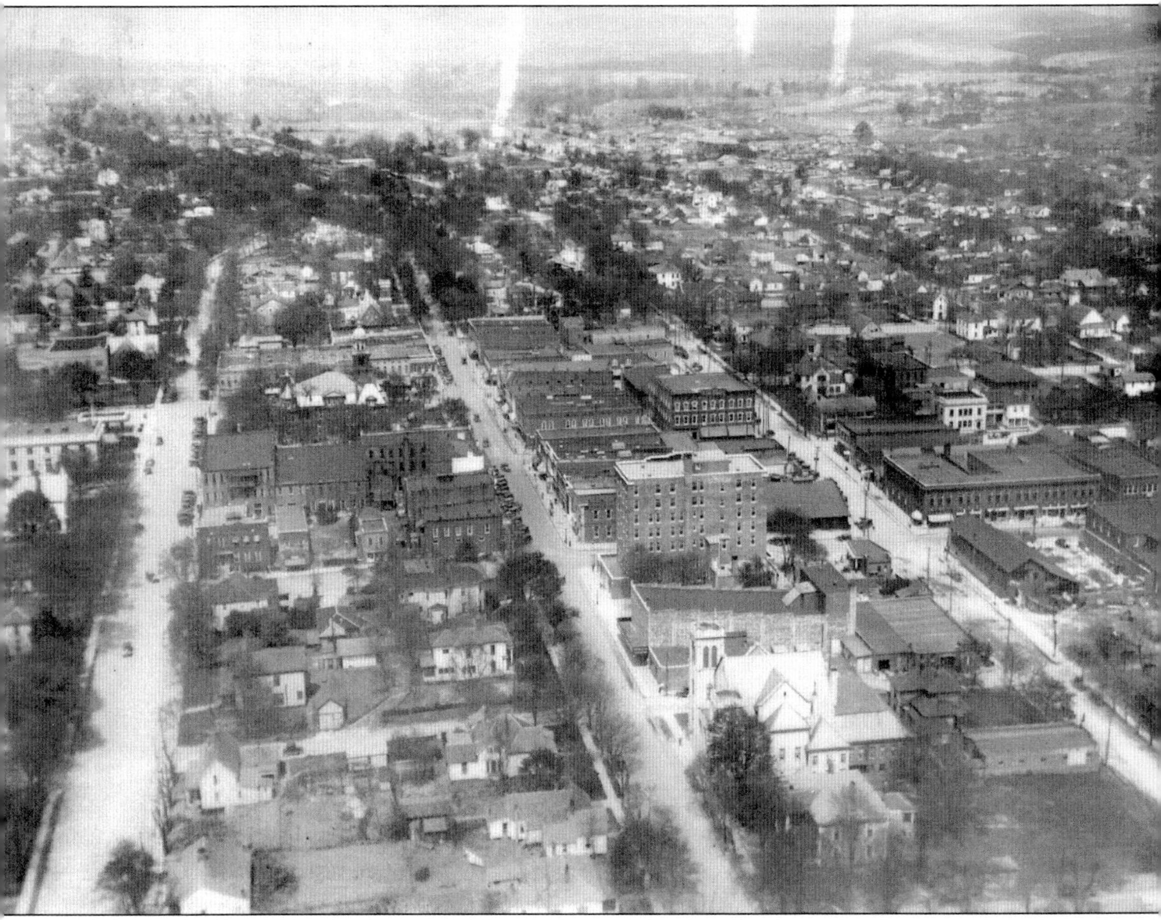

This photograph shows an airplane view of Cleveland in June 1928. In the center, notice the number of houses where Johnston Park is now located.

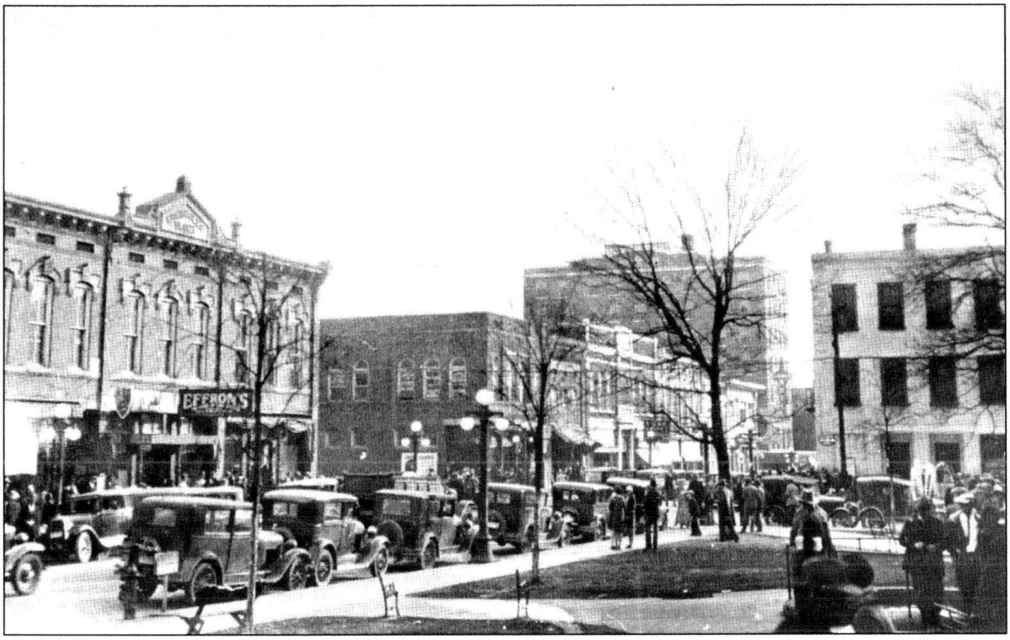

The east view from the courthouse shows the Cherokee Hotel in the distance and the Masonic Hall in the middle of the block. The building on the far right is the Ocoee House, a 19th-century hostelry.

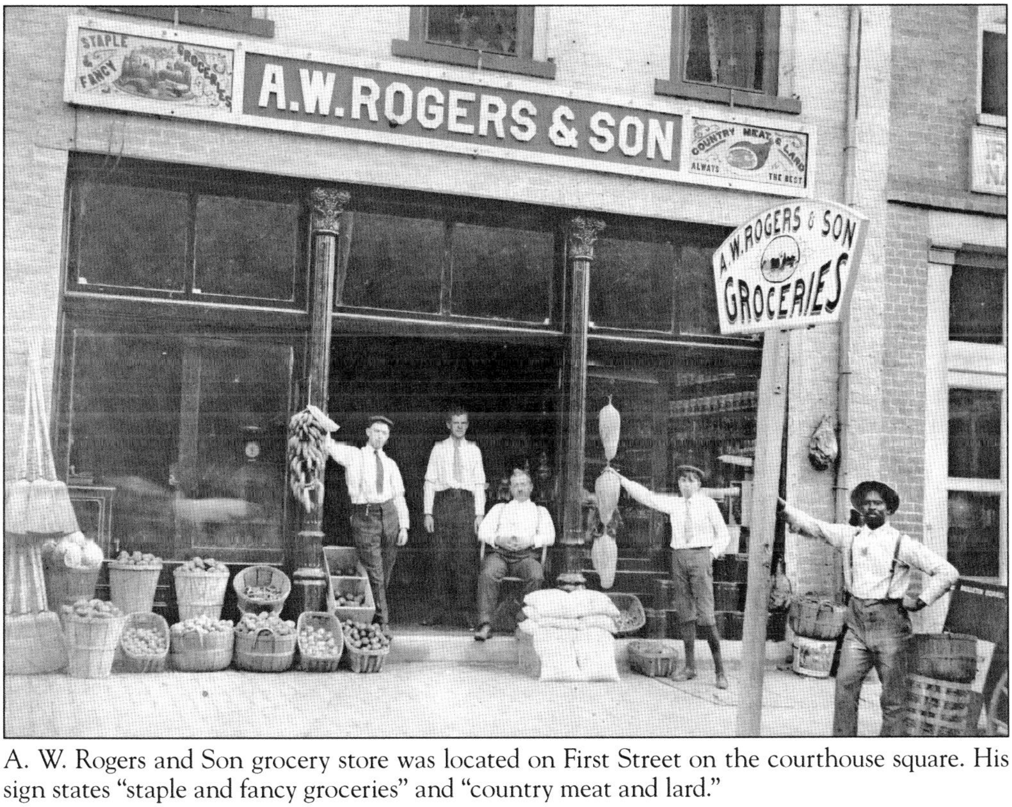

A. W. Rogers and Son grocery store was located on First Street on the courthouse square. His sign states "staple and fancy groceries" and "country meat and lard."

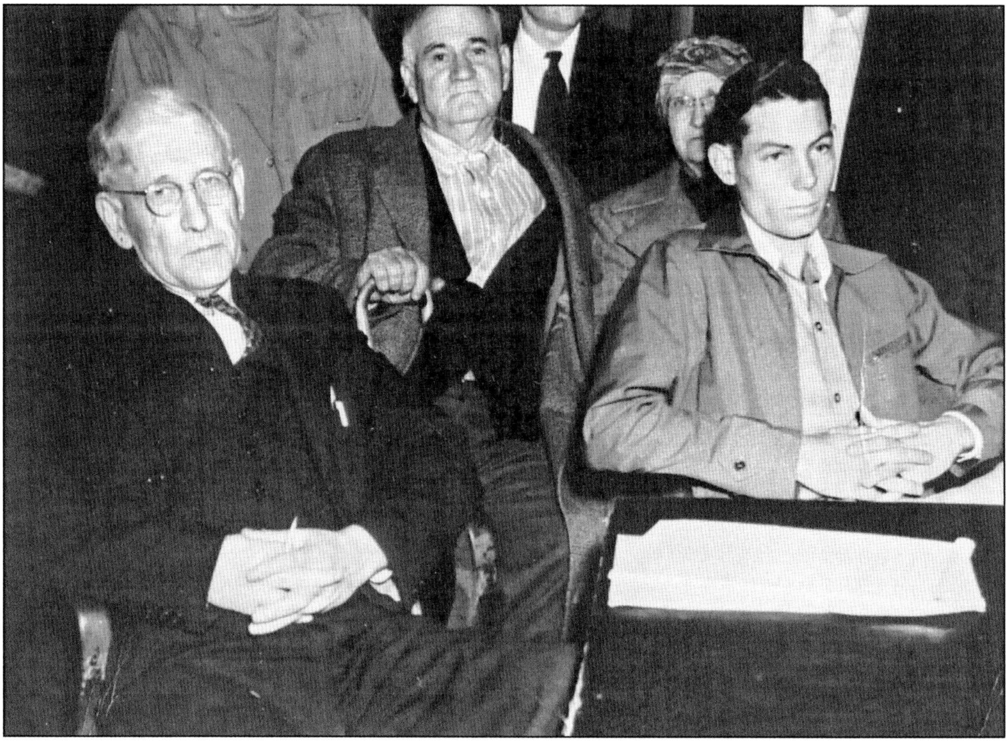

George E. Westerberg (left), later a distinguished judge, defended many clients in his legal career, as shown in this 1951 trial.

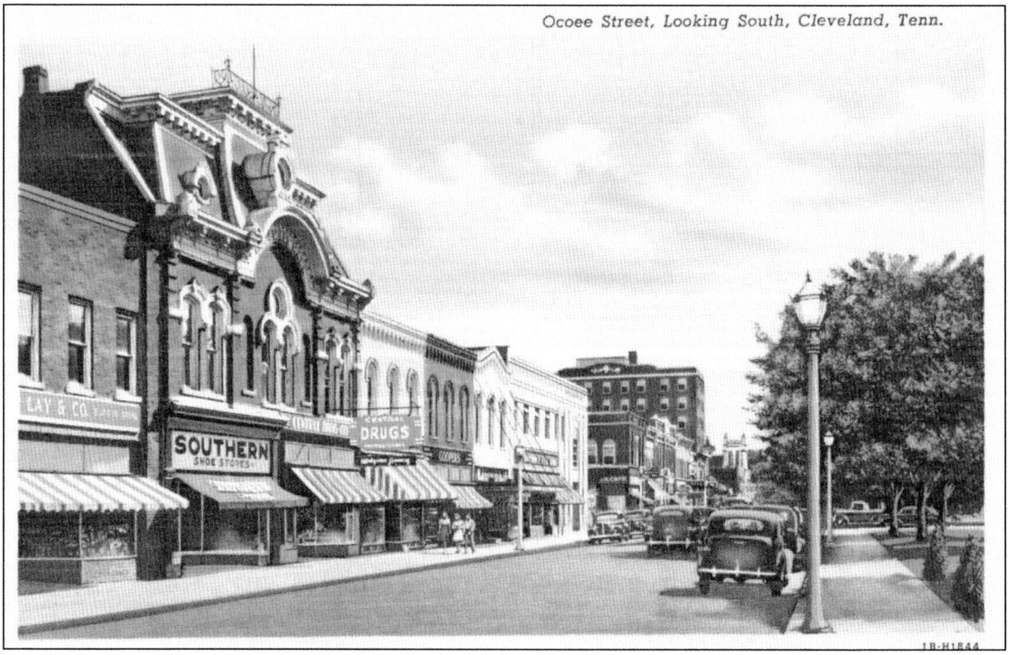

In the 1940s, Ocoee Street was the "main street" of Cleveland. Businesses shown are Lay and Company, Southern Shoe Stores, Central Drug Store, and Cooper's Book Store.

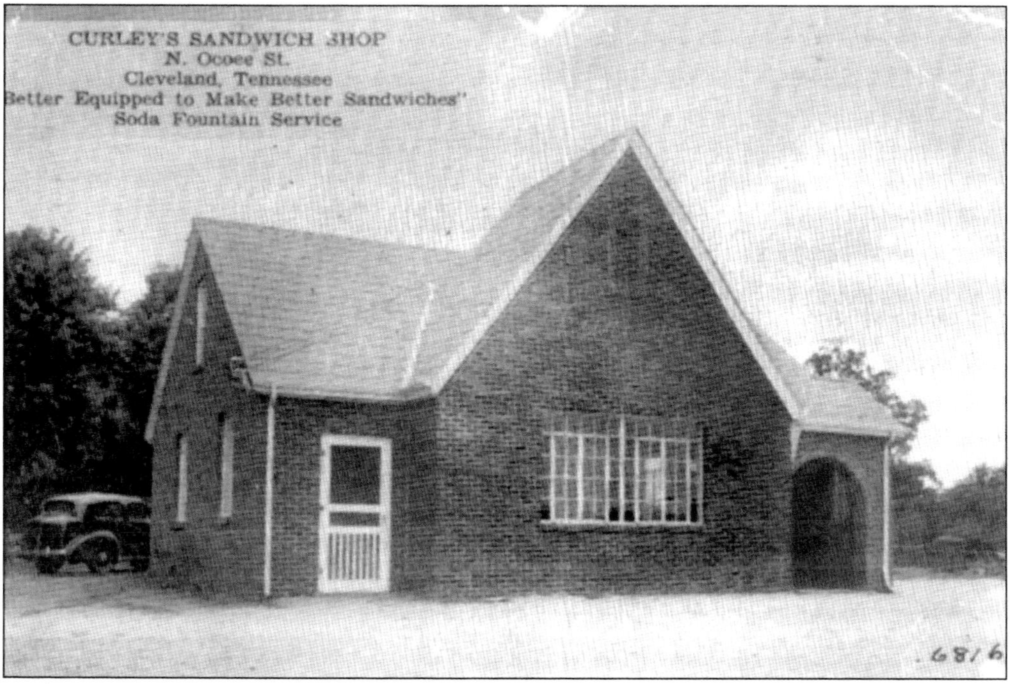

Curley's Sandwich Shop was built on North Ocoee Street about 1935. It was a popular hangout for students. The building later was used as a fire hall for many years, then a retail store, the Accent Mark. The building, at the corner of Ocoee and Twenty-fifth Streets, no longer exists.

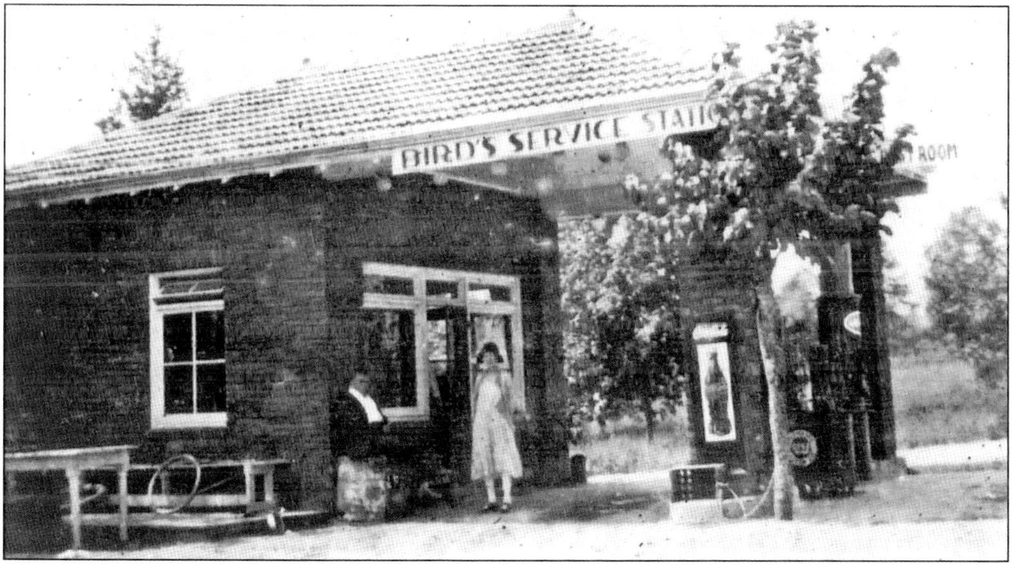

This photograph from the 1920s shows Bird's Service Station, which was located on South Lee Highway.

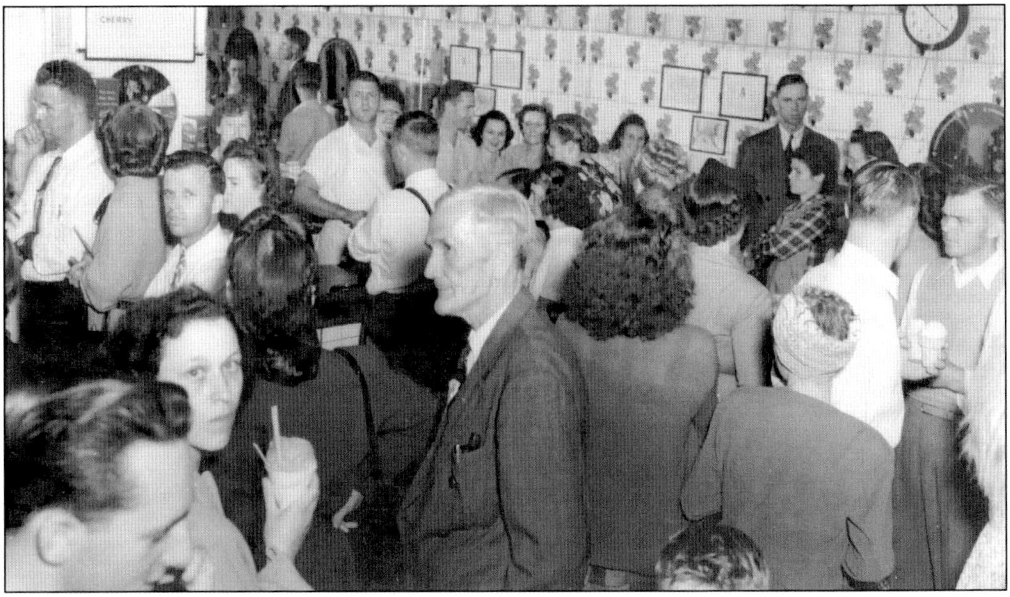

Dooley's Ice Cream Bar was owned by Bill and Beulah O'Neal Dooley. Located on Central Avenue, the ice cream parlor is a favorite memory of many Clevelanders. During the annual Church of God of Prophecy Assembly, delegates from all over the United States and other countries would enjoy Dooley's homemade ice cream. Shown around 1936 are delegates being served ice cream and snowballs by Billy (white shirt), Evelyn (dark hair), and Beulah (glasses) Dooley.

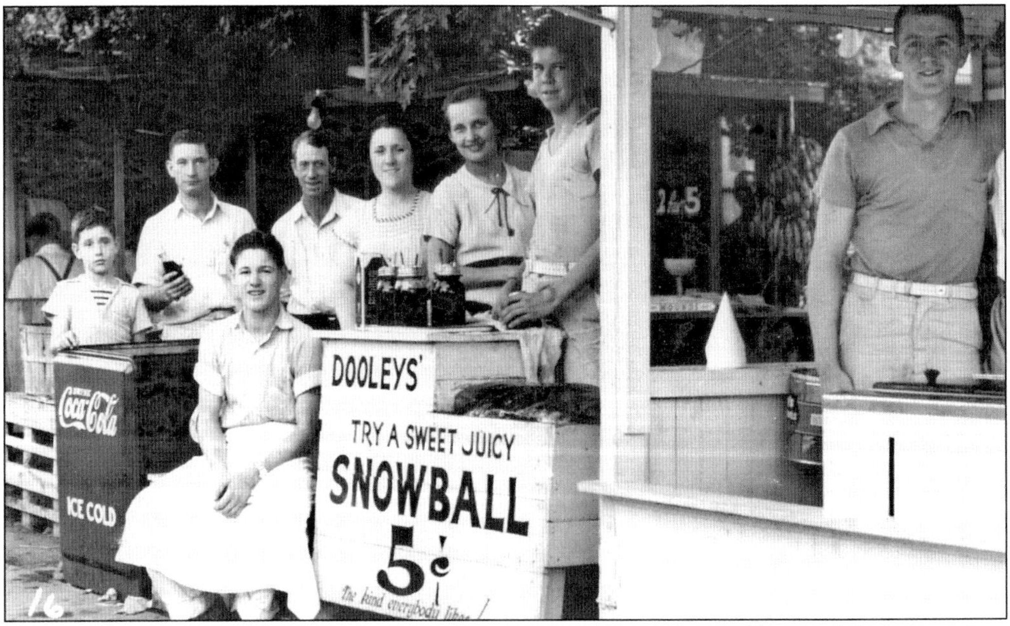

Dooley's also sold ice cream and snowballs from a pony-drawn wagon all around the city and on Saturdays on the courthouse square. Among the drivers were Billy Dooley and Jimmy Cooke. They started the day with 15 gallons of ice cream and usually sold out at 5¢ per three-scoop cone. Dooley had stands selling hot dogs and peanuts also at ballgames. Shown in 1934 are, from left to right, (standing) Bob Riden, Ralph Riden, Luck Logans, Edith O'Neal, Katherine Rose, Fred Elrod, and Billy Dooley; (seated) Knox Riden.

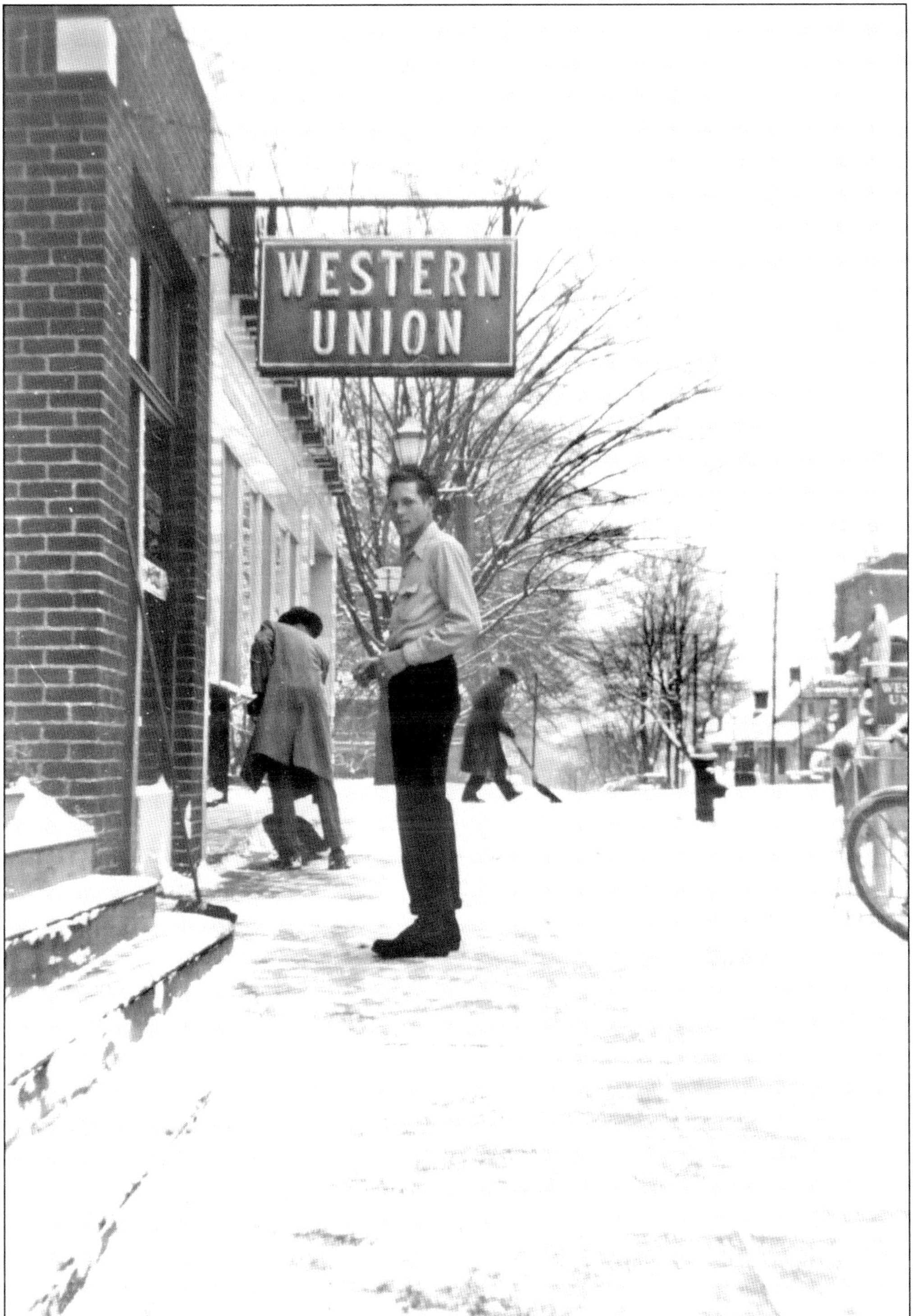

On January 24, 1948, William Bennett was a messenger for Western Union. At that time, the telegram was a speedy means of communication and wiring money.

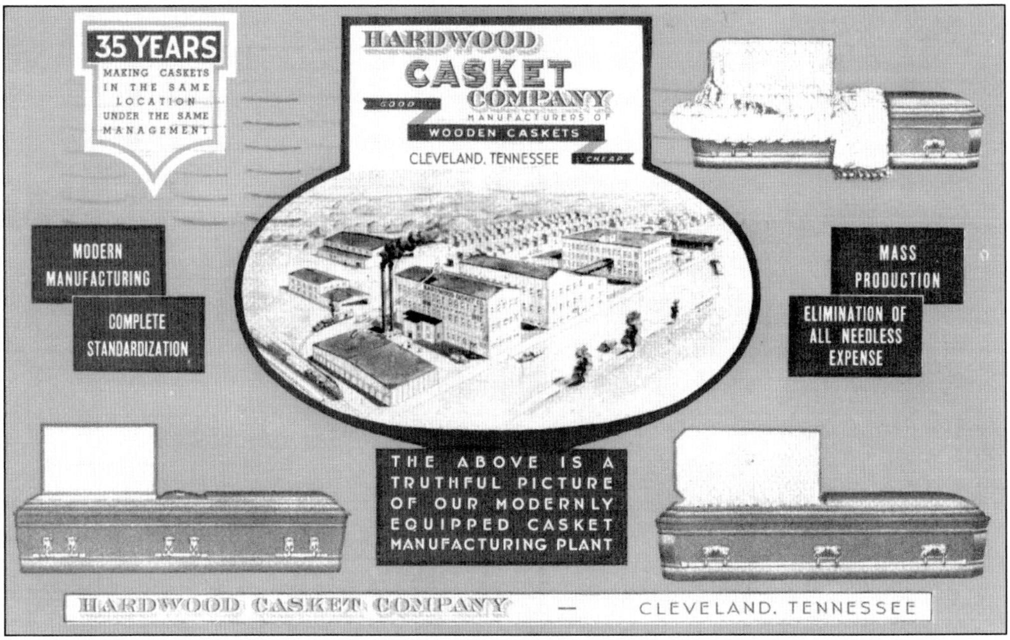

The Hardwood Casket Company was founded in 1901 by R. M. Neil and Charles Itzel. During World War II, it became the largest wood-only casket company in the United States.

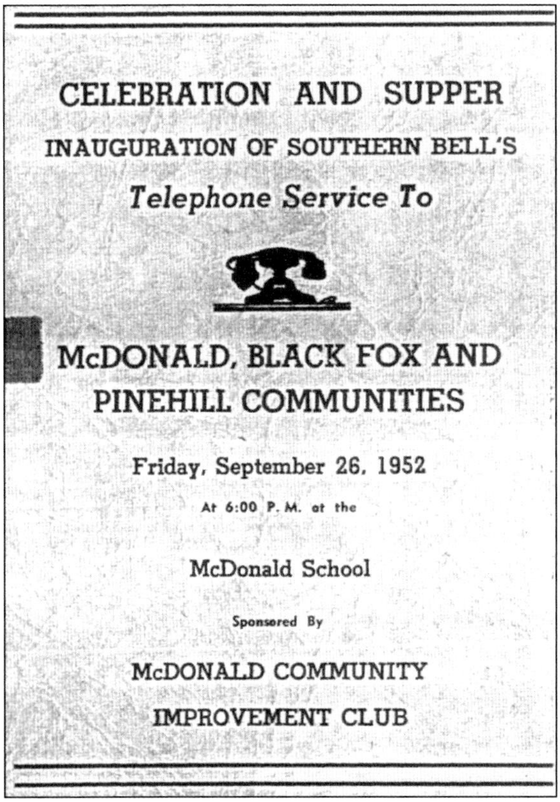

Progress in the form of telephone service came to the communities of McDonald, Black Fox, and Pine Hill in 1952.

Boykin Auto Supply was located at 3205 Ocoee Street, next door to the Hotel Ocoee. They carried Goodrich tires and batteries.

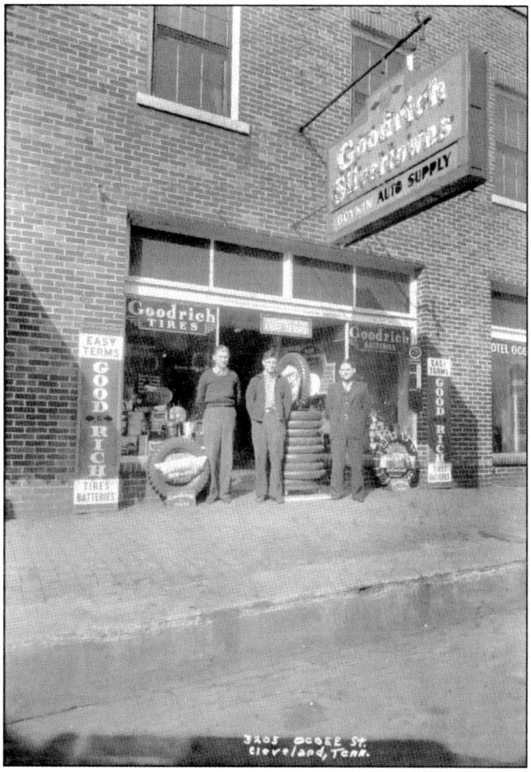

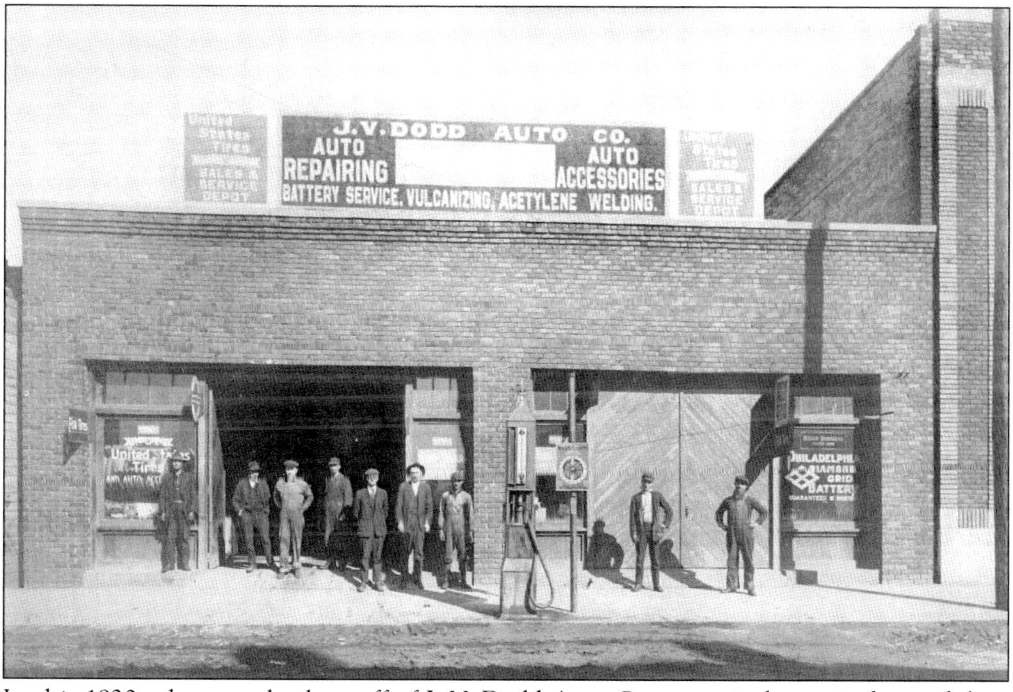

In this 1930s photograph, the staff of J. V. Dodd Auto Company is shown in front of their automobile shop. Dodd carried United States tire and auto accessories, Philadelphia Diamond Grid batteries, as well as the Dodge Brothers Motor Cars.

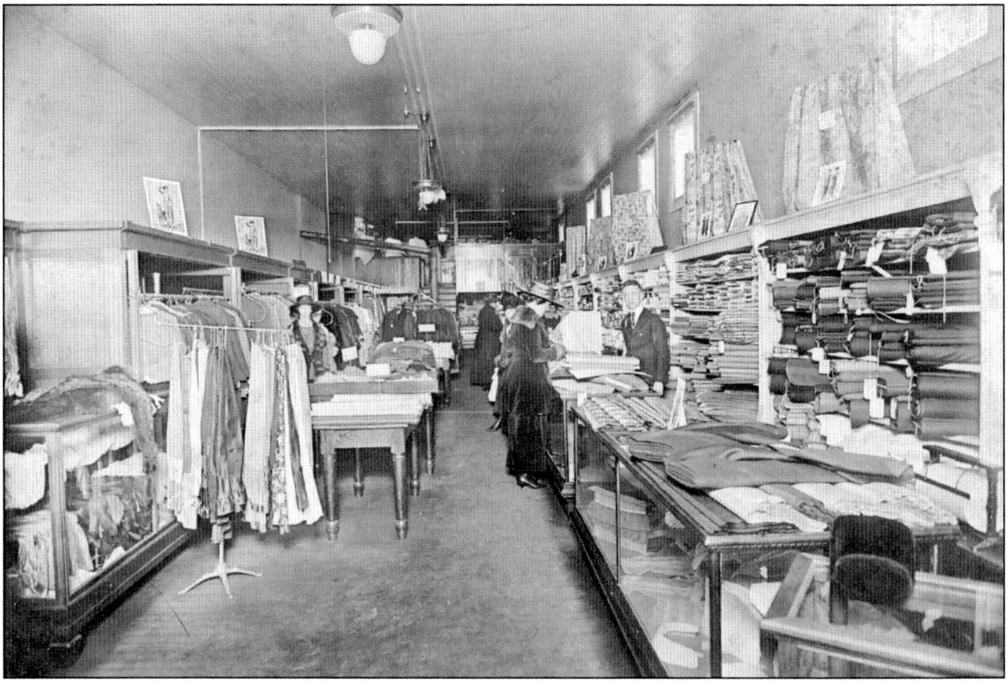

An early dry goods store is shown in this photograph. Merchants stacked their clothing stock in piles on counters for shoppers to examine and make their selections for purchase. Woe to the young boy that got the stacks out of order!

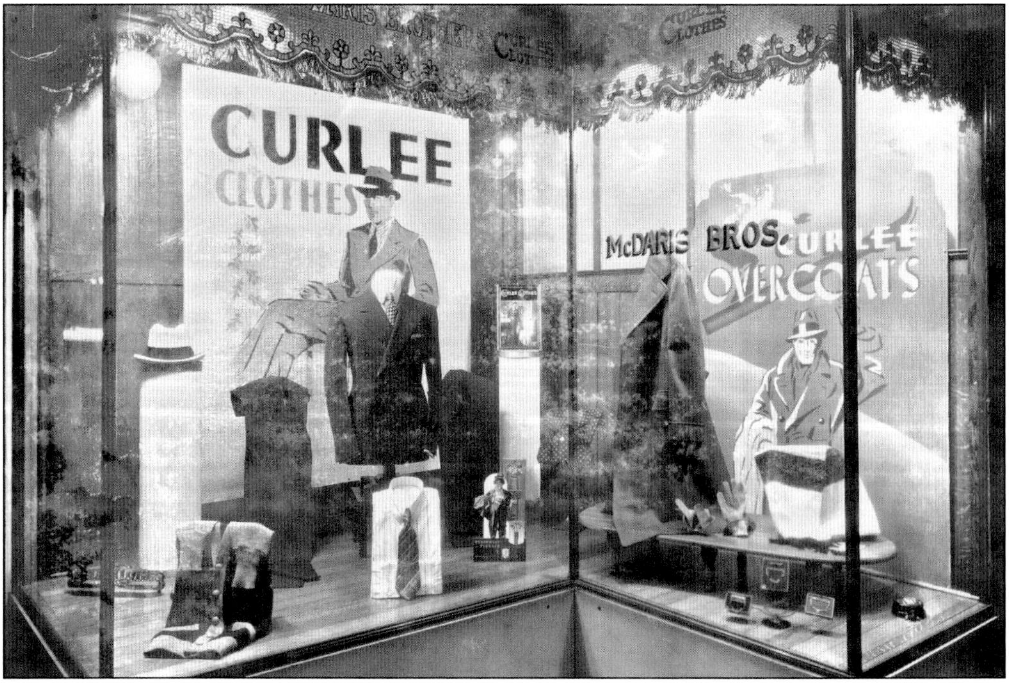

McDaris Brothers Clothiers, shown about 1947, was located on Ocoee Street. It always carried a popular line of men's clothing. Their display windows on the courthouse square were colorful and enticing.

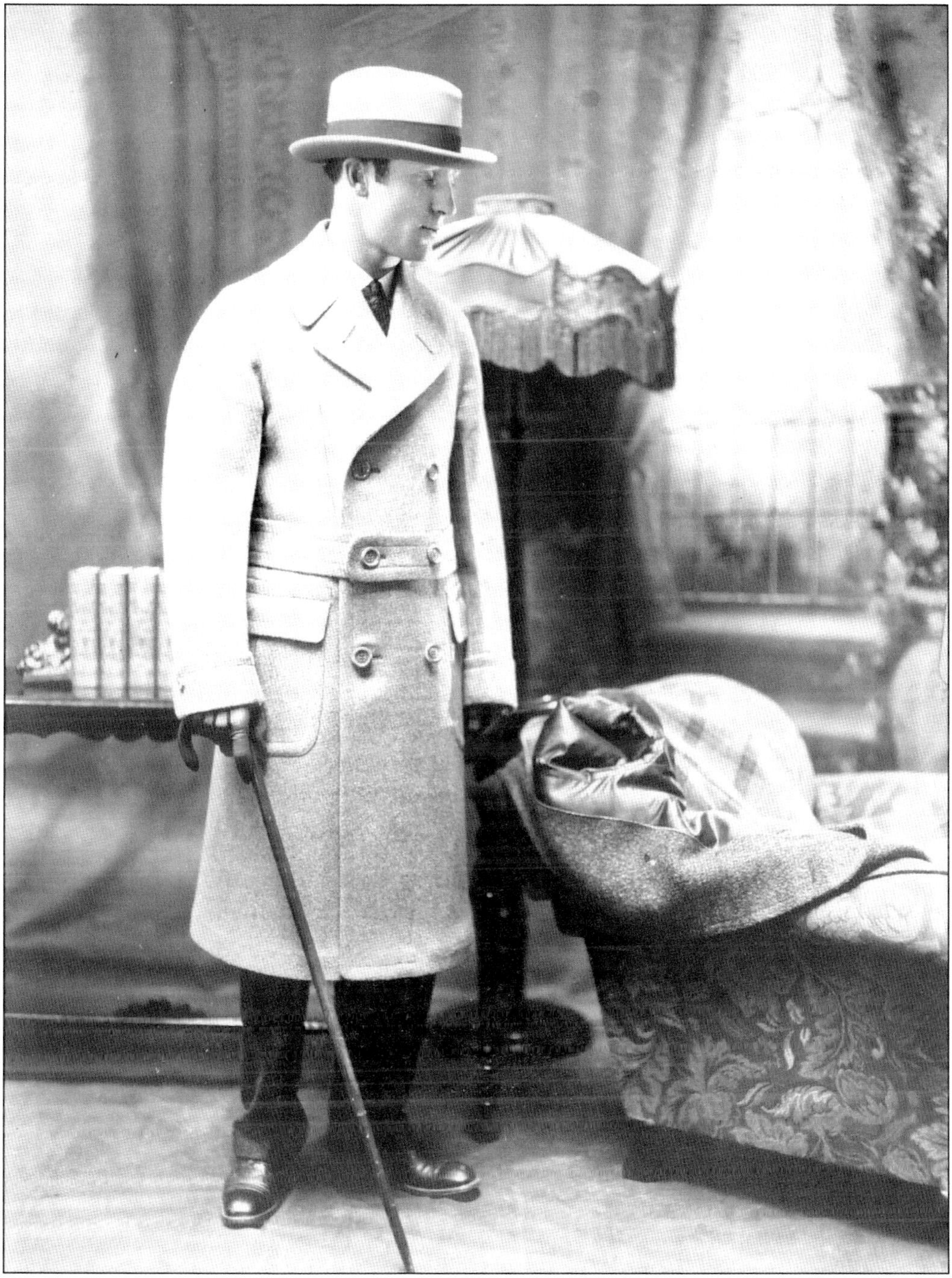

Sharon Tipton is shown modeling a coat for inclusion in a catalog of Hardwick Woolen Mills. Models were photographed so that the pictures could be shown by salesmen to solicit orders from retail stores for clothing to be manufactured by the mill.

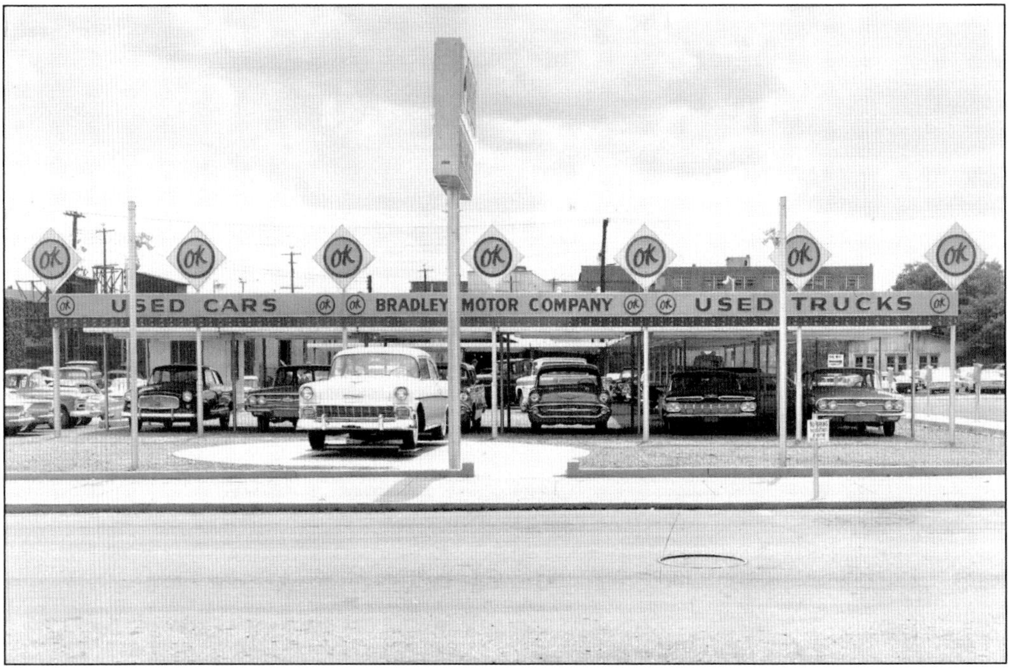

In 1941, Merle A. Hall started Bradley Motor Company, a Chevrolet dealership. It was located at Five Points. The name changed to Hall Chevrolet in 1965, and the dealership later moved to Twenty-fifth Street. The Hall family has been selling Chevrolets in Cleveland for 65 years.

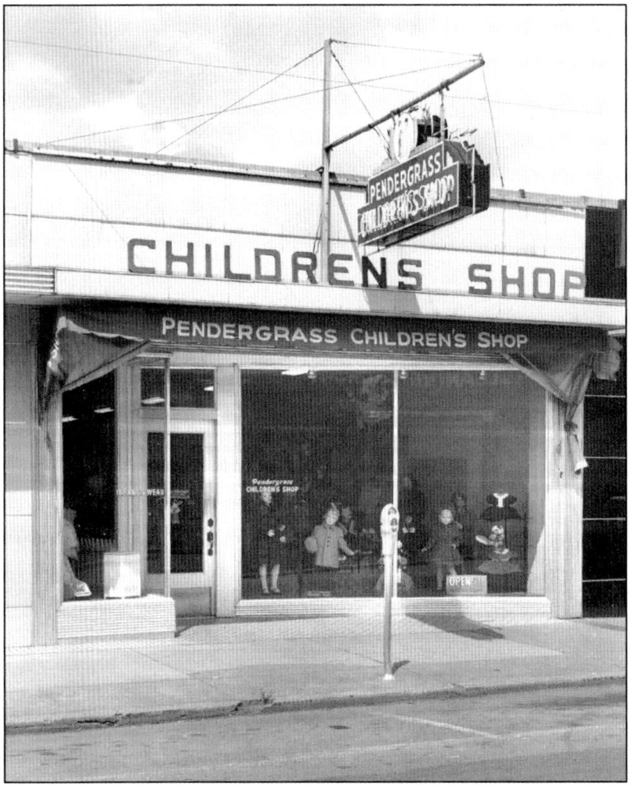

The Pendergrass Children's Shop, located on East Inman Street, was the place for area children to find just the right clothing. It was owned by Roy and Beatrice Pendergrass.

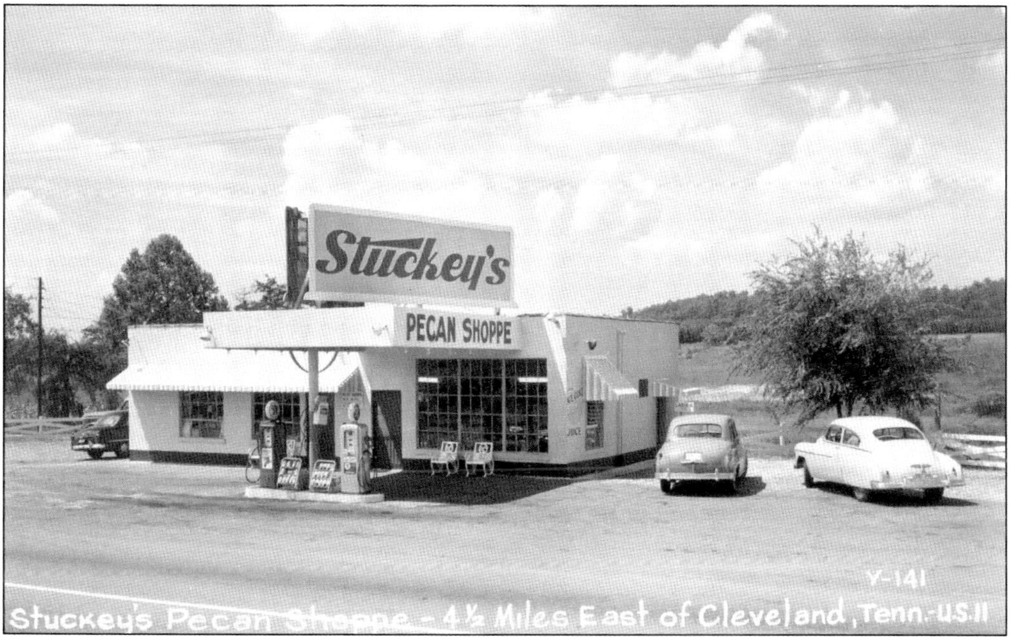

This is a postcard of the Stuckey's Pecan Shoppe located on North Lee Highway near Tasso Lane. Lots of travelers enjoyed stopping here in the 1950s for gas and cooling refreshments.

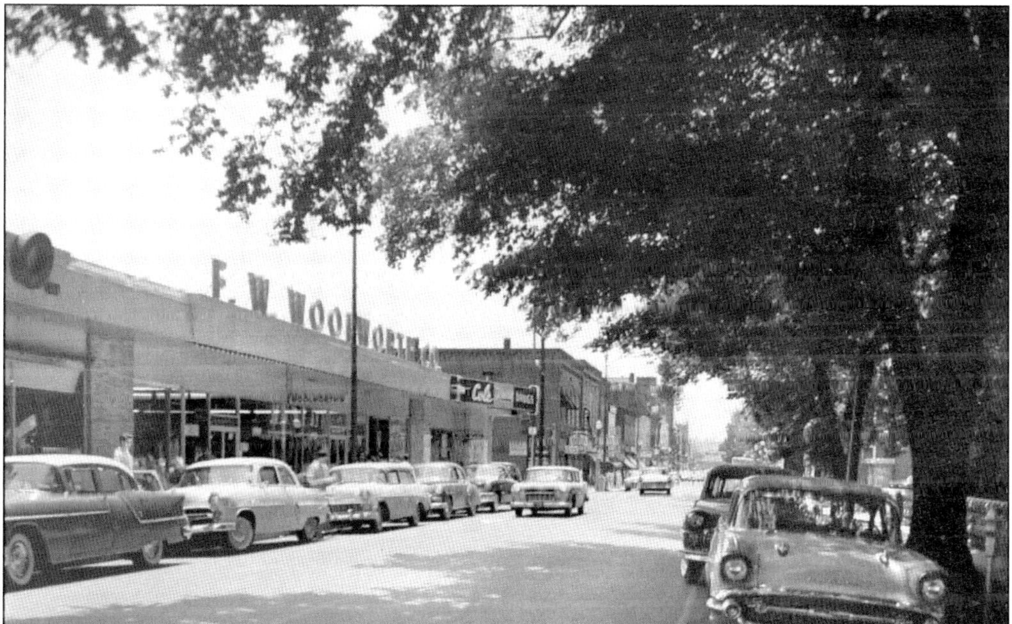

This photograph is of F. W. Woolworth Company in the 1950s. It was located on Ocoee Street across the street from St. Luke's Episcopal Church. Prior to moving to this site, Woolworth's had been on Ocoee Street in the building now occupied by the Odd Fellows Lodge.

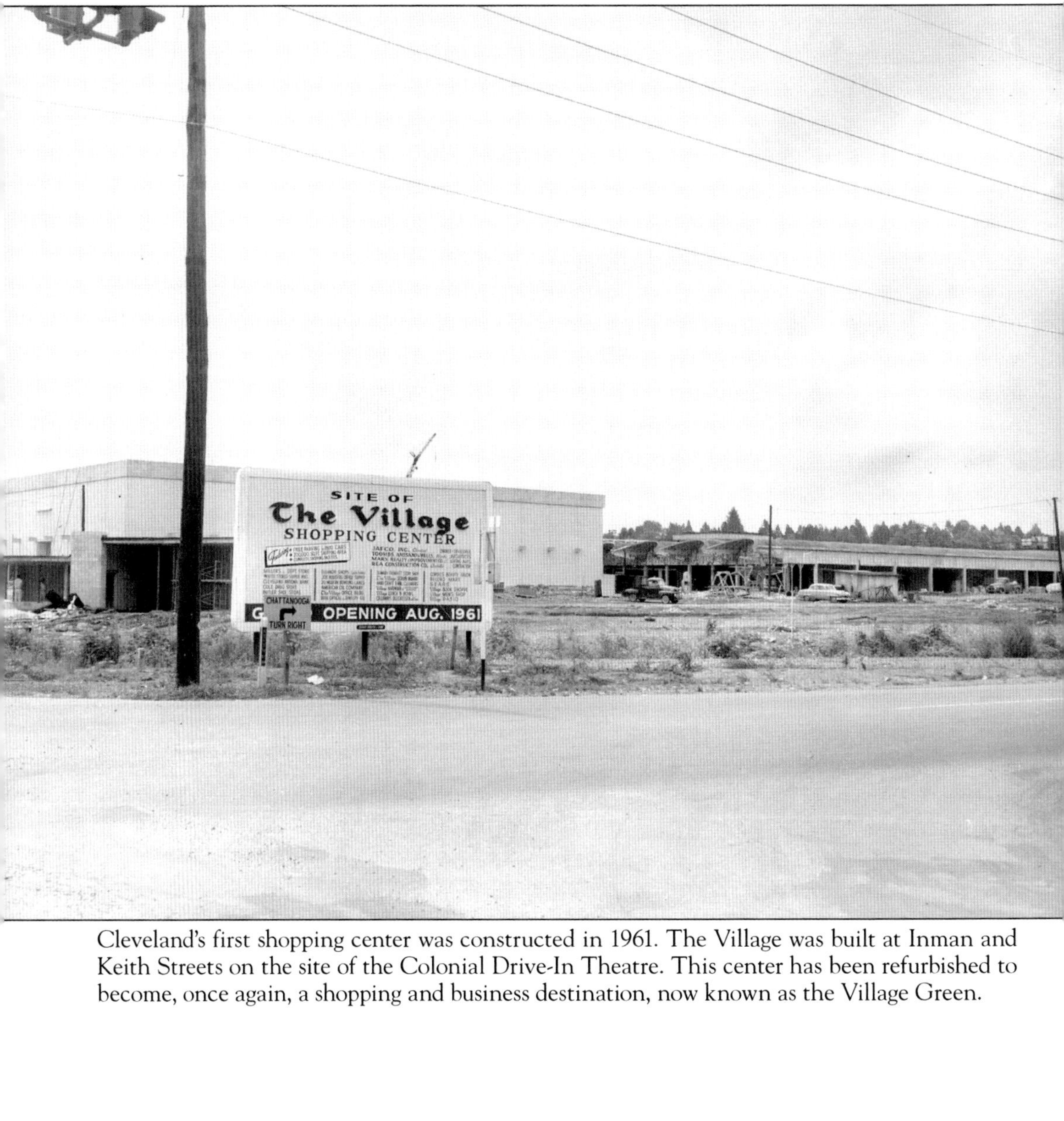

Cleveland's first shopping center was constructed in 1961. The Village was built at Inman and Keith Streets on the site of the Colonial Drive-In Theatre. This center has been refurbished to become, once again, a shopping and business destination, now known as the Village Green.

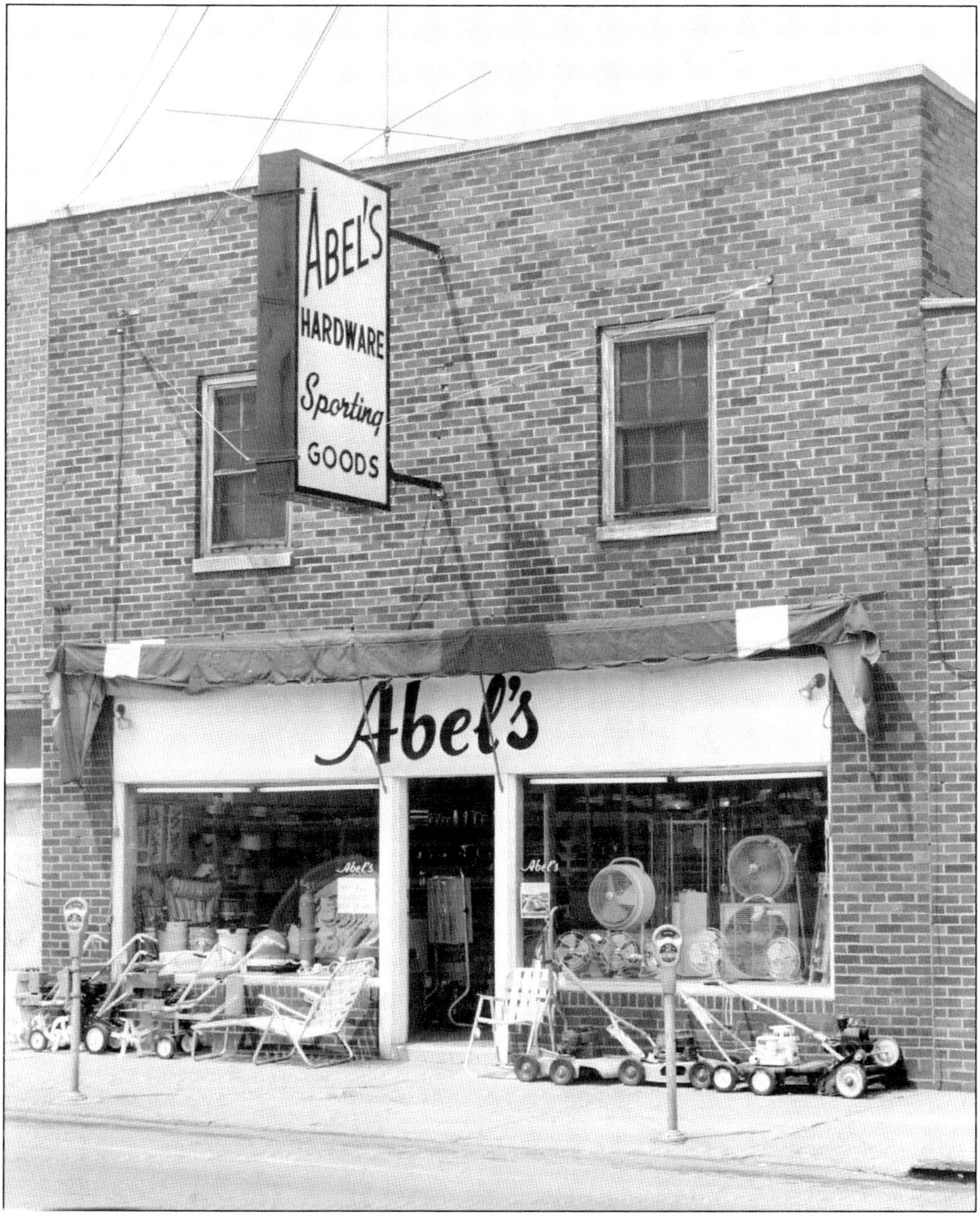

Abel Hardware Company was established in 1916 by Frank H. Abel on Ocoee Street adjacent to Cooper's Book Store and across from the courthouse. Frank Abel was joined in the hardware business by his sons, Paul and Raleigh. In 1922, they purchased the Fillauer Hardware Company and moved to its larger, First Street location, still on the courthouse square. In 1929, they bought J. M. Bennett and Son Hardware. "Abel's On the Square" was the slogan used in the 1960s. Paul Abel died in 1968, and Raleigh Abel died in 1974. The store was closed in December 1974.

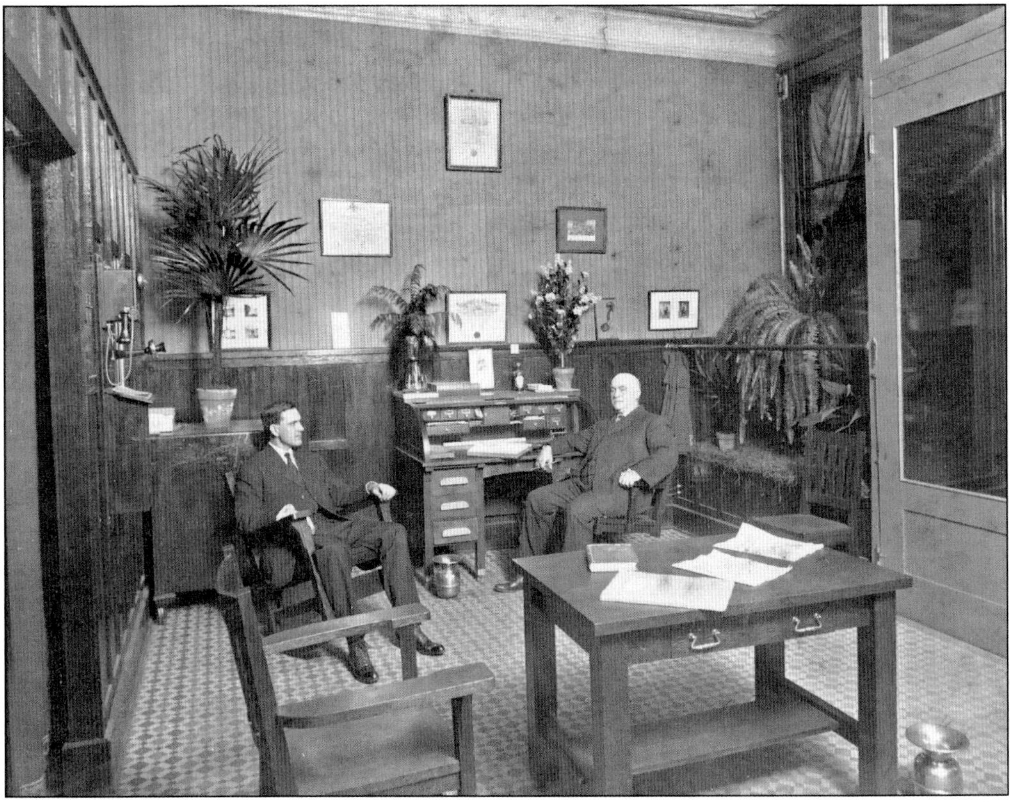

Rogers and Tipton Funeral Home was also a furniture store. Shown here in their office in the 1890s are M. Rogers (left) and Horace S. Tipton. This business was the predecessor of Fike Funeral Home and Furniture.

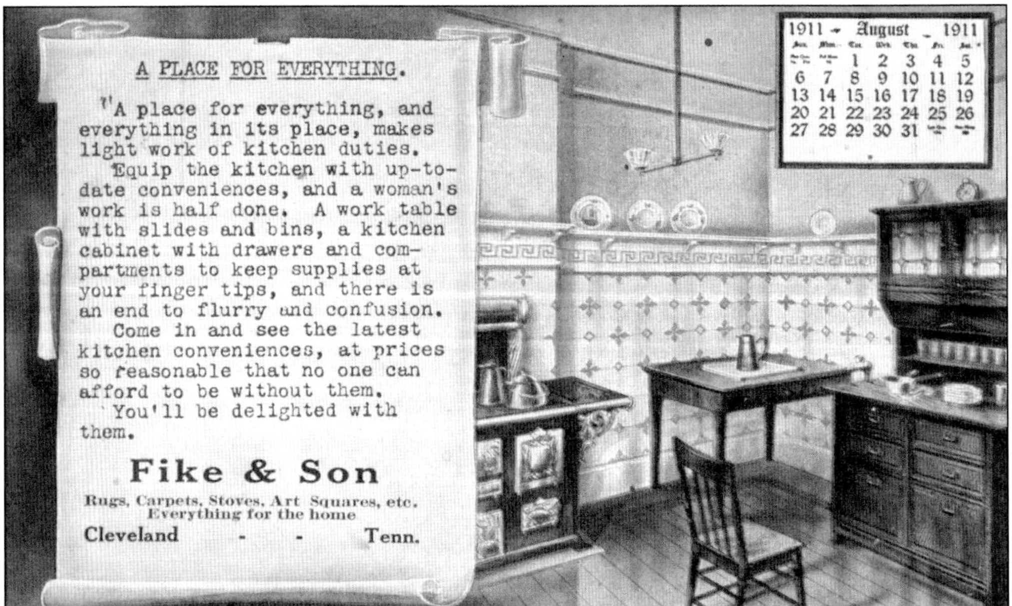

This 1911 postcard advertises Fike and Son, a furniture store as well as an undertaker.

Six

GETAWAYS

Several of our citizens are talking of spending the summer months at different watering places, in order to get out of the city and enjoy the fresh country air and fine spring water.

—W. S. Tipton, May 2, 1884
Editor of the *Cleveland Herald*

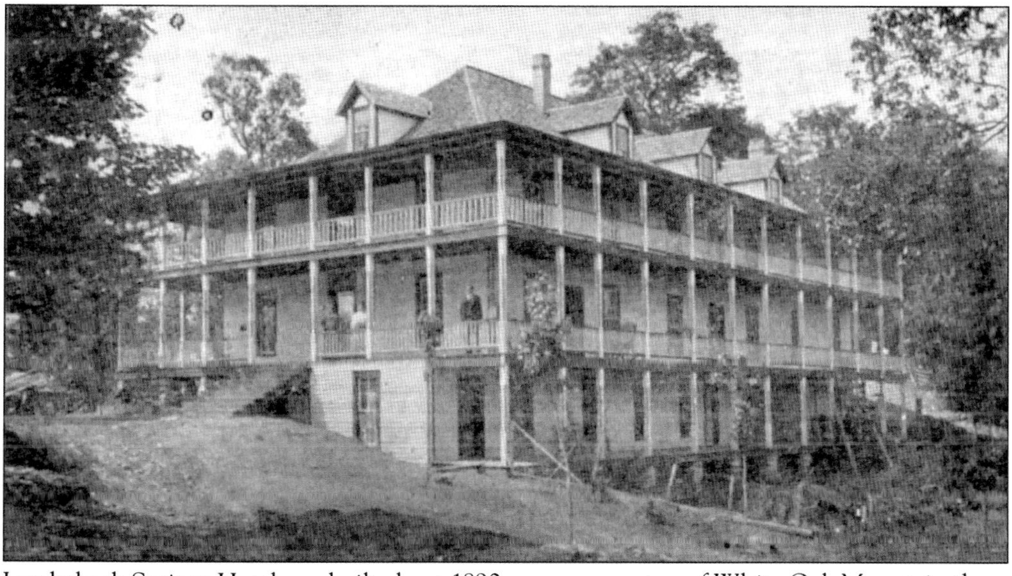

Lauderback Springs Hotel was built about 1890 on a spur on top of White Oak Mountain three miles southwest of McDonald. Sallie Lauderback Everhart owned and operated the hotel, which was built by Elisha Everhart (Sallie's second husband) and Luther Cooper of McDonald. The hotel was a two-story building with 29 rooms. In 1889, an individual could stay in the hotel for $18 per month. Without electricity, the hotel did have one crank-telephone and a conveyor belt with small, attached buckets stretching to a spring. Using a crank in the hotel, guests could dip the buckets in the water and bring the water inside. The hotel operated until 1942 and was destroyed by fire July 29, 1960.

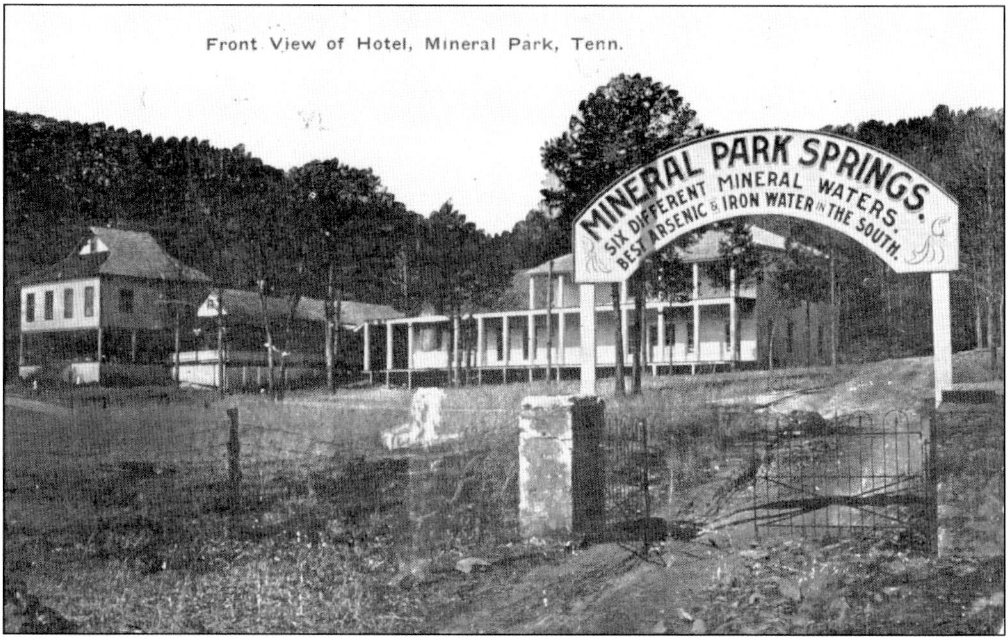

Mineral Park was built about 1910 west of McDonald. It contained the Mineral Springs Inn with 23 rooms, a dance pavilion, and several cabins. There were more than 40 springs in the Mineral Springs Park. Often guests were ill and came to drink the mineral water for their health. From 1910 to 1912, Mineral Park was the site of the encampment of the Ocoee Baptist Association.

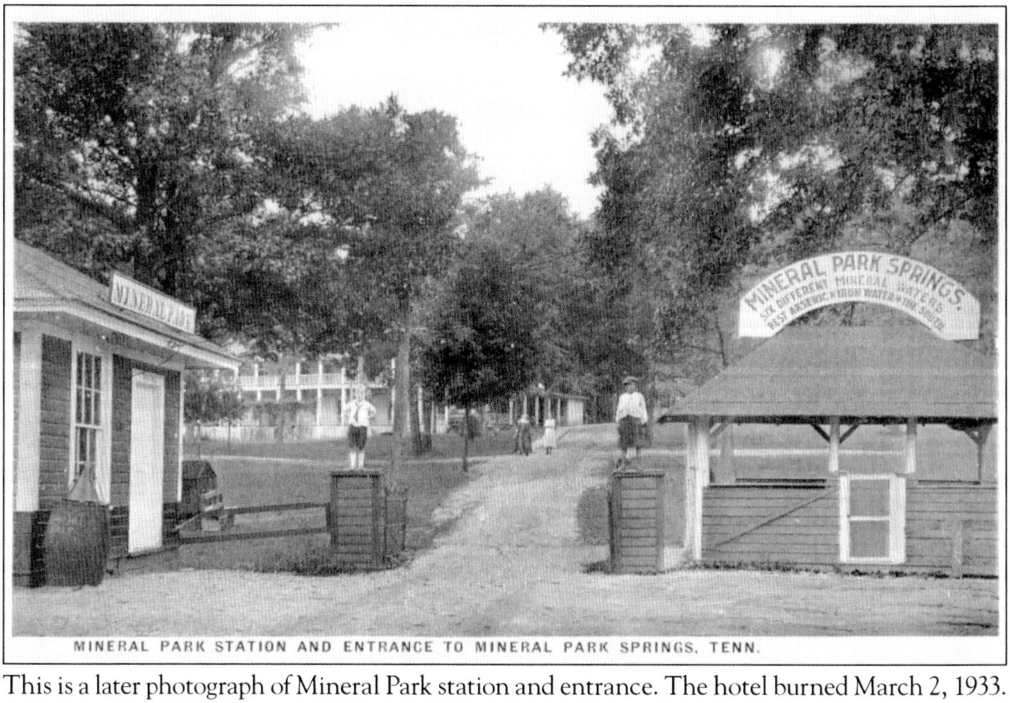

This is a later photograph of Mineral Park station and entrance. The hotel burned March 2, 1933. The springs have been covered, leaving only a trickle of their former abundance.

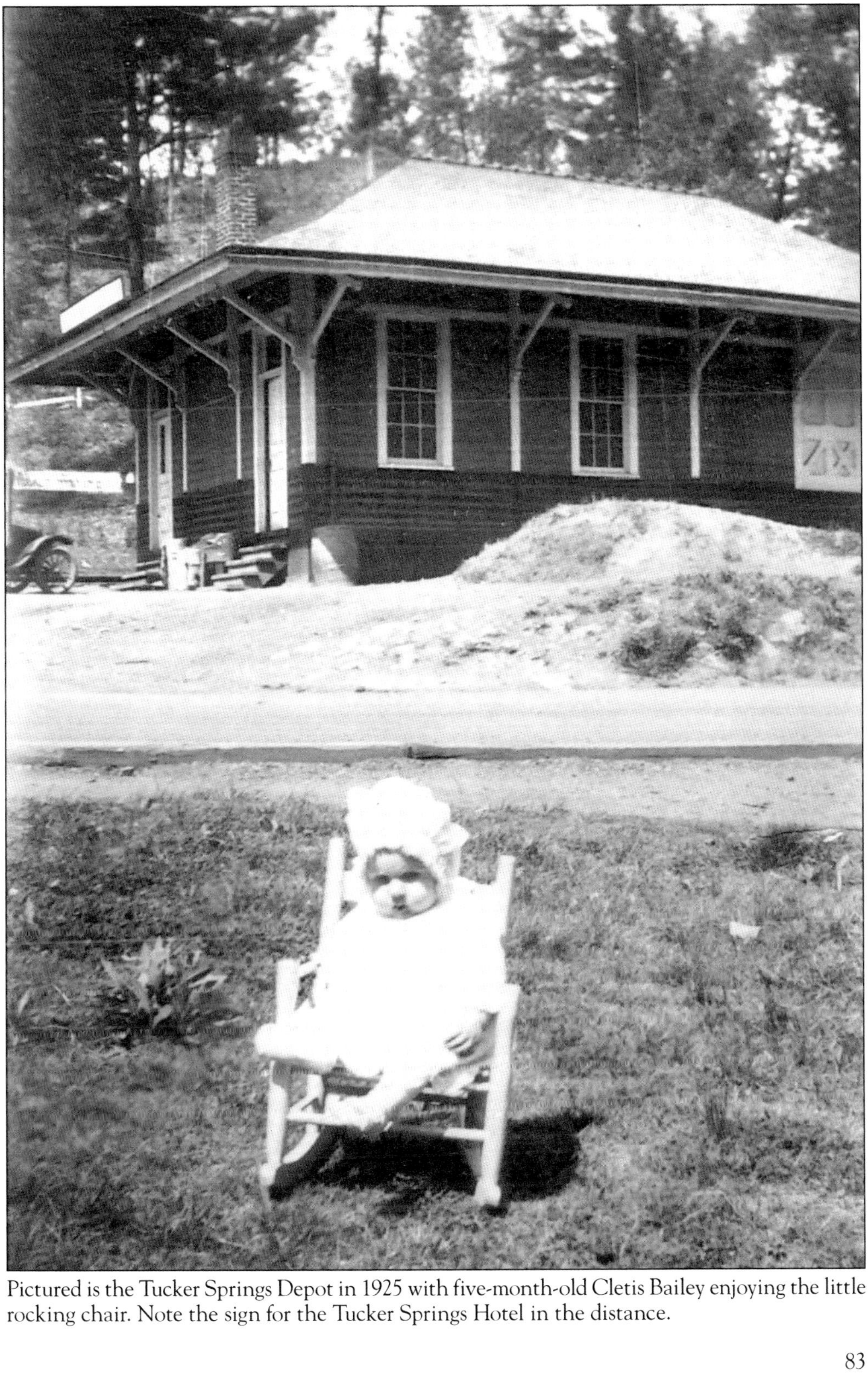

Pictured is the Tucker Springs Depot in 1925 with five-month-old Cletis Bailey enjoying the little rocking chair. Note the sign for the Tucker Springs Hotel in the distance.

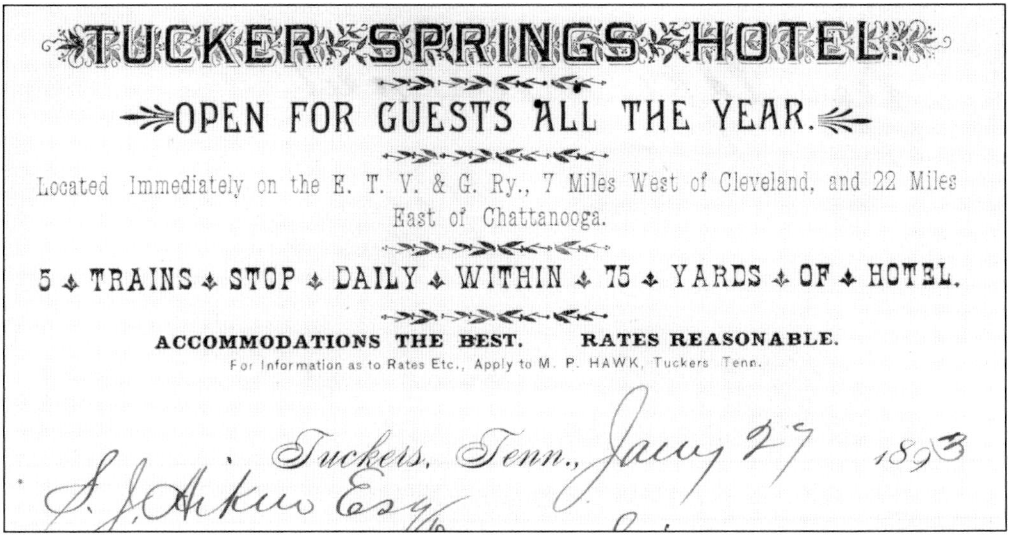

TUCKER SPRINGS HOTEL.

OPEN FOR GUESTS ALL THE YEAR.

Located Immediately on the E. T. V. & G. Ry., 7 Miles West of Cleveland, and 22 Miles East of Chattanooga.

5 TRAINS STOP DAILY WITHIN 75 YARDS OF HOTEL.

ACCOMMODATIONS THE BEST. RATES REASONABLE.

For Information as to Rates Etc., Apply to M. P. HAWK, Tuckers Tenn.

Tuckers, Tenn., Jany 27 1893

S. J. Aiken Esq.

Tucker Springs was used by the Cherokee for drinking and bathing. It is mentioned in 1861 in Myra Inman's diary. The Tucker Springs resort consisted of the hotel, dance pavilion, bowling alley, tennis court, store, post office, coach house, livery stable, and depot. This stationery for the Tucker Springs Hotel was used in 1893.

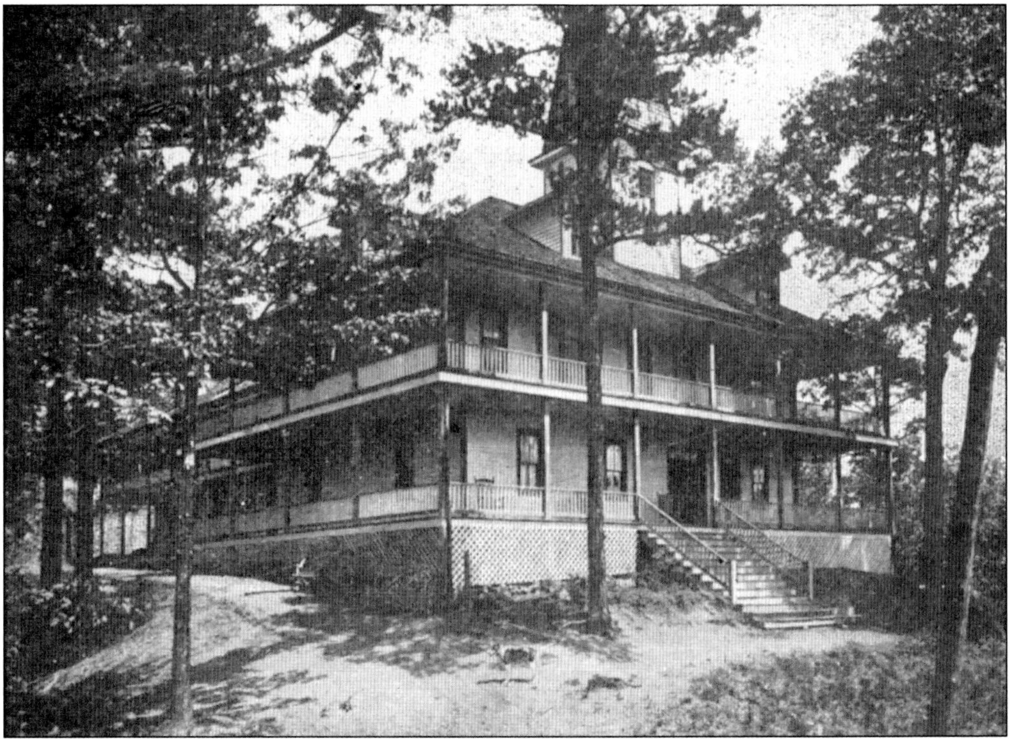

The Tucker Springs Hotel was built in 1885. Advertised rates in 1887 were $4.50 per week. Today nothing remains of the hotel, which was located on what is presently Bendabout Farm.

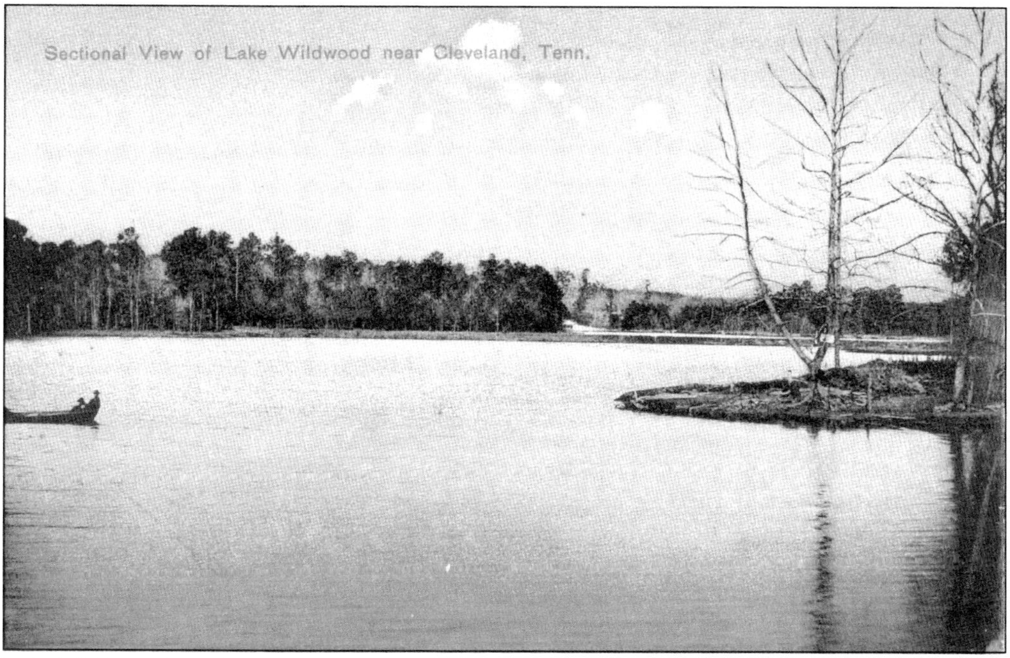

Lake Wildwood was located southeast of Cleveland and was popular for outings and picnics in the late 1800s.

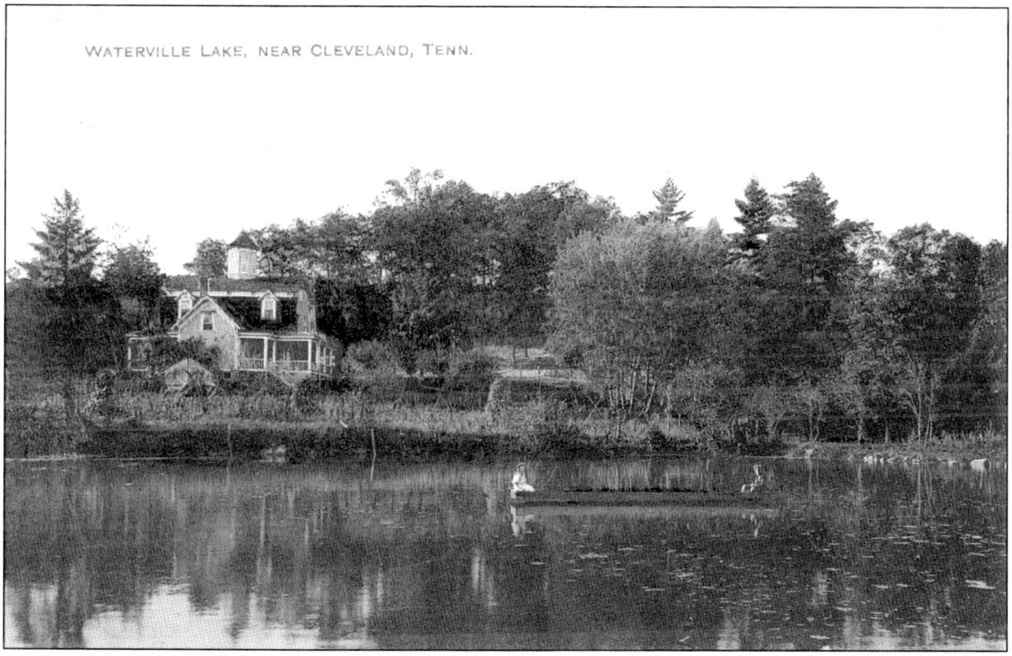

Waterville Lake was located southeast of Cleveland and was the scene for large picnics and gatherings in the early 20th century. This postcard of a 1908 view of the lake shows the home of W. M. Bryant, who owned the property. Today the lake is on the site of Cherokee Springs Golf Course.

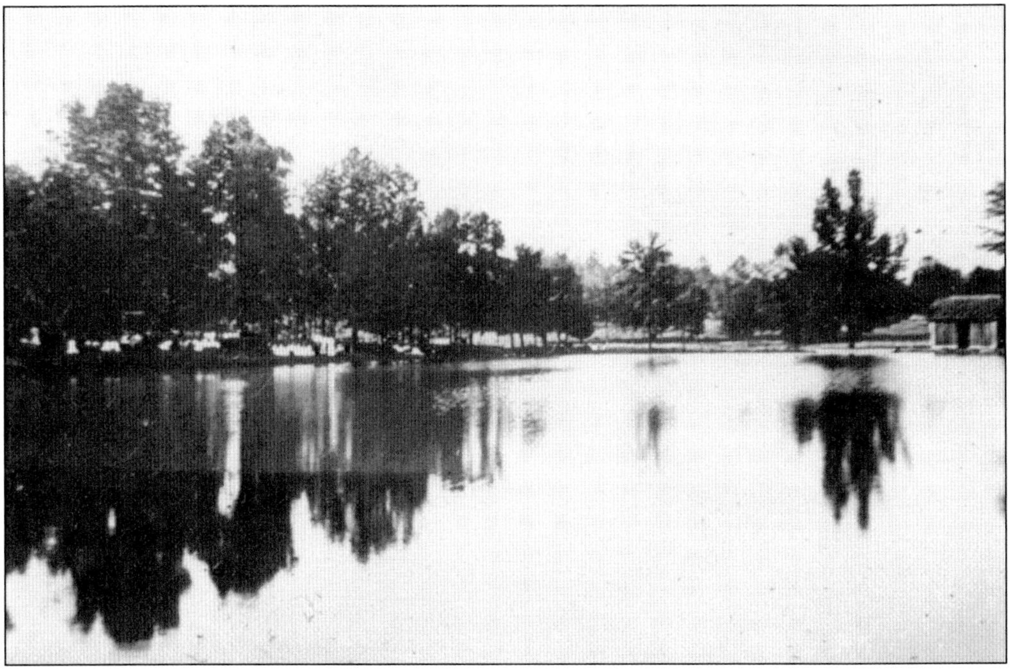

Stuart Lake was located at Seventeenth Street and Keith Street near the George R. Stuart home.

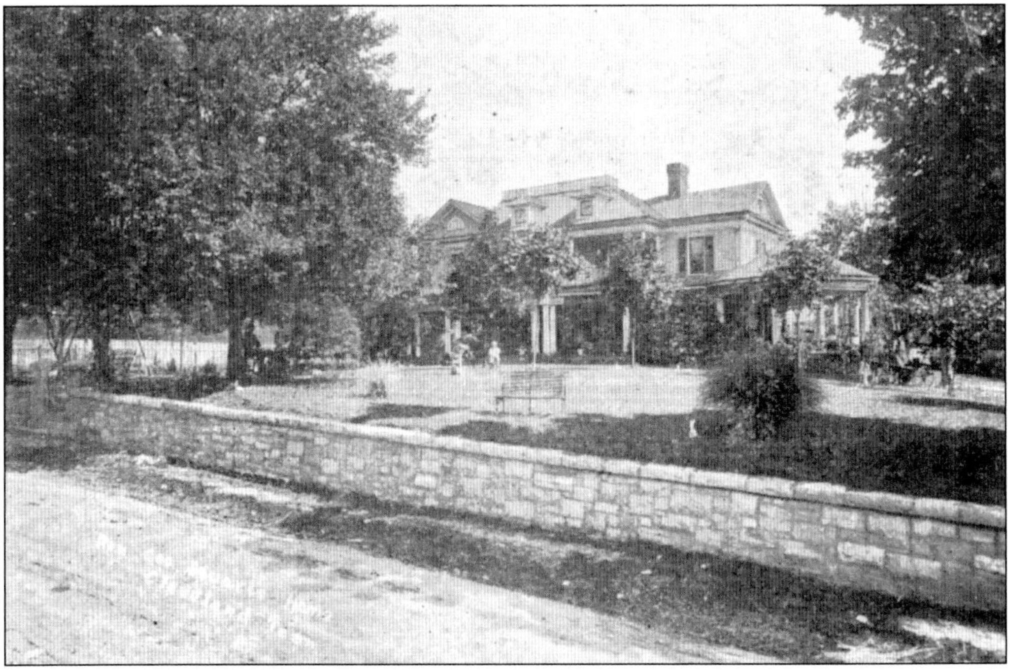

The Reverend George R. Stuart was pastor of Lea Street Methodist Episcopal Church, South, founder of Centenary Female College, and a national evangelist in the 1890s with Sam Jones of Cartersville, Georgia. Shown in this postcard is his residence, which later became the site of Faith Memorial Church.

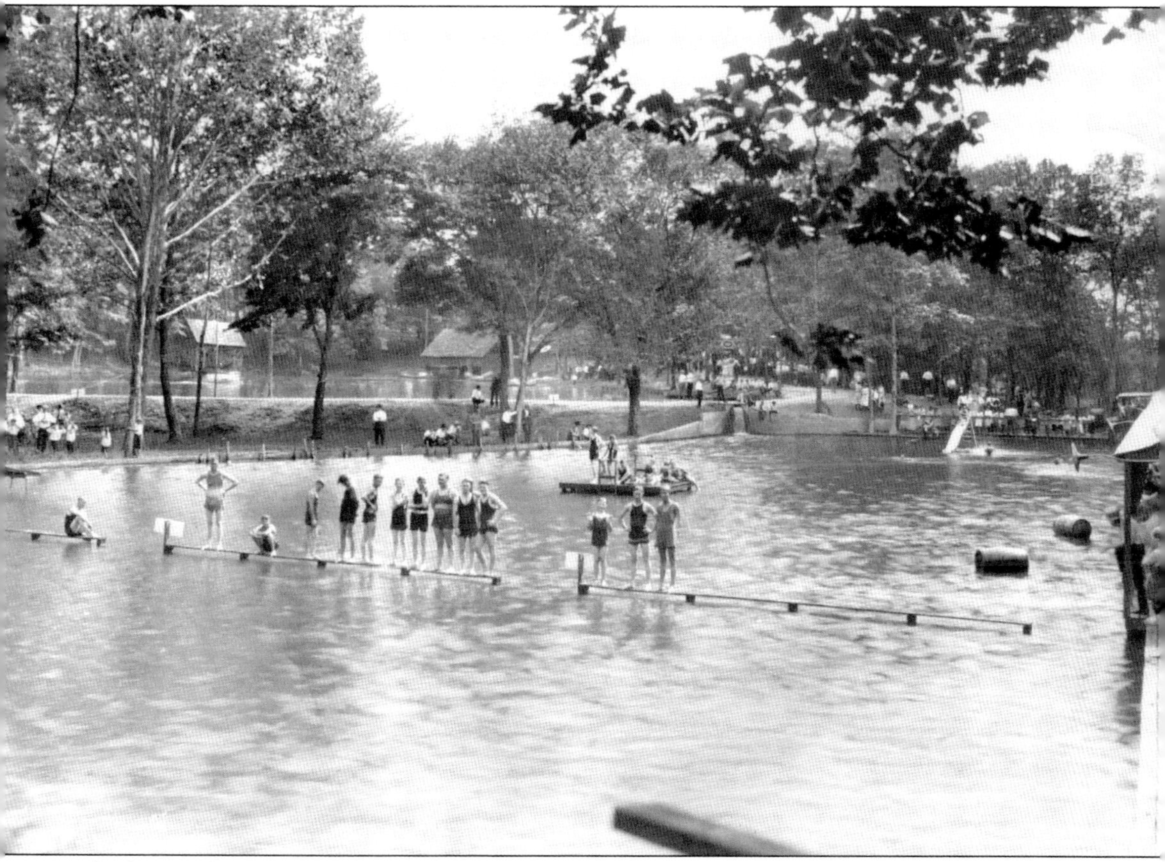

In the late 19th century, W. M. Craigmiles owned a lake with land that became a favorite site for picnics. The Fillauer family purchased the farm and later opened a park to the public in 1922. Shown are patrons enjoying the pool area of the park.

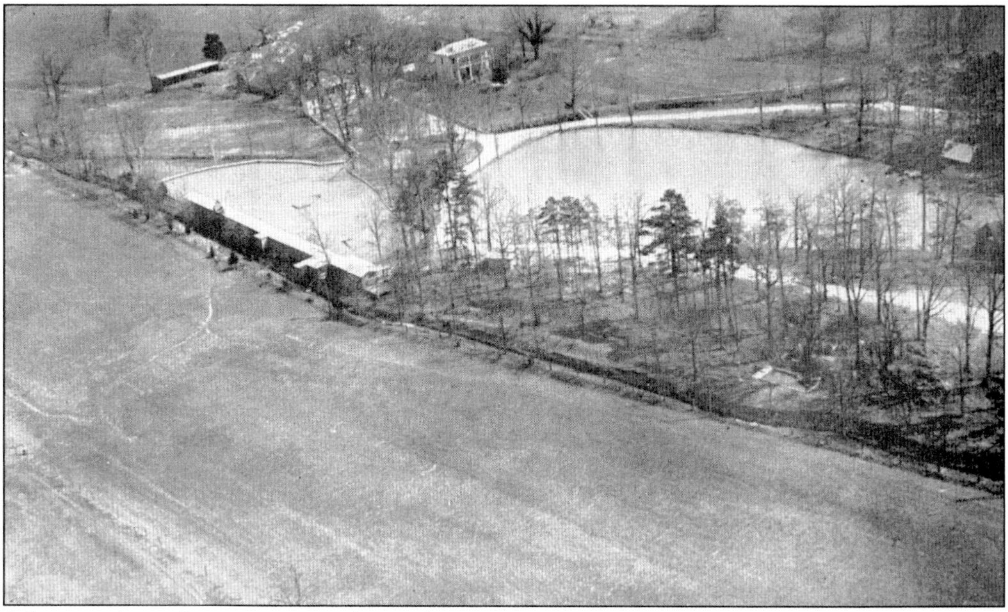

Fillauer Lake and swimming pool were located off Lee Highway. The new Mayfield School is currently being constructed on part of this site.

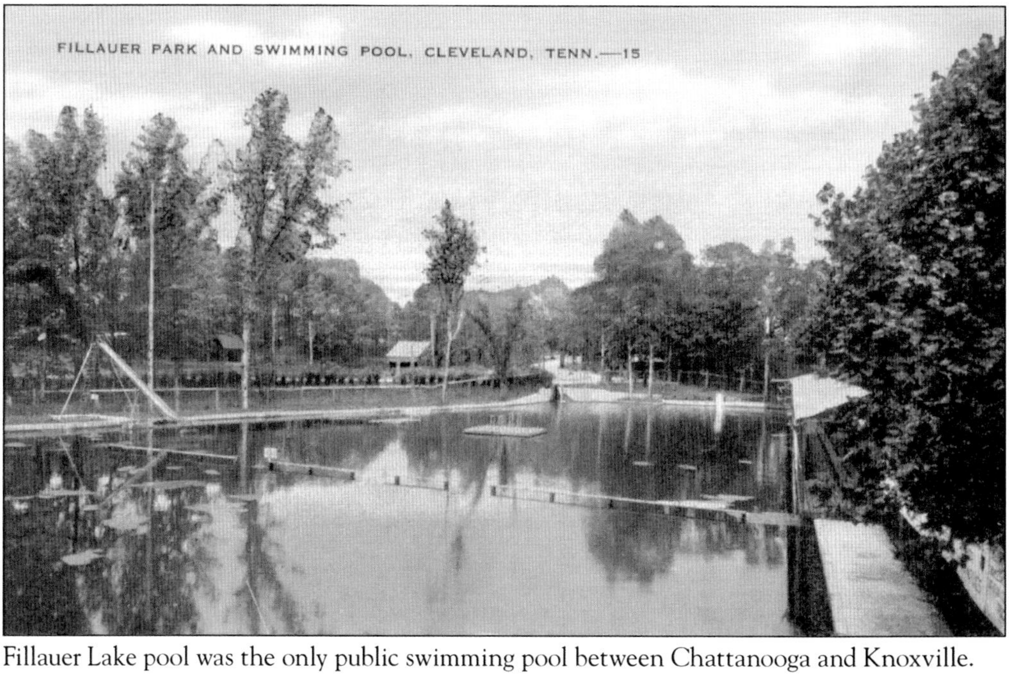

Fillauer Lake pool was the only public swimming pool between Chattanooga and Knoxville.

Hollywood was located near Fillauer Lake. A popular hang-out for young people, it had games and rides.

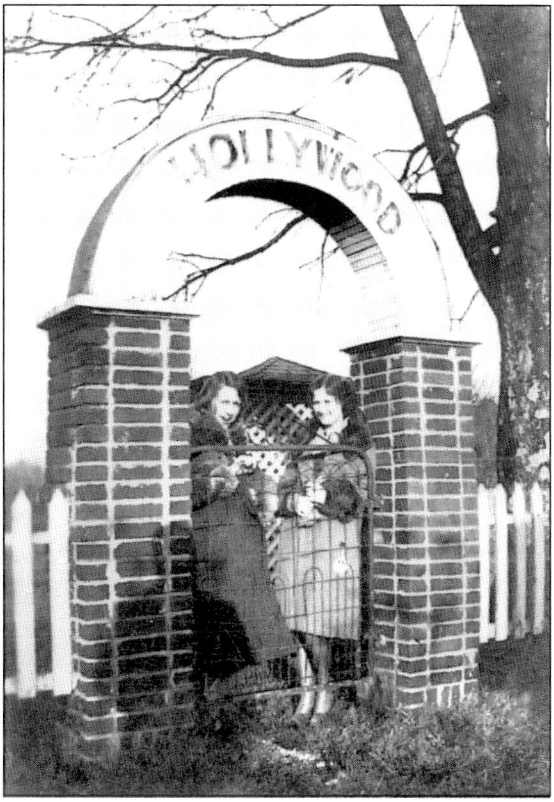

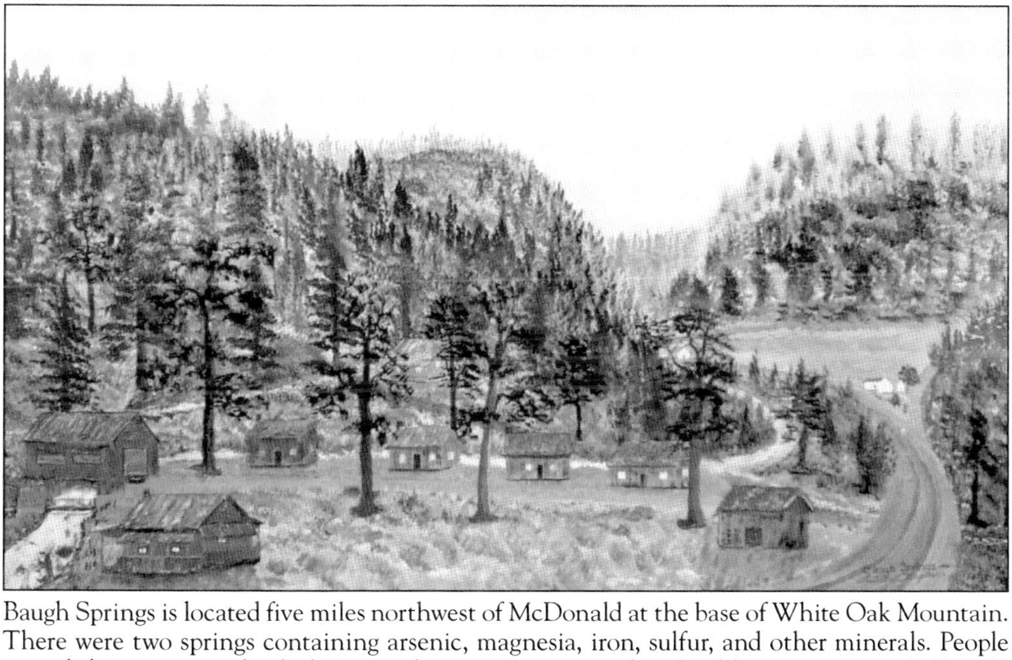

Baugh Springs is located five miles northwest of McDonald at the base of White Oak Mountain. There were two springs containing arsenic, magnesia, iron, sulfur, and other minerals. People visited the springs to drink the water, hoping to improve their health. In 1922, Marshall Ingle bought the land and built a pavilion and cabins on Harris Creek to rent for summer vacations. Many enjoyed picnics, square dances, and turkey hunts there. Only one cabin remains today.

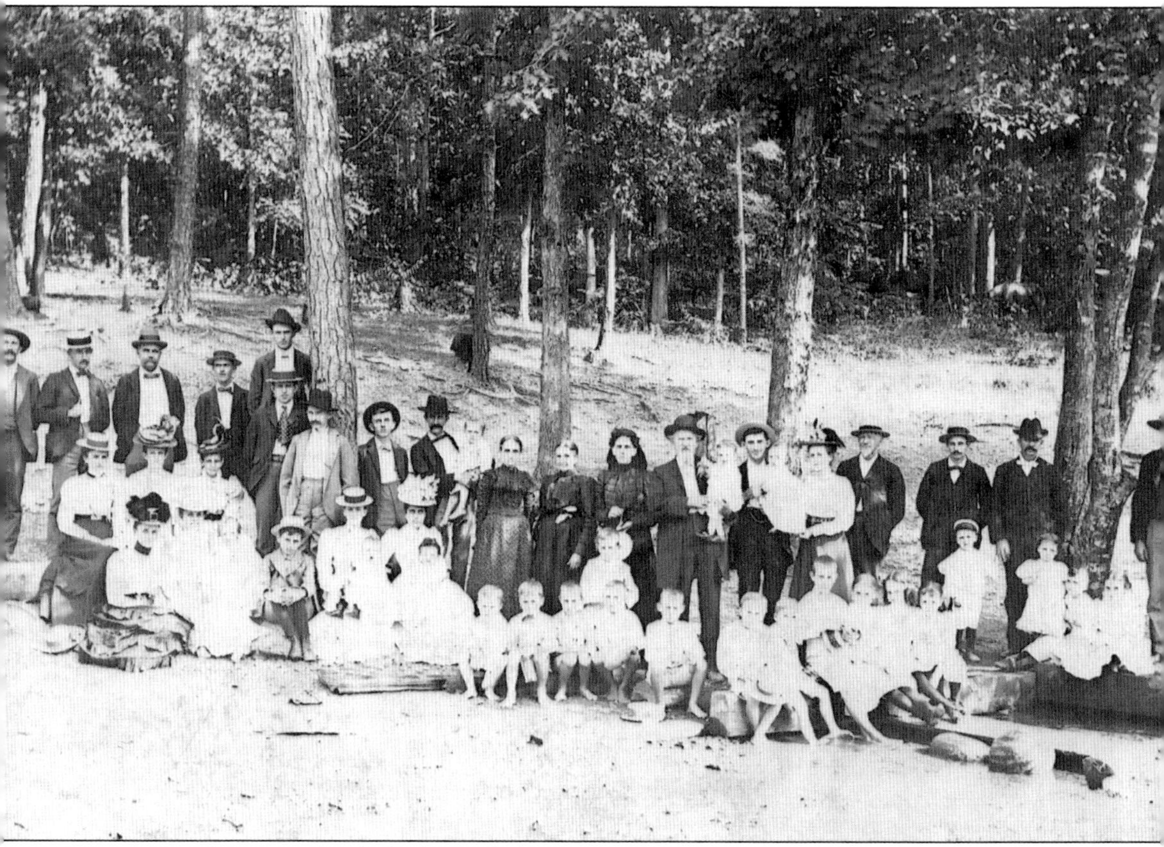

In 1899, the Knox family had a gathering at Bellfounte Spring, located between Tasso and Charleston. The Bellefounte community had a Methodist and a Baptist church.

Seven

Old-Time Religion

Church bells, Sunday School, and fanning through an un-air-conditioned sermon defined the seventh day of the week.

—Jane Foster Kendrick
A 1950s resident of Charleston

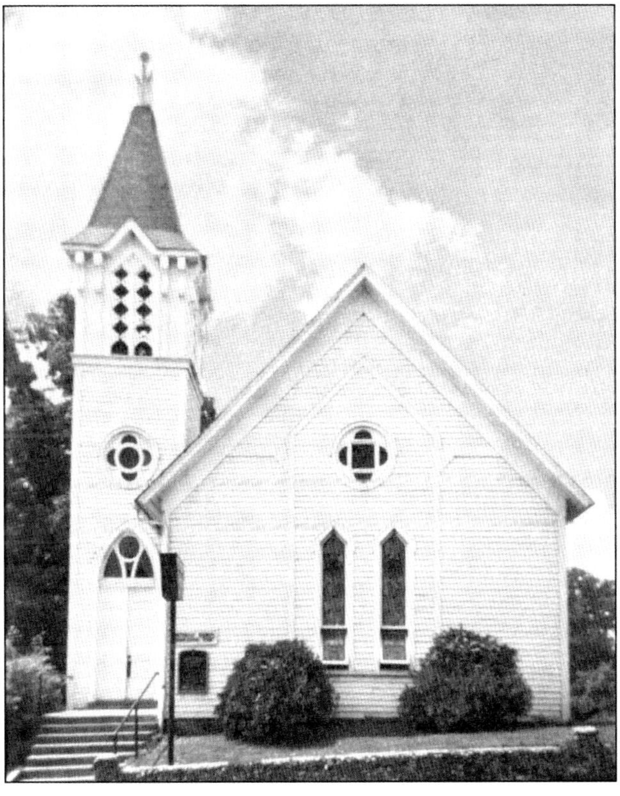

The Methodist Episcopal Church at Charleston was formed in 1825 near the Cherokee Indian Agency. This is the oldest continuing congregation in Bradley County. The congregation worshipped in this building from 1887 until 1963. While a student at Bob Jones College in 1936, Billy Graham preached his first sermon to this Methodist congregation.

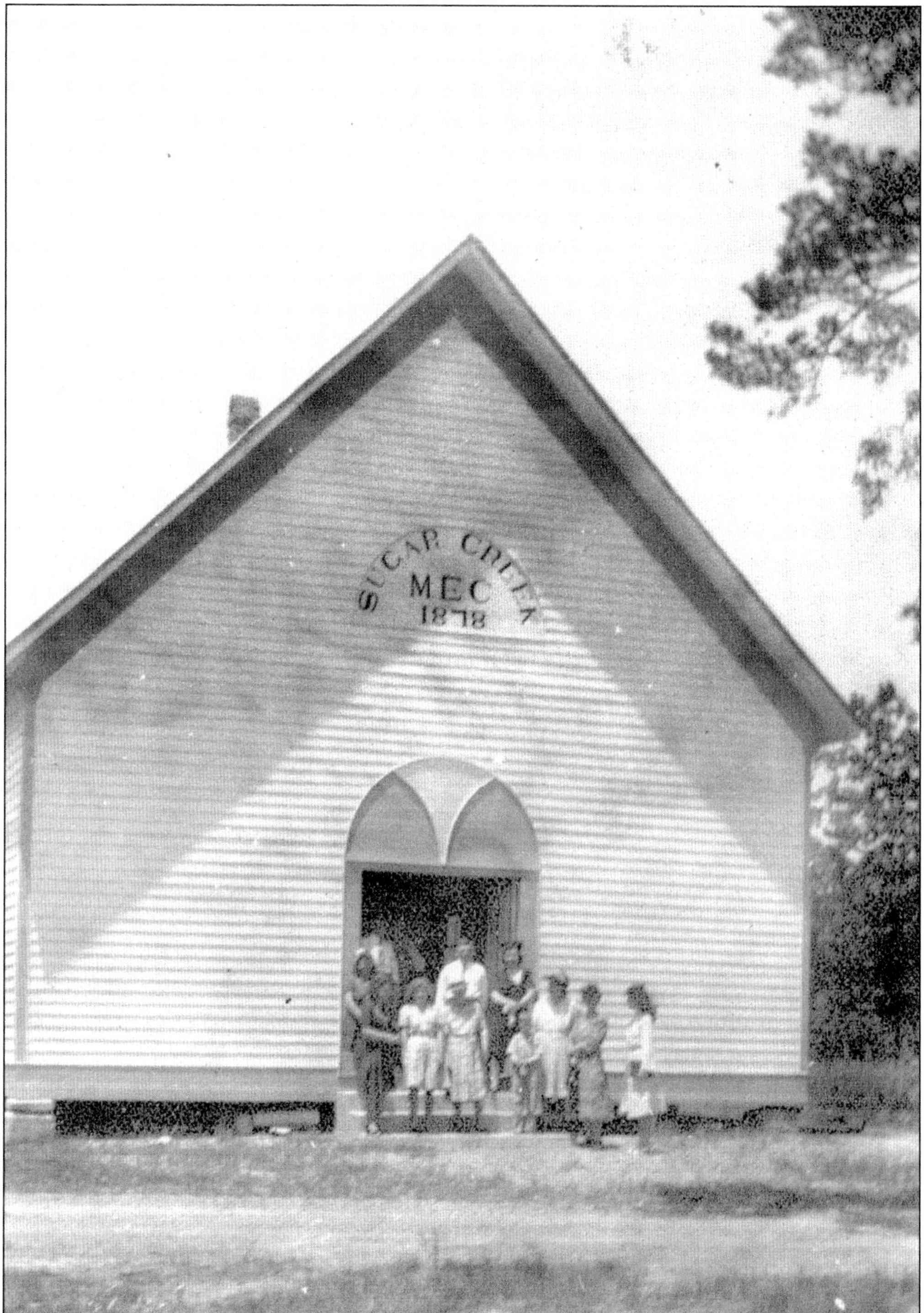

Sugar Creek Methodist Episcopal Church was organized in 1840. A large cemetery adjoins the sanctuary. The church is located off Hughes Lake Road near the Georgia state line. This building was later replaced, and the congregation worships in the new building today.

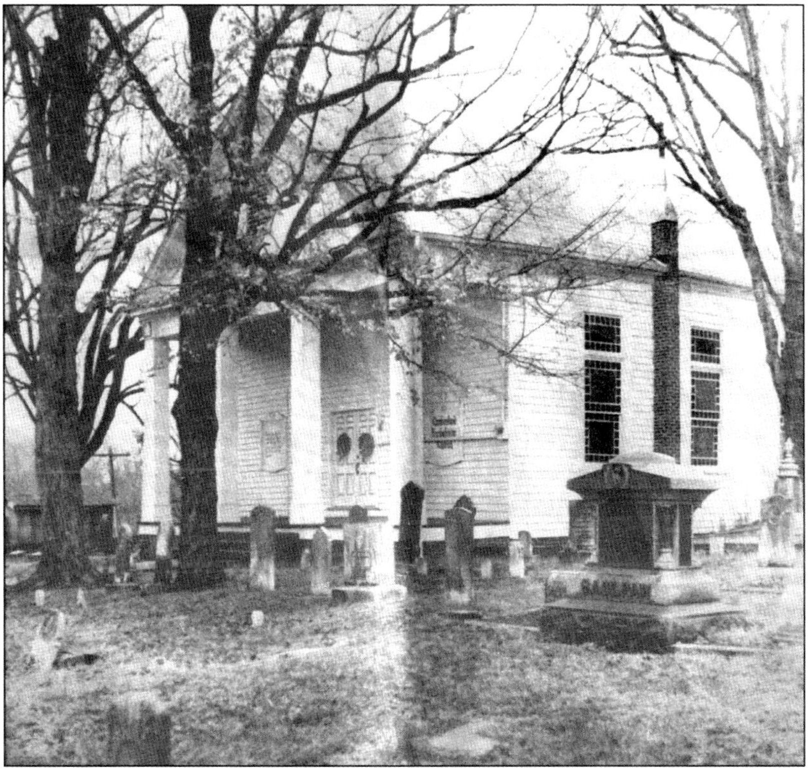

The Cumberland Presbyterian Church at Charleston was built about 1860. Union and Confederate soldiers used the building as a hospital during the Civil War. Markings on the windowsills show where horses chewed the wood while tied outside waiting to be fed. Today this congregation worships in a modern brick building on Highway 11.

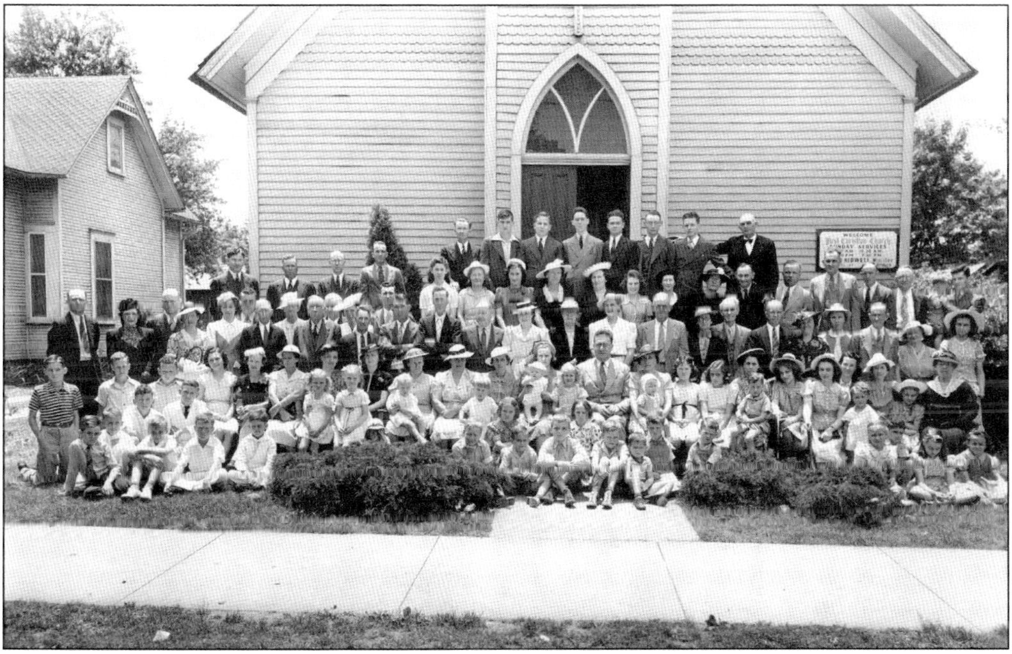

First Christian Church (Disciples of Christ) was organized in 1897 with 19 charter members. The church purchased the wooden building erected by the Evangelical Association on Berry Street, later renamed Central Avenue. In 1961, First Christian moved to North Lee Highway, and the wooden structure was dismantled.

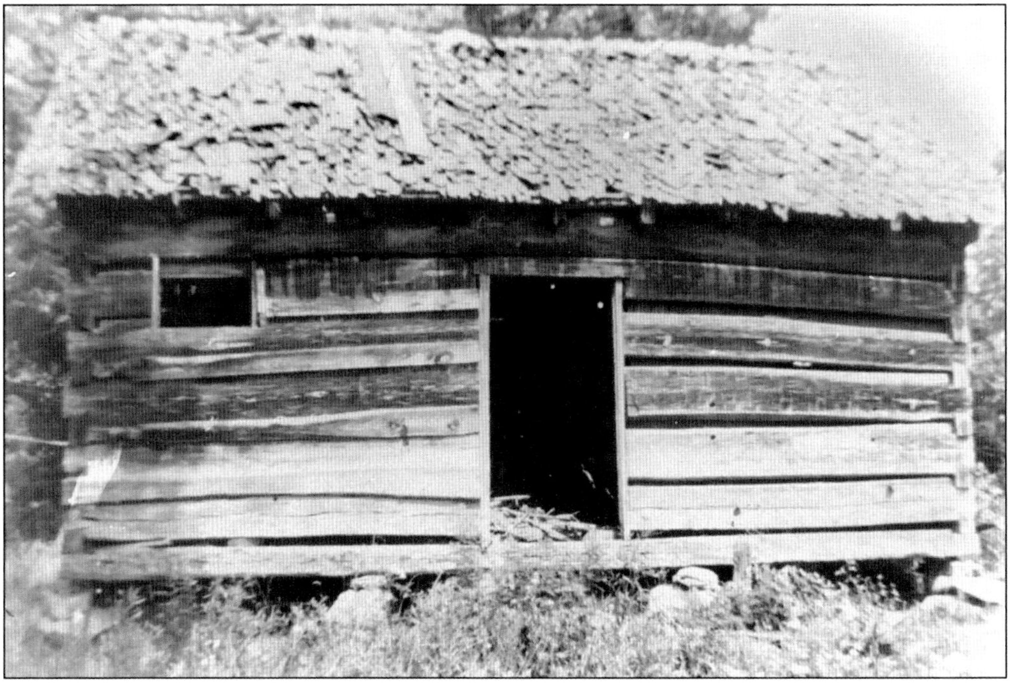

This log cabin served the Pleasant Grove Methodist Episcopal Church until the current building was completed around 1885. Pleasant Grove began as Price Chapel campground in the 1830s during camp meetings conducted by the Reverend Henry Price. Located on Pleasant Grove Church Road, the congregation remains active today.

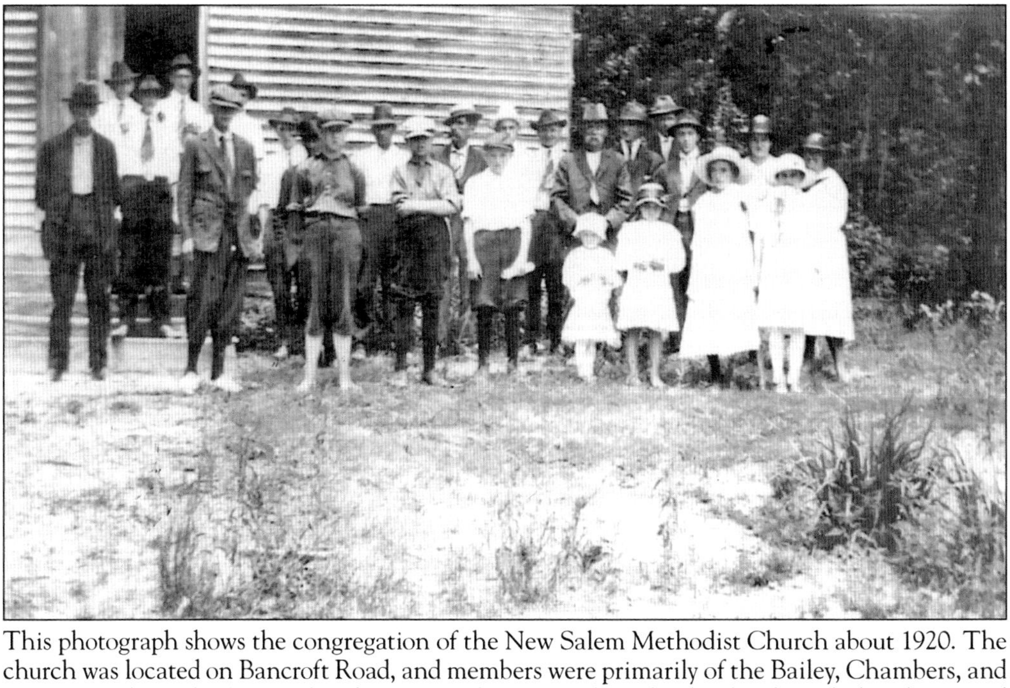

This photograph shows the congregation of the New Salem Methodist Church about 1920. The church was located on Bancroft Road, and members were primarily of the Bailey, Chambers, and Trotter families. Charles Roark, a former member, remembers that his family took their horse and buggy to church and would tie the horses in the nearby shade trees.

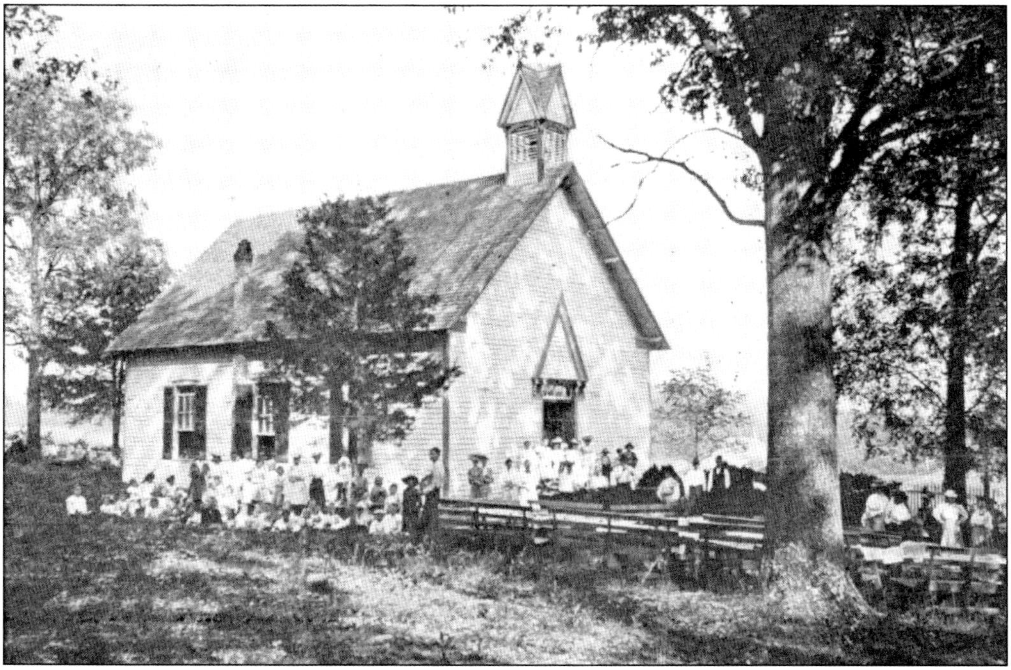

This postcard, from about 1910, shows Tasso Christian Church. This church remains active today as an Independent Church of Christ.

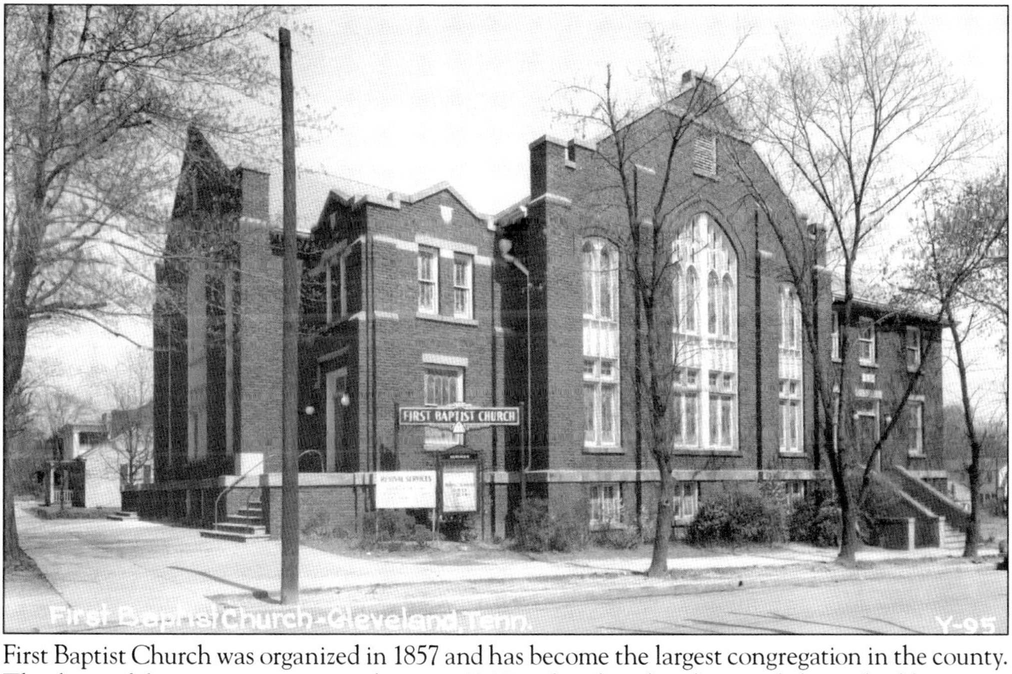

First Baptist Church was organized in 1857 and has become the largest congregation in the county. This beautiful sanctuary was torn down in 1966 and replaced with a much larger building.

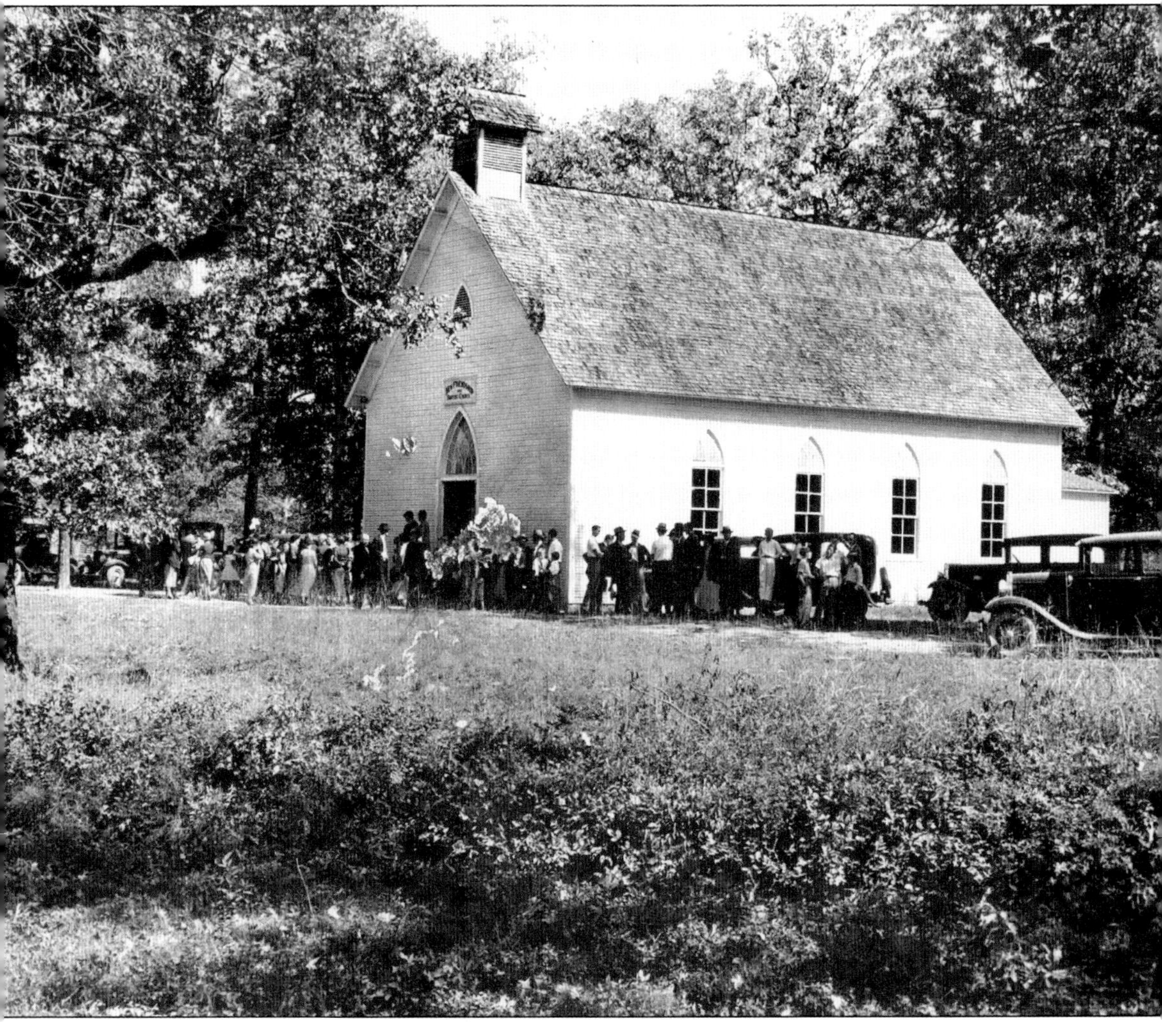

New Friendship Baptist Church was organized in 1835 and is the second oldest Baptist church in the county. The first act of the new church was to ordain John B. Cate deacon. The building shown was erected in 1913 and was located in the beautiful hills of Chatata Valley.

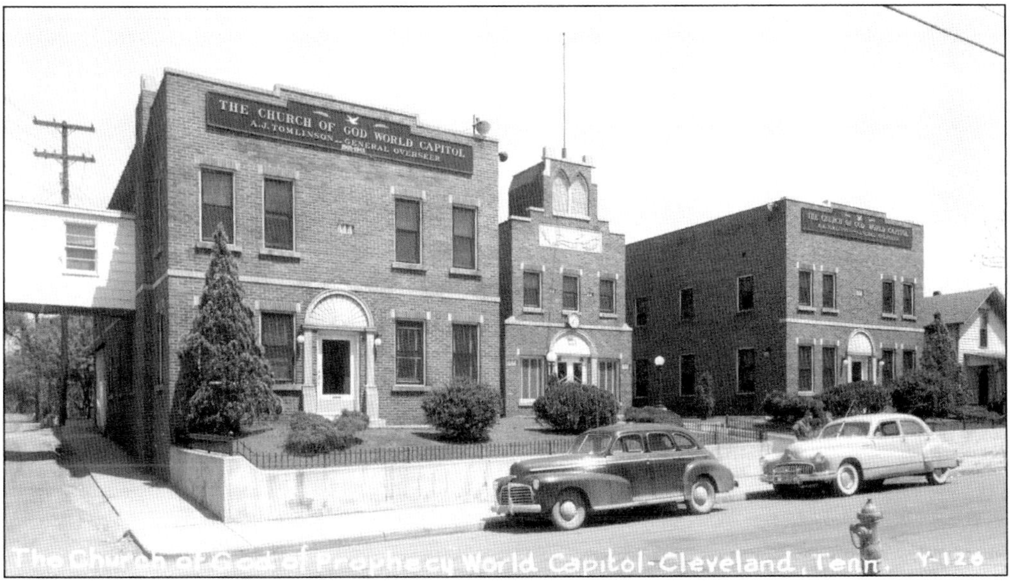

A. J. Tomlinson was the first general overseer of the Church of God. He moved to Cleveland before any congregation existed here. Under his leadership, the Church of God became an international Pentecostal denomination.

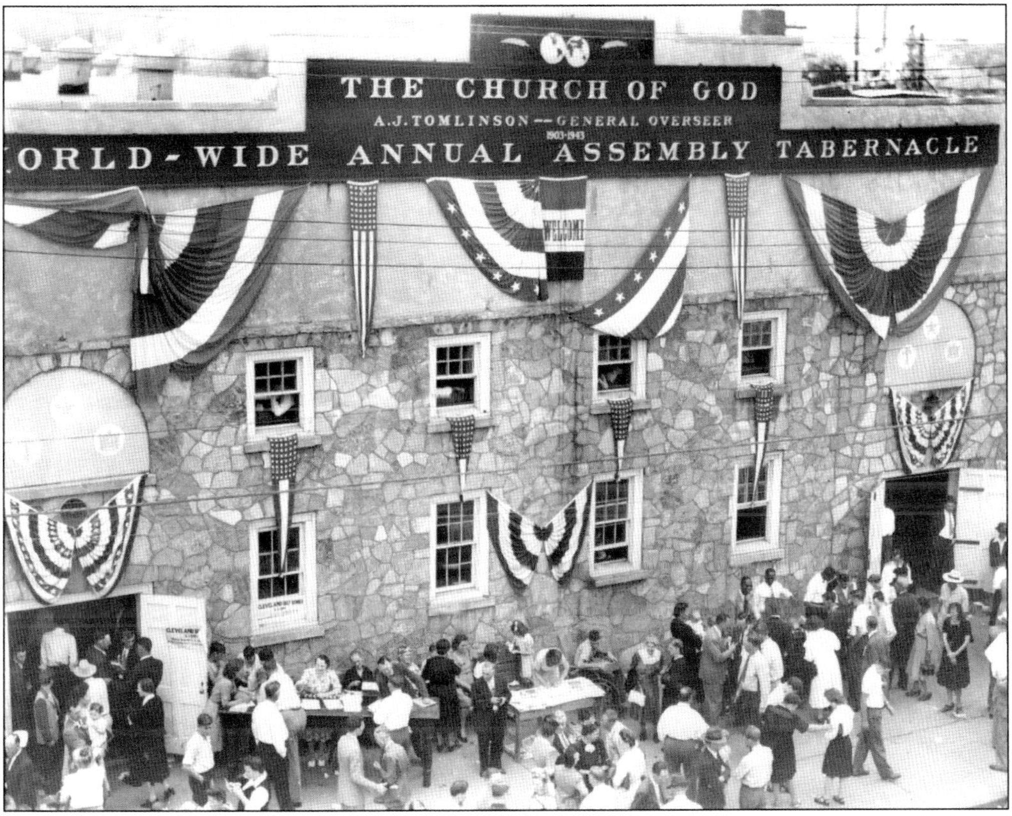

The annual assembly of the Church of God of Prophecy was a very important event in the life of Cleveland, with the population of the city more than doubling during assembly week.

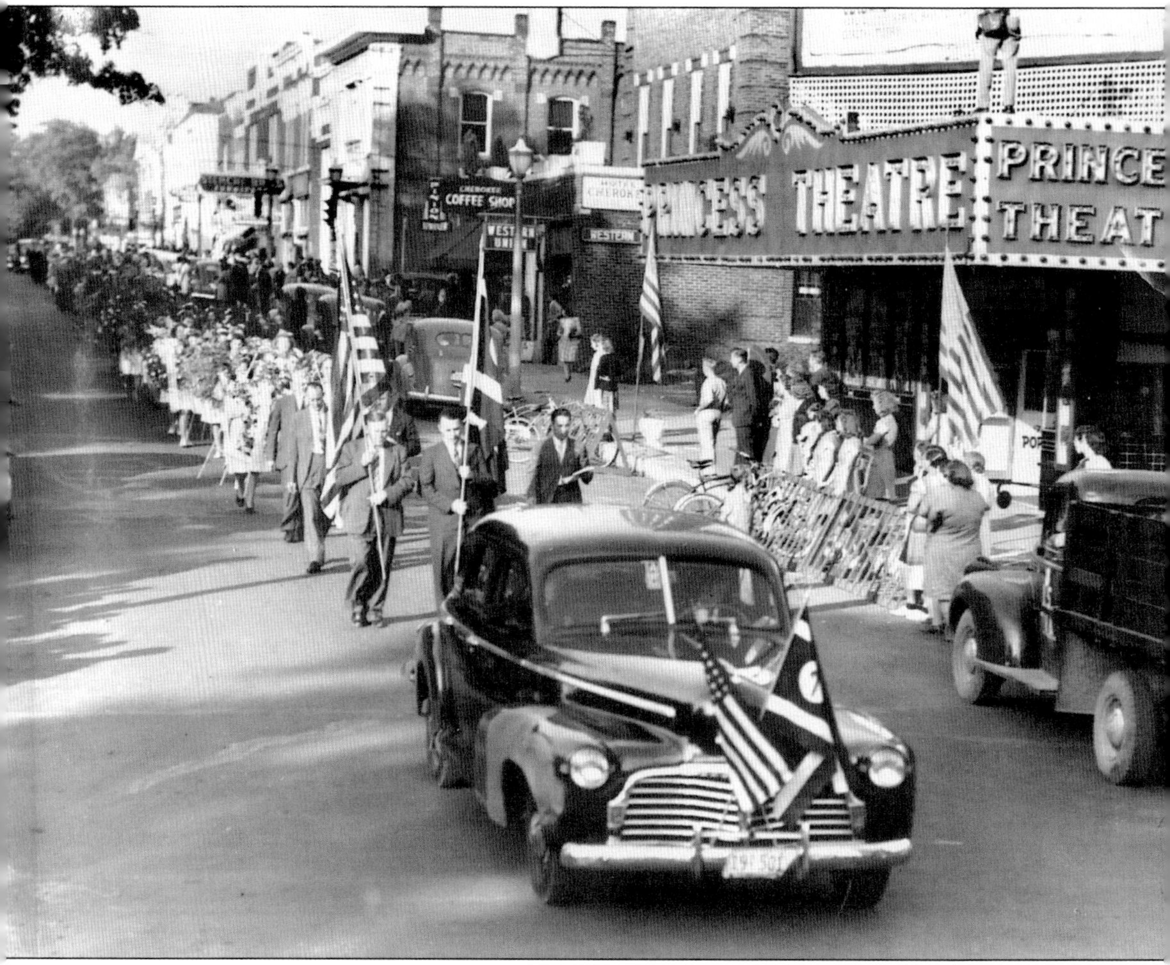

Ambrose Jesup Tomlinson came to Cleveland in 1904 soon after the Fire Baptized Holiness Church failed to build its School of Prophecy in nearby Beniah, Tennessee. Under his leadership as general overseer, the Church of God flourished until the great disruption in 1923. Then Tomlinson led the Church of God of Prophecy for 20 years. He died in 1943, and his funeral procession, as shown, reached from the tabernacle at Bible Place to Fort Hill Cemetery.

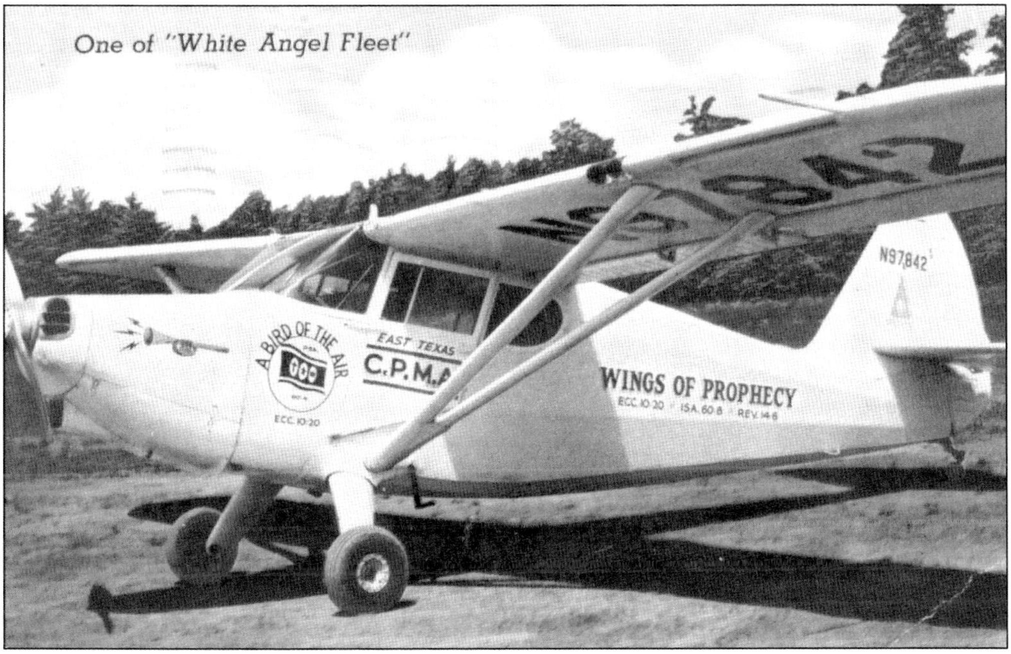

The Church of God of Prophecy, headquartered in Cleveland, had quite a ministry with airplanes due to their founding in the year 1903, which coincided with the year the Wright brothers first flew an airplane at Kitty Hawk, North Carolina.

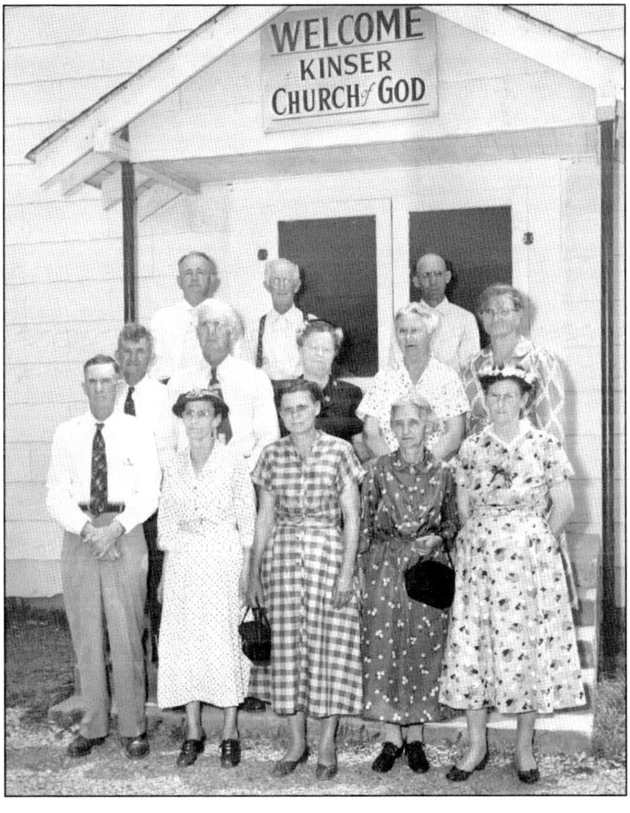

The Kinser Church of God was an early congregation of this Pentecostal denomination. Pictured are some members at their old church off Waterlevel Highway about 1950.

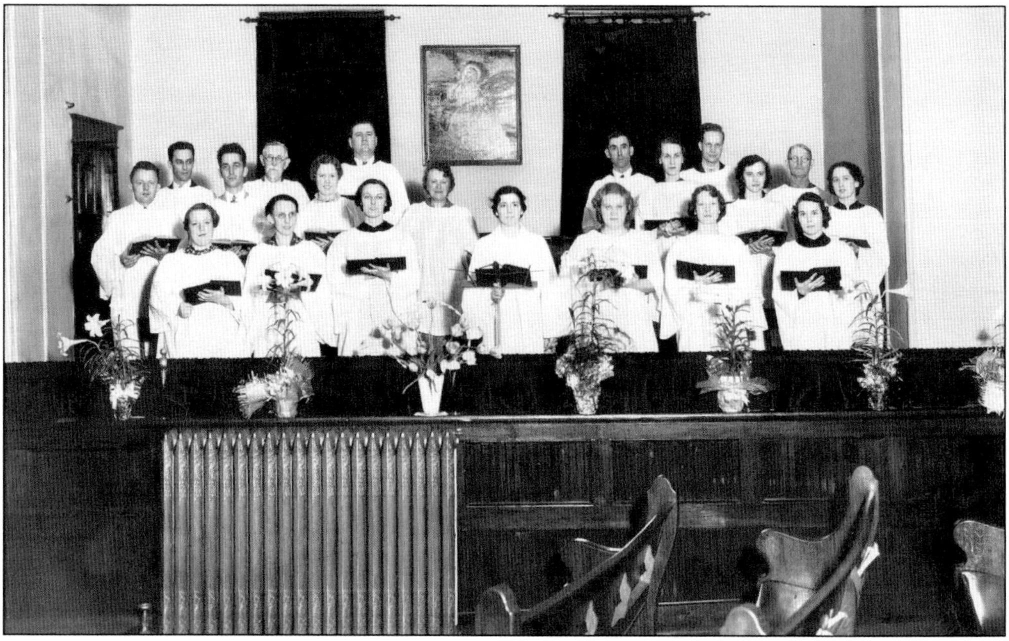

Shown is the First Methodist choir on an Easter Sunday in the sanctuary of the South Ocoee Street location. From left to right are (first row) Helen Brown, Rose Kinder, Mara Sue Simmons, Becky Jordan, Rachael Frazier, Frances Hudson, and unidentified; (second row) unidentified, Hazel Gannaway, Mrs. E. J. Frazier, unidentified, and Ruth Jones; (third row) Bayse Jordan, Hubert Miller, unidentified, Jewel Gannaway, Walter Lawson, Sara Lou Simmons, Harry Garnsey, and O. W. Hudson.

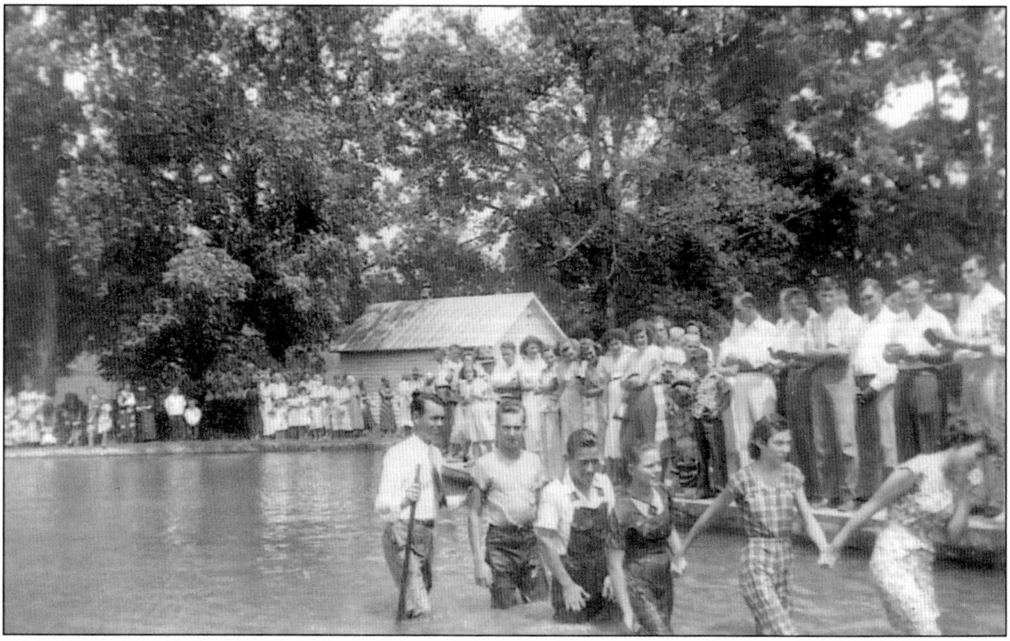

This photograph shows a baptism in 1951 held by Strawhill, now Coahulla, Baptist Church at Flint Springs. In the foreground from left to right are the Reverend Cecil Fortenberry, Harold Hawkins, Earl Sprayberry, Mary Jo Clayton, Margaret Reagan, and Kathleen Tipins.

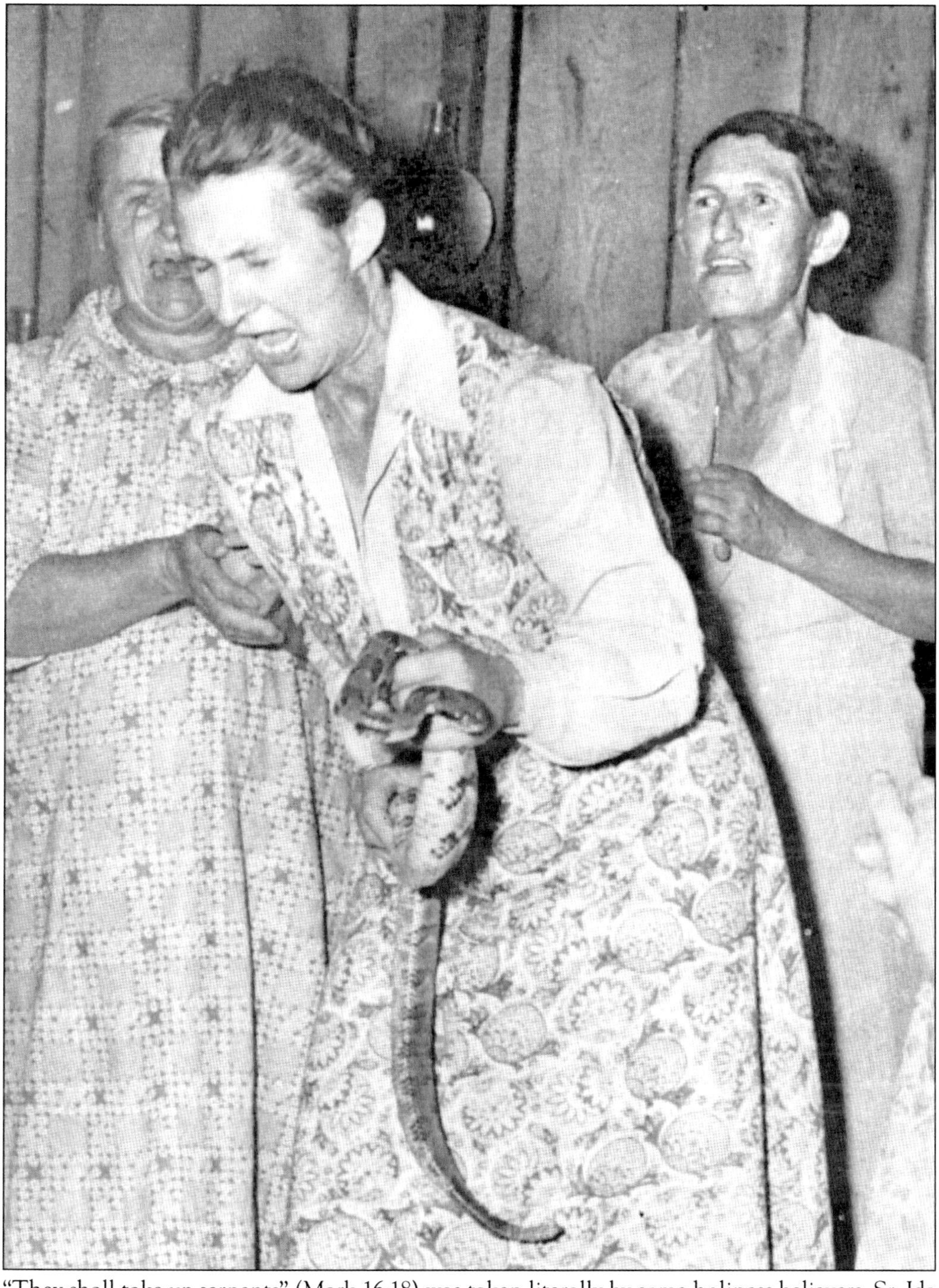

"They shall take up serpents" (Mark 16:18) was taken literally by some holiness believers. Sr. Ida Mae Hardin is in ecstasy while holding a rattlesnake in a worship service in 1946. George Henley of Grasshopper Valley introduced snake handling to the Tennessee believers in 1916. On Saturdays while shoppers thronged the downtown, Sister Hardin and other believers handled snakes on the courthouse square. In 1946, three men of Bradley County died from handling poisonous rattlesnakes. In 1947, Tennessee passed a law prohibiting the handling of poisonous snakes.

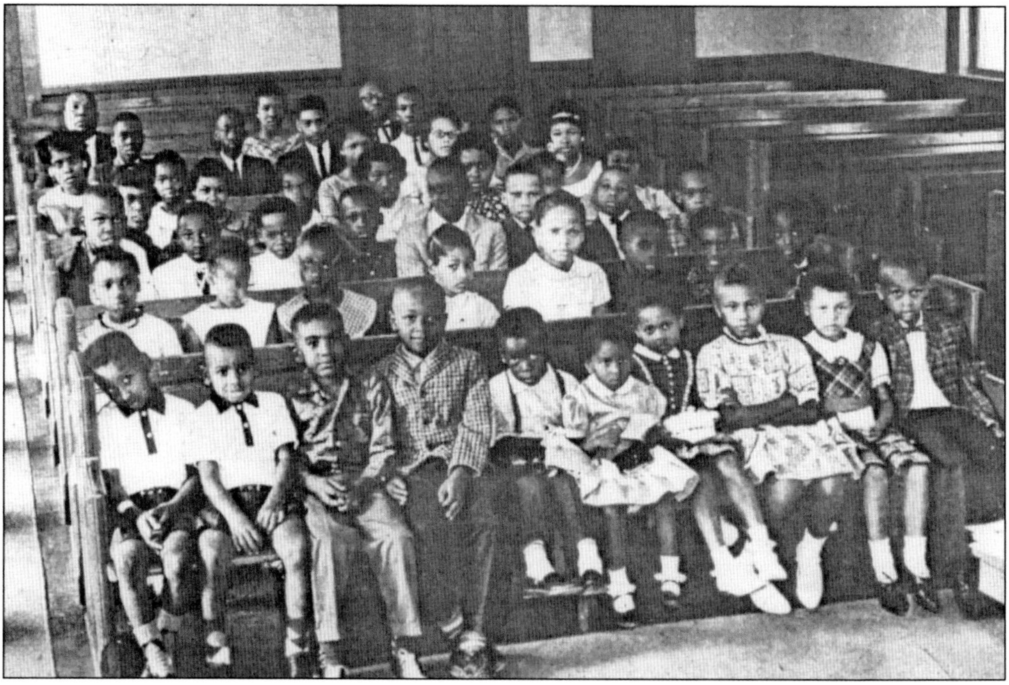

The Sunday school is an important ministry of a church. Several young scholars of Pleasant Grove Baptist Church are shown in this photograph about 1930.

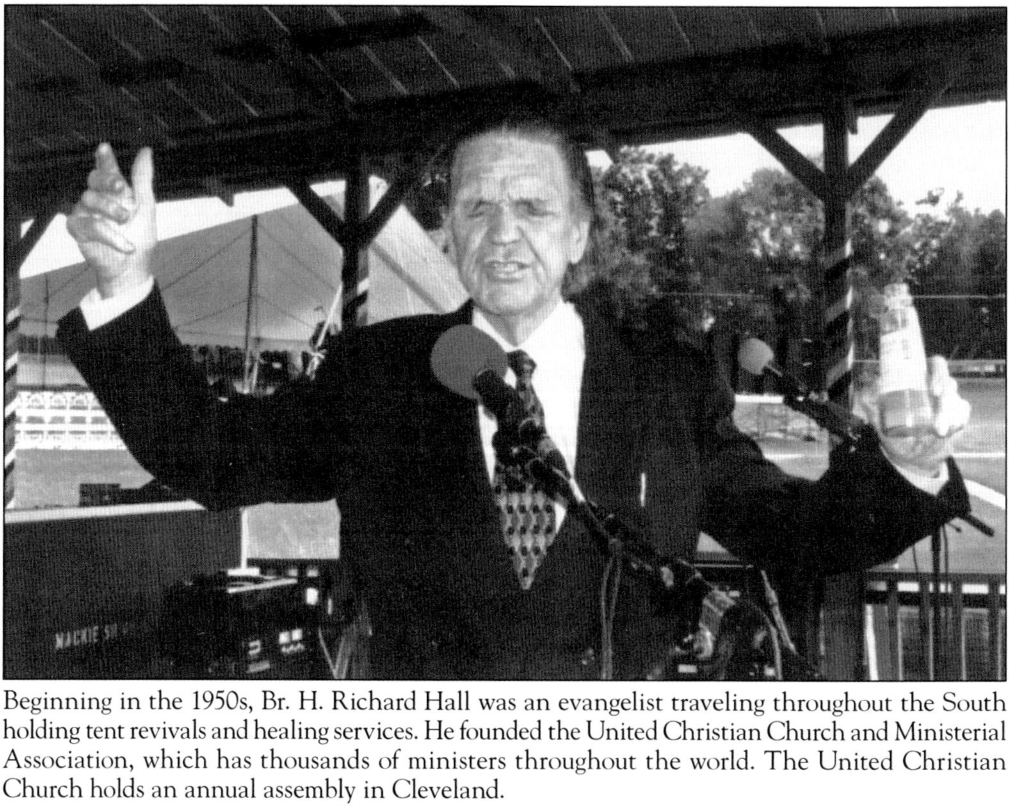

Beginning in the 1950s, Br. H. Richard Hall was an evangelist traveling throughout the South holding tent revivals and healing services. He founded the United Christian Church and Ministerial Association, which has thousands of ministers throughout the world. The United Christian Church holds an annual assembly in Cleveland.

Eight

We Belong, Too

No grand idea was ever born in a conference, but a lot of foolish ideas have died there.

—F. Scott Fitzgerald
Author

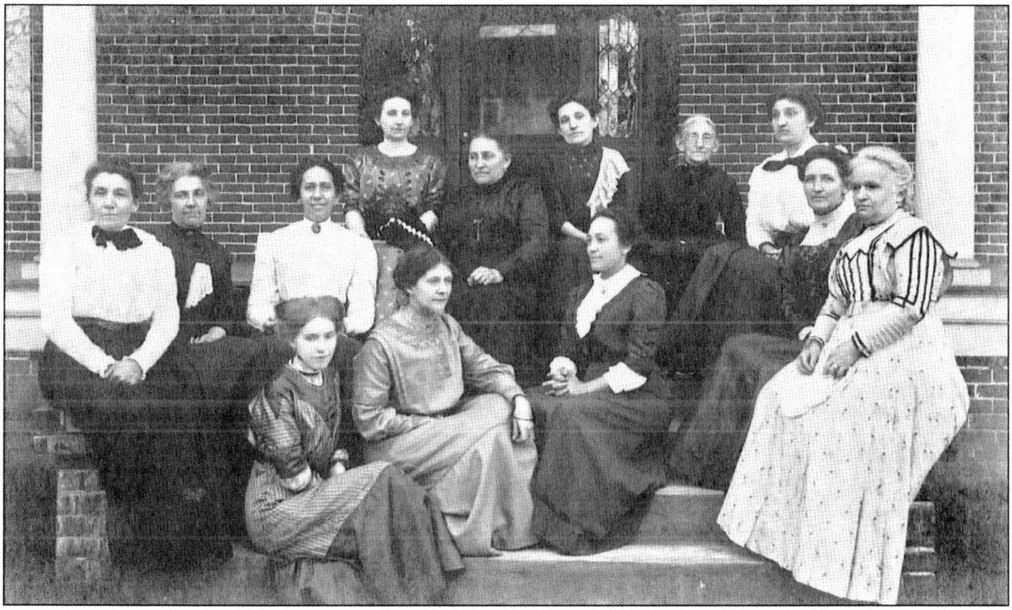

The Embroidery Club was organized in 1904 and is Cleveland's oldest continuously active social club. Membership is limited to 12 and, when possible, handed down from mother to daughter or daughter-in-law. The women gather socially and work on needlework or other crafts. Shown at the home of Hattie McNabb Pearson on Central Avenue about 1910 are Florence Lusk, Virgie Horner, Grace Rogers, Bessie Keys, Christina Fillauer, Lizzie Itzel, Mrs. Bryant, Ethel McDaris, Lizzie Rogers, Mrs. Thurston, Lizzie Fillauer, Bess Herman, and Hattie McNabb Pearson.

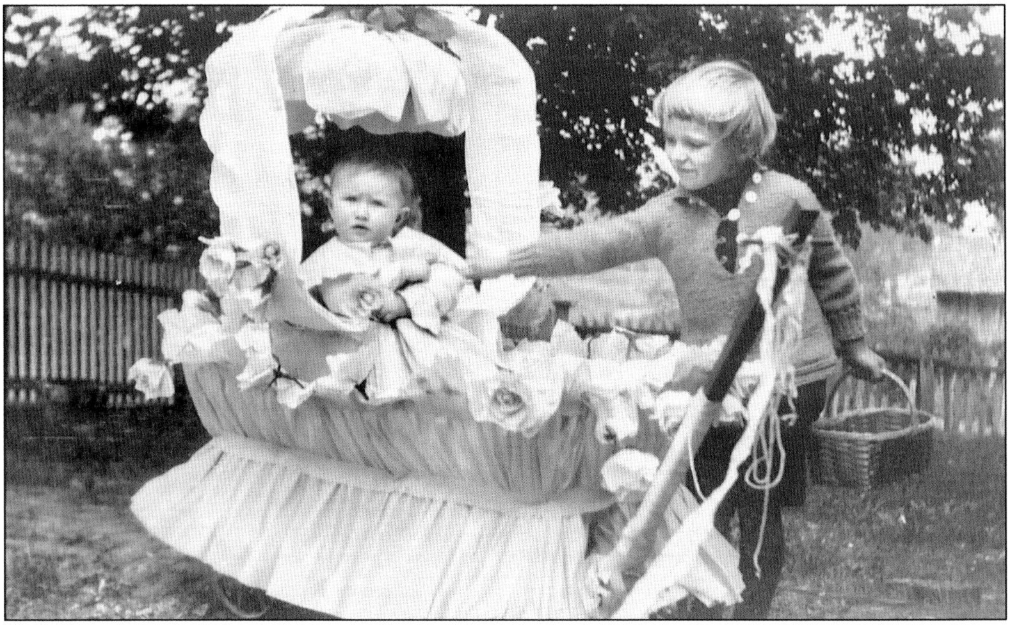

An annual event drawing large crowds was the Children's Flower Parade, sponsored by the garden department of the Woman's Club. The children paraded around the courthouse square on floats, wagons, and tricycles decorated with crepe-paper flowers. Prizes were awarded. This entry in 1924 was entitled "Roses;" the baby is Ellen Ann Westerberg with her brother, George Davis Westerberg.

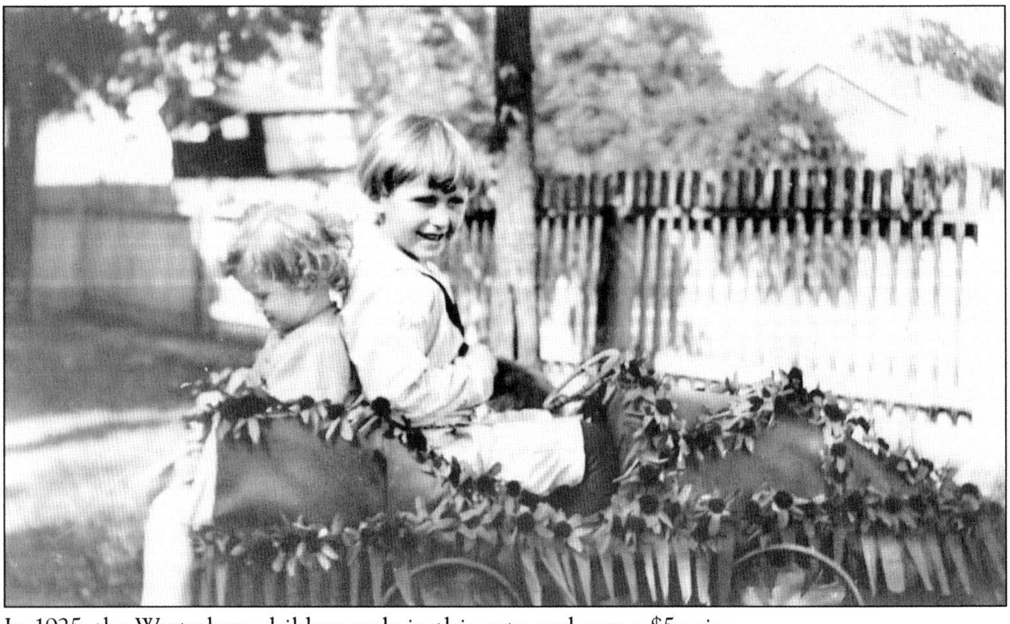

In 1925, the Westerberg children rode in this auto and won a $5 prize.

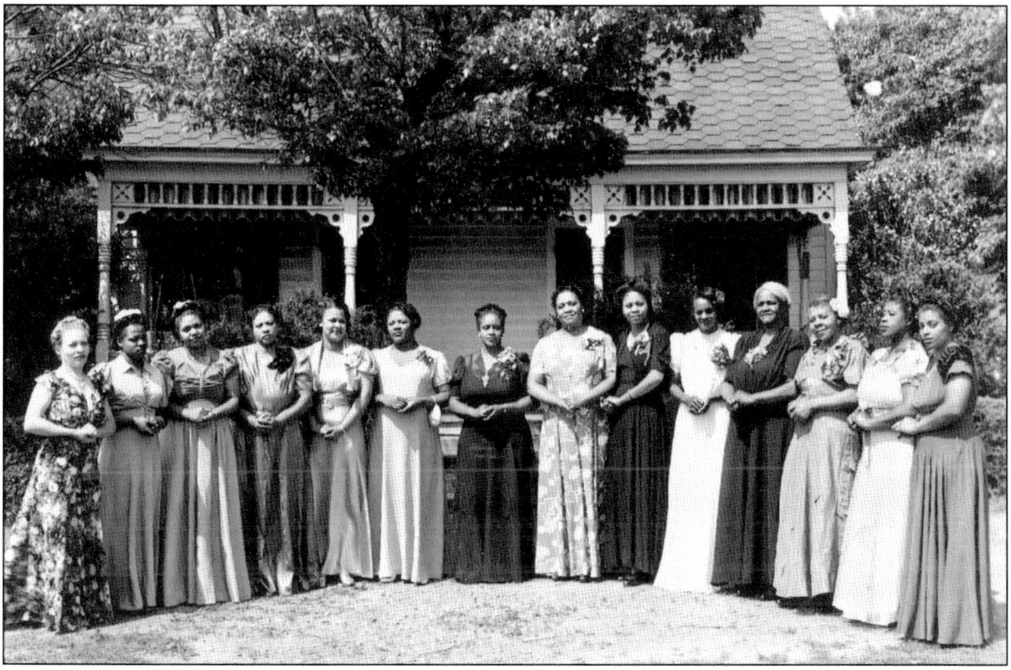

Sorority members gathered for a meeting. From left to right are Mae E. Carr, Gloria Russell, Della Tiller, Bell Hill, Inez Wood, Alice Sharp, Hattie Mae Osment, Anna Russell, Teula Miles, Louvenia Johnson, Sarah Tillery, Daisy Little, Francis Baine, and Willie Mae Tillery.

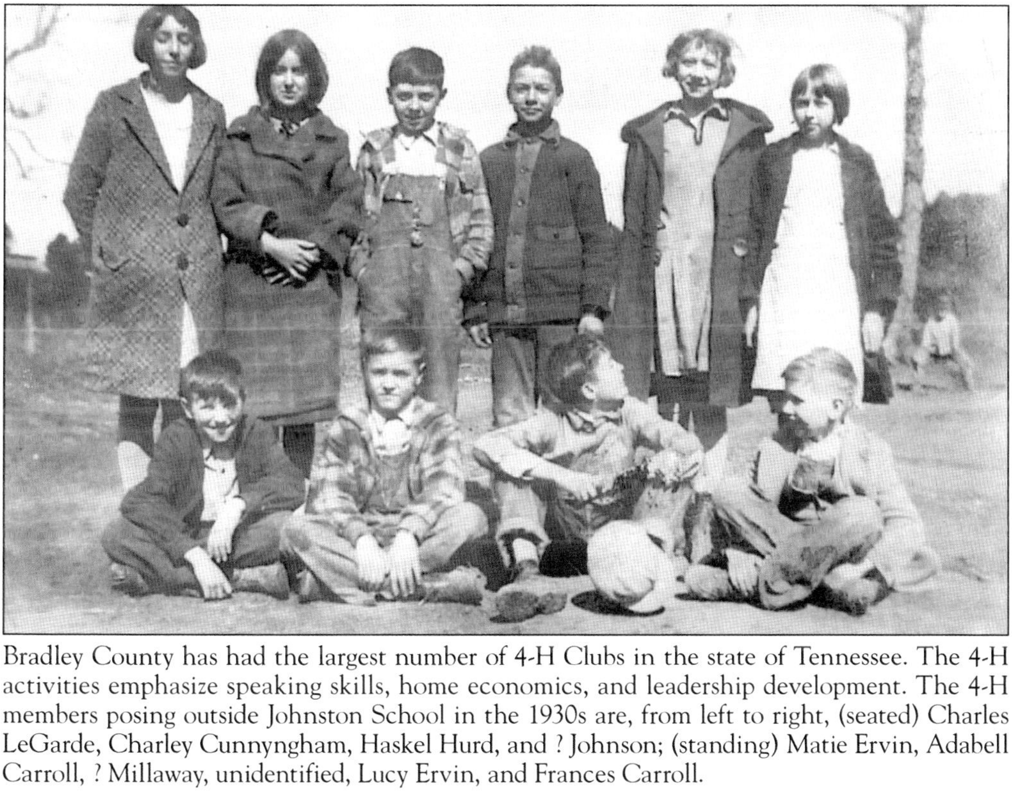

Bradley County has had the largest number of 4-H Clubs in the state of Tennessee. The 4-H activities emphasize speaking skills, home economics, and leadership development. The 4-H members posing outside Johnston School in the 1930s are, from left to right, (seated) Charles LeGarde, Charley Cunnyngham, Haskel Hurd, and ? Johnson; (standing) Matie Ervin, Adabell Carroll, ? Millaway, unidentified, Lucy Ervin, and Frances Carroll.

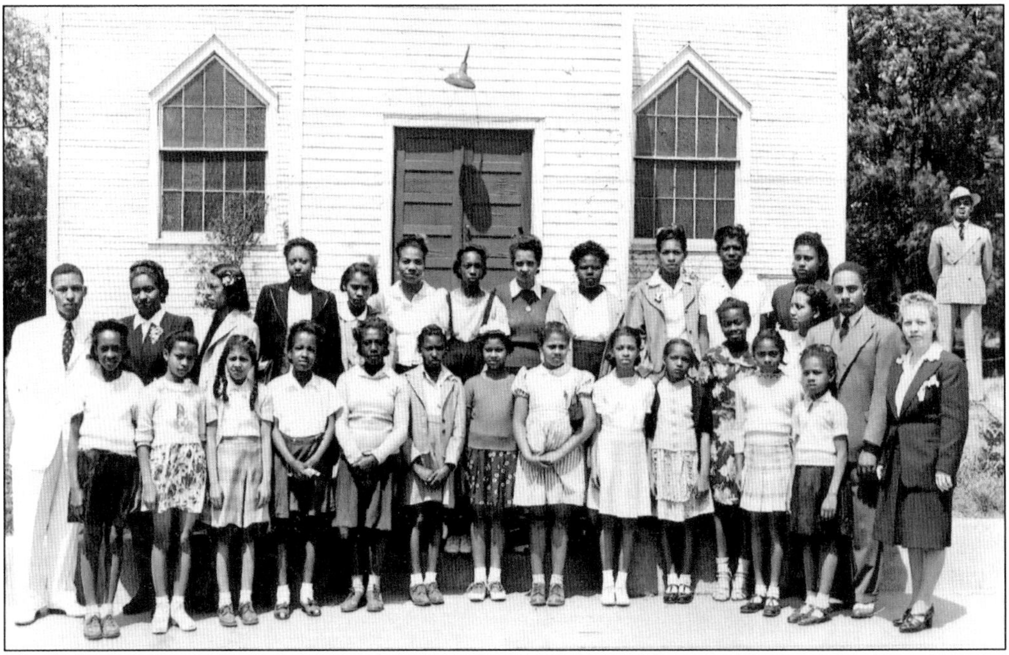

About 1946, Pleasant Grove Baptist pastor B. W. Bickers organized the first black Girl Scout troop in Cleveland. Members of the troop were girls between the ages of 12 and 19. Advisors to the troop were faculty members of College Hill High School: Juliet Bond, Sue O'Connor, Sally Smith, Mae Carr, Pauline Bradford, and Oscar Johnson.

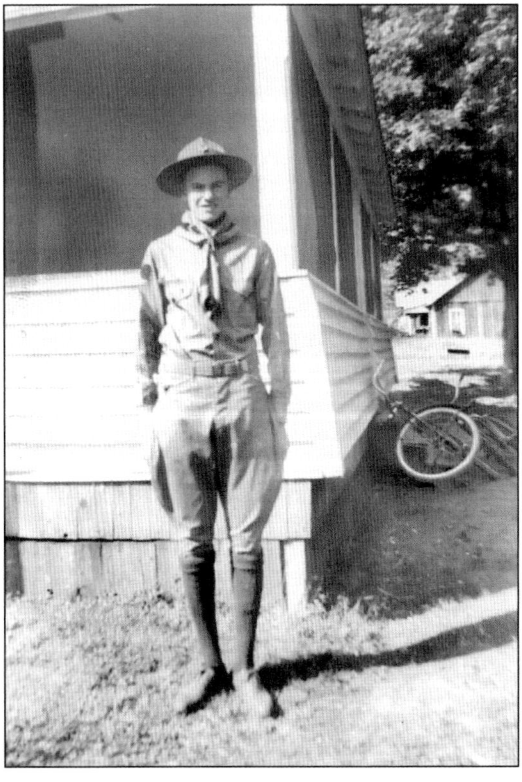

Boy Scout Second Class Cletis Bailey of McDonald was a member of Troop 75 in the 1930s.

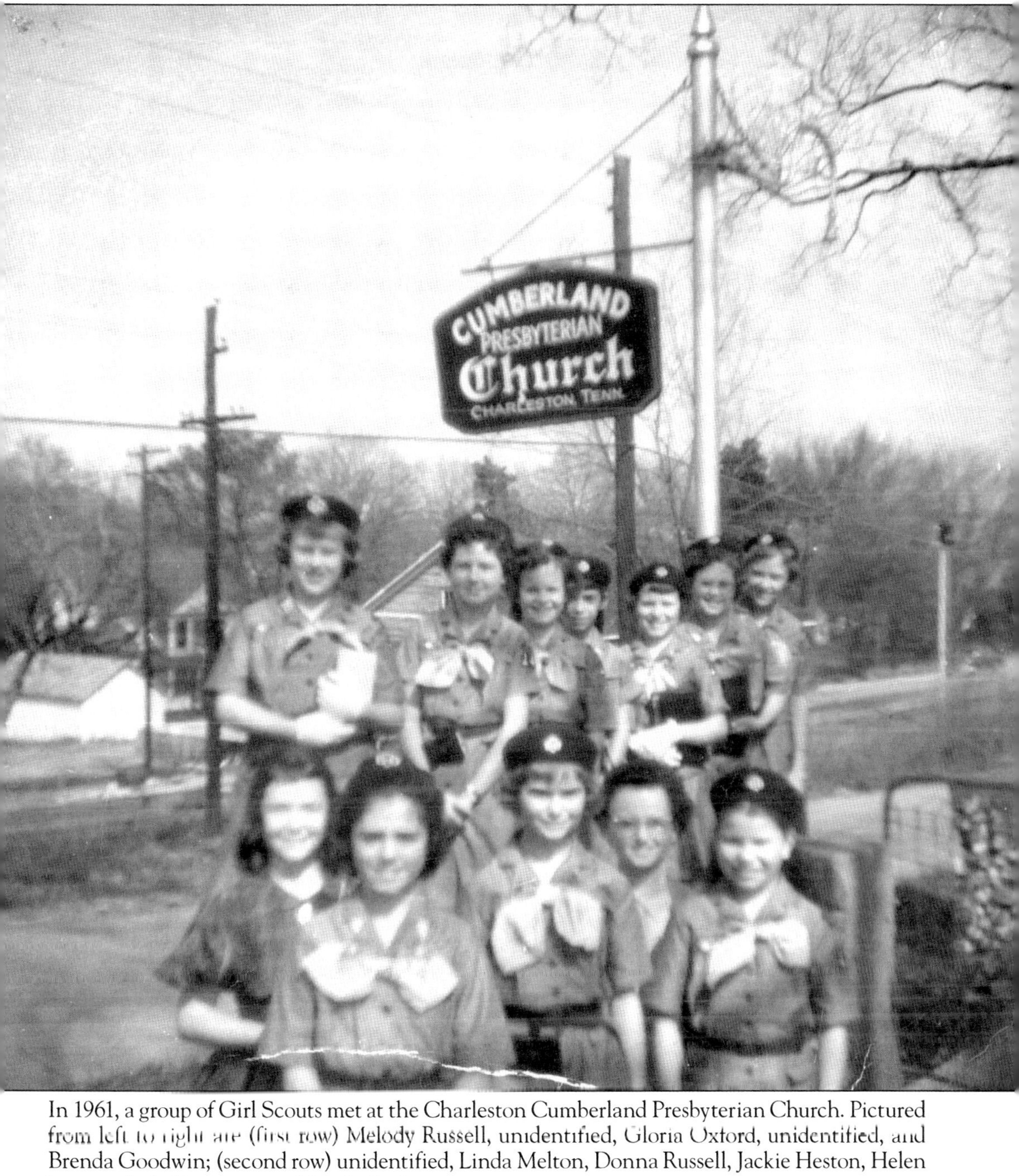

In 1961, a group of Girl Scouts met at the Charleston Cumberland Presbyterian Church. Pictured from left to right are (first row) Melody Russell, unidentified, Gloria Oxford, unidentified, and Brenda Goodwin; (second row) unidentified, Linda Melton, Donna Russell, Jackie Heston, Helen Lowery, Jody Bozeman, and Linda Peck.

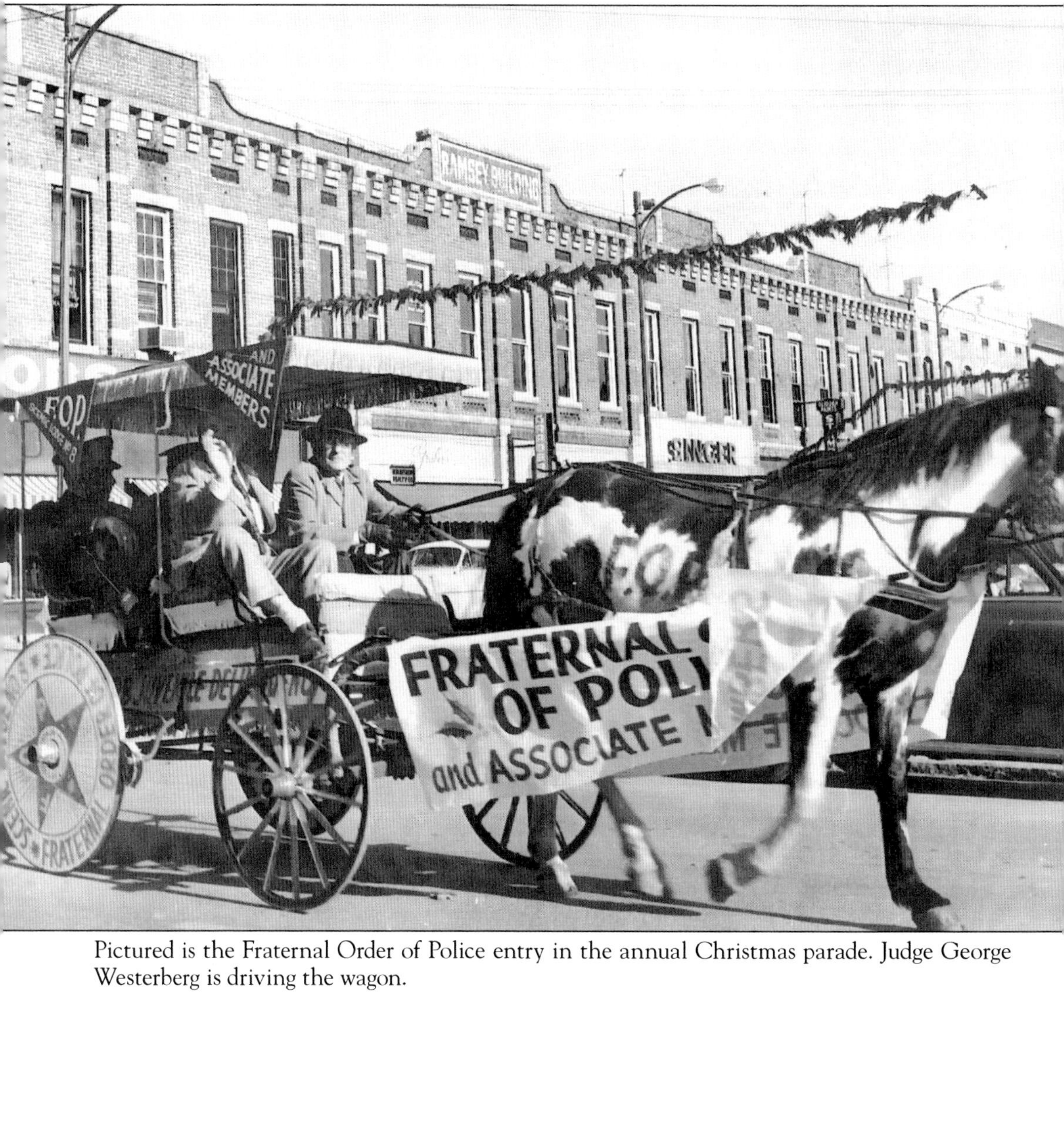

Pictured is the Fraternal Order of Police entry in the annual Christmas parade. Judge George Westerberg is driving the wagon.

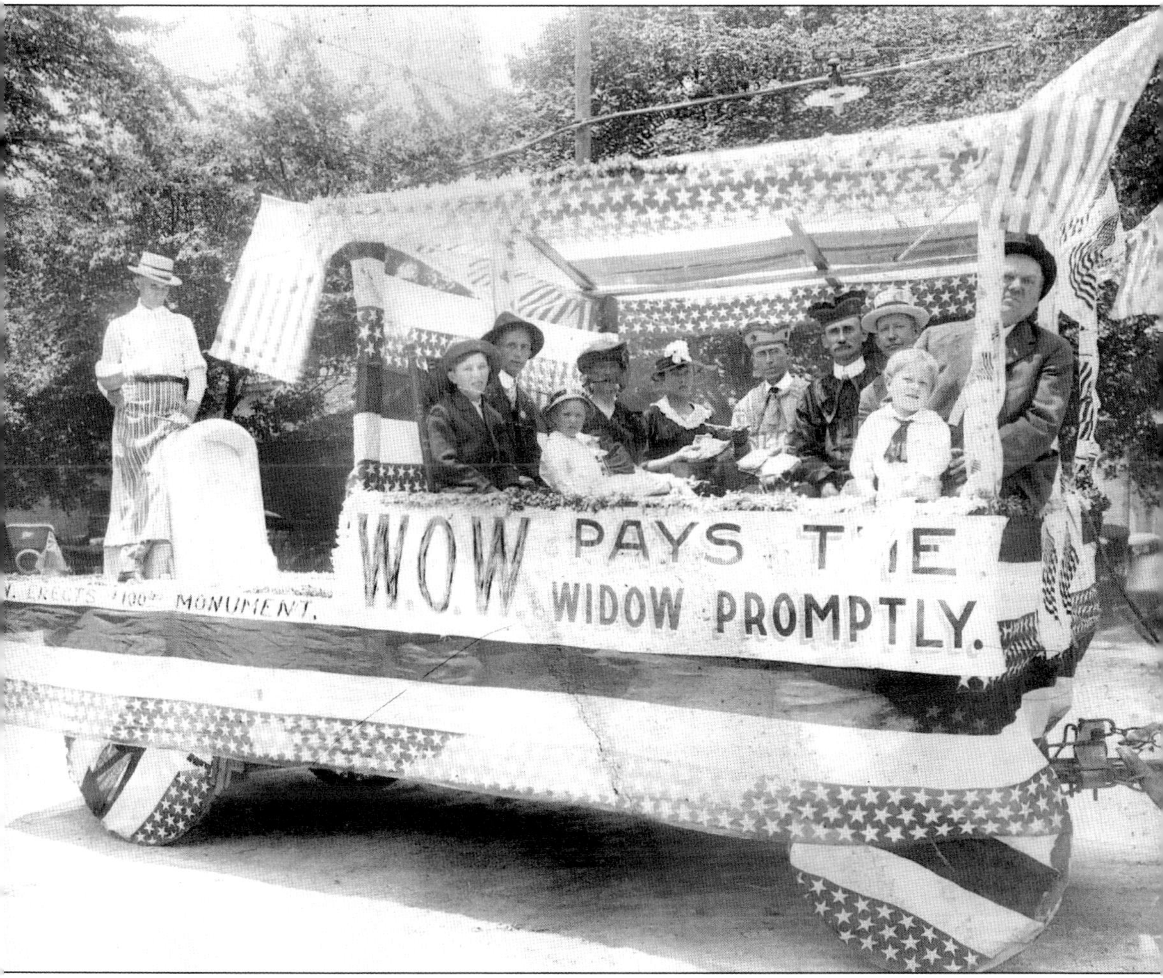

Shown is a parade float in the 1920s of the Wildwood Camp Number 16 of the Woodmen of the World. At that time, the fraternal group gave a cemetery marker to the family of each deceased member. The lodge is still active today. Among the float riders are J. P. Lawson, Frank Lawson, Clarence Lawson, Tina Lawson, Benna Lawson, and Louella Lawson. Lodge members are shown in their ritual regalia.

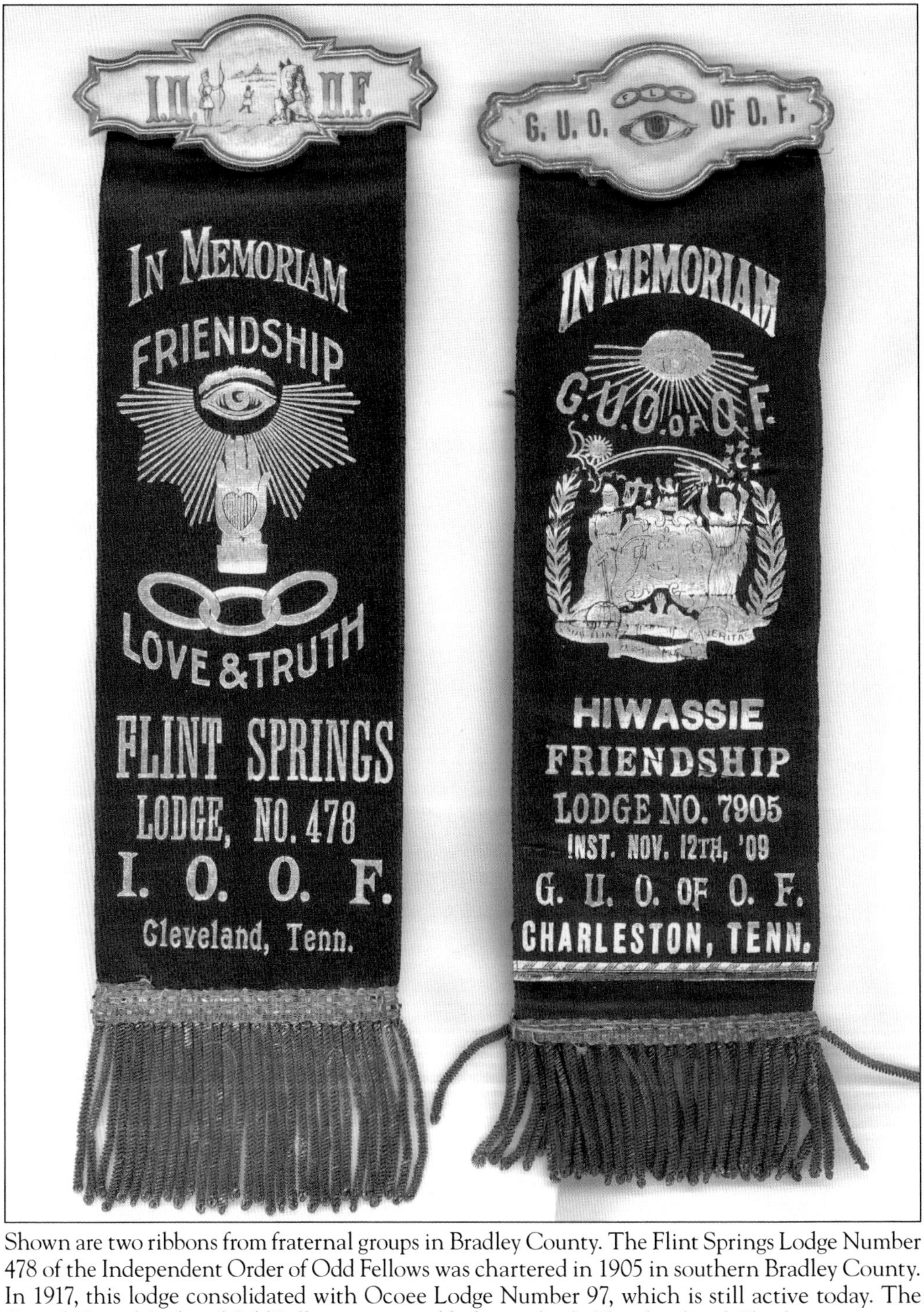

Shown are two ribbons from fraternal groups in Bradley County. The Flint Springs Lodge Number 478 of the Independent Order of Odd Fellows was chartered in 1905 in southern Bradley County. In 1917, this lodge consolidated with Ocoee Lodge Number 97, which is still active today. The Grand United Order of Odd Fellows organized lodges in both Cleveland and Charleston to serve the blacks of Bradley County. Shown is a memorial ribbon of the Hiwassee Friendship Lodge Number 7905, which was organized November 12, 1909. Neither of the black lodges is in existence today in Bradley County.

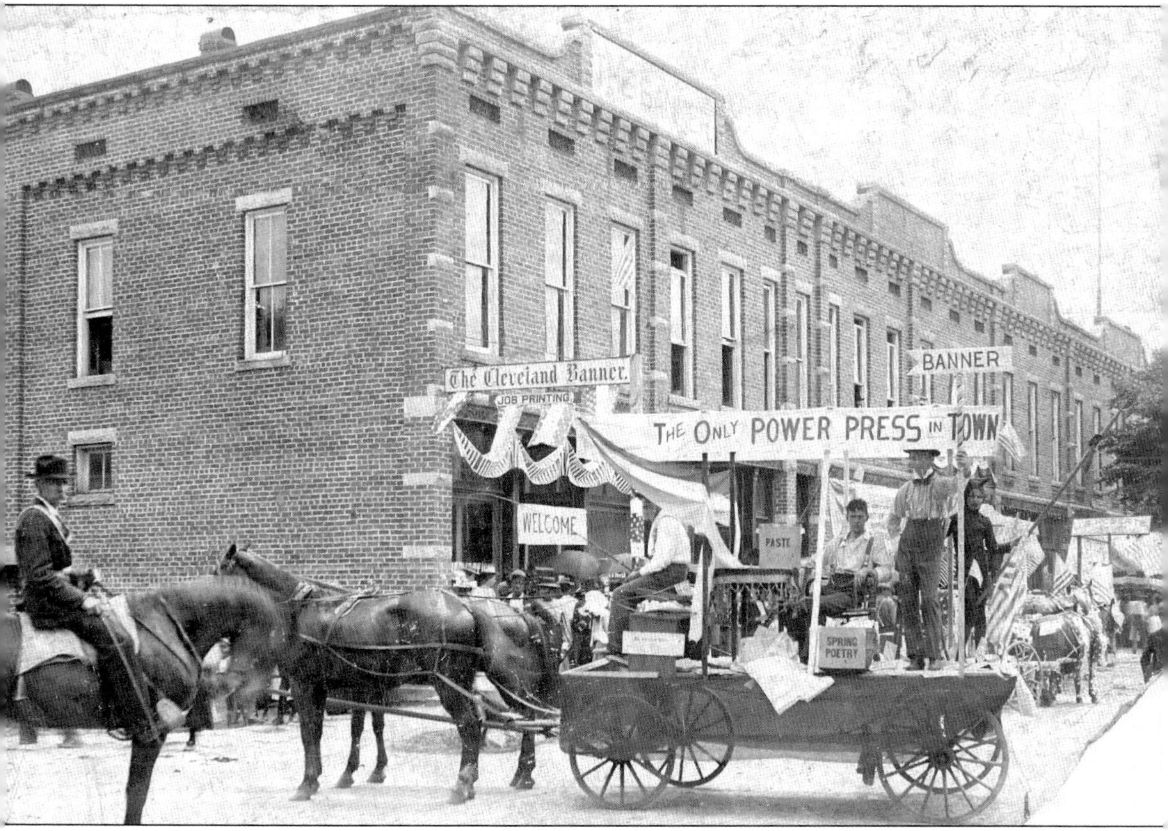

Pictured is a patriotic parade on the courthouse square in the 1890s. A local paper, the *Cleveland Daily Banner*, has a float boasting that it has "the only power press in town."

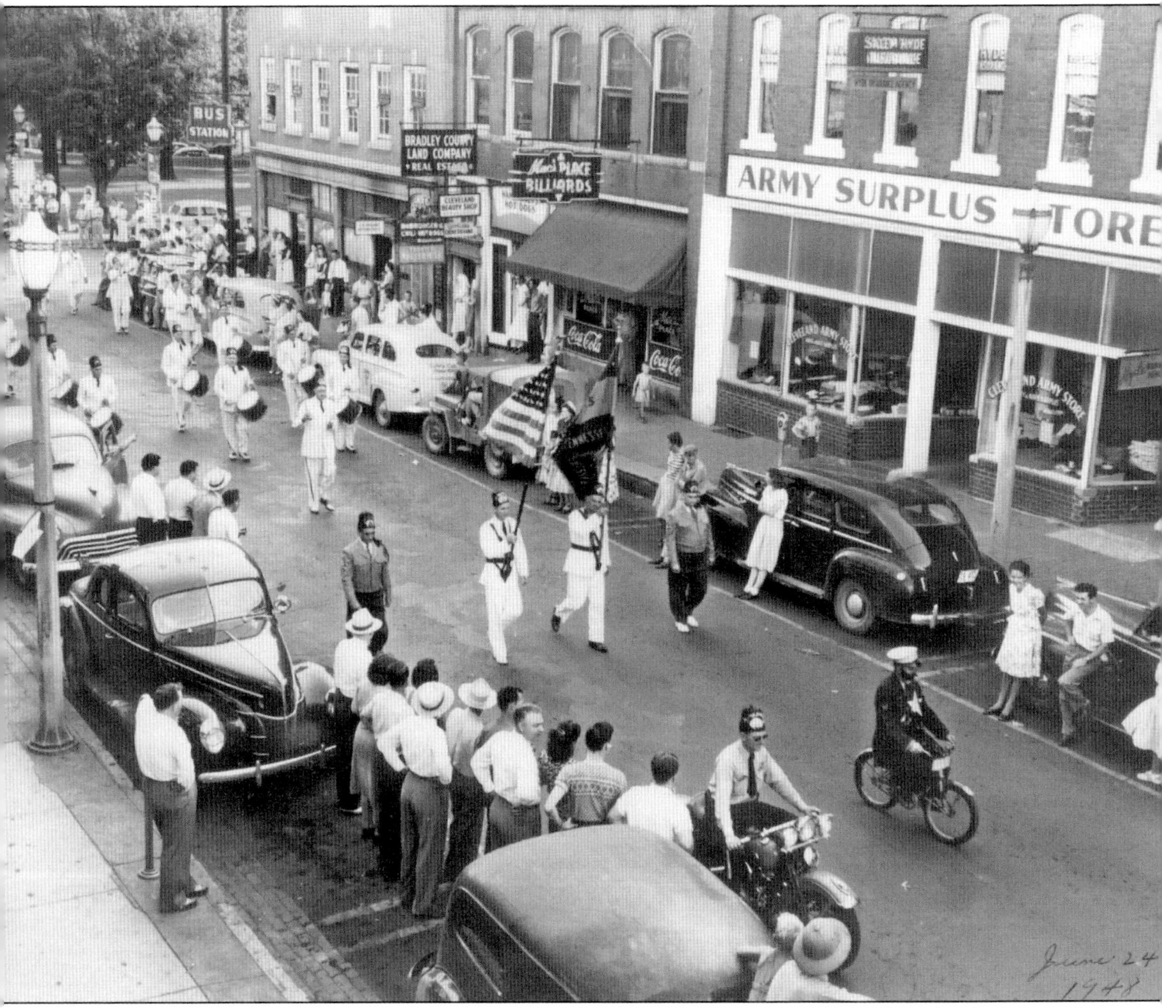

In 1948, a parade was held in downtown Cleveland. The Shriners marching band is shown in this photograph taken on Ocoee Street, one block south of the courthouse. Businesses shown include the Spot, the bus station, Mac's Place Billiards, Hyde Insurance, Cleveland Credit Exchange, and the Cleveland Army Store.

Nine

Just for Fun!

Oh Would I were a boy again, when life seemed formed of sunny hours,
When all the heart knew then of pain was swept away in transient showers.

—R. M. Edwards, 1883
Recollections of 60 Years Ago

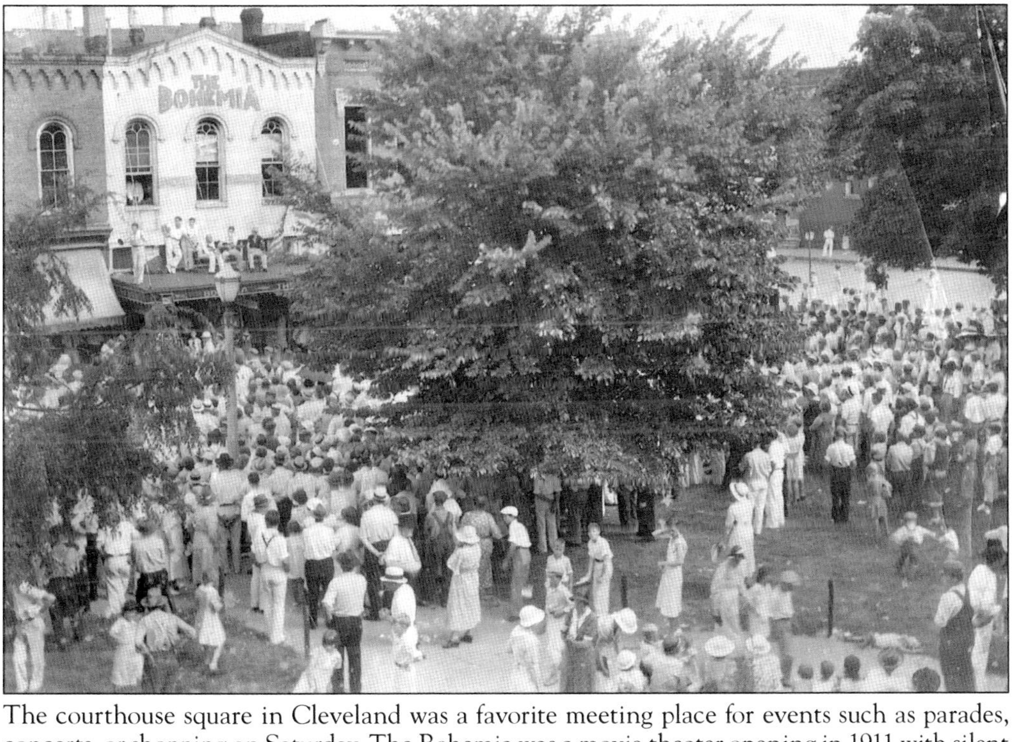

The courthouse square in Cleveland was a favorite meeting place for events such as parades, concerts, or shopping on Saturday. The Bohemia was a movie theater opening in 1911 with silent films. When it closed in 1955, the price of admission was 15¢ for children and 35¢ for adults.

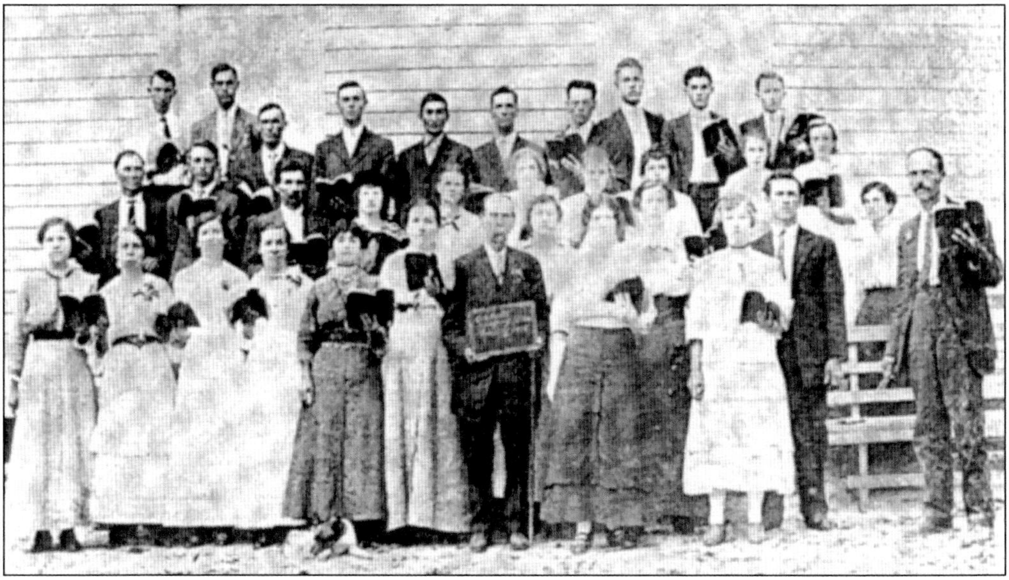

An old-time gospel singing school was held November 7, 1915, at Chilcutt's Chapel Methodist Church. Singing schools were conducted by gospel music publishers such as A. J. Showalter, James D. Vaughan, R. E. Winsett, Kieffer-Ruebush, and Stamps-Baxter. Teachers traveled throughout the South to teach the shape note manner of reading music and at the same time to sell their publishers' songbooks.

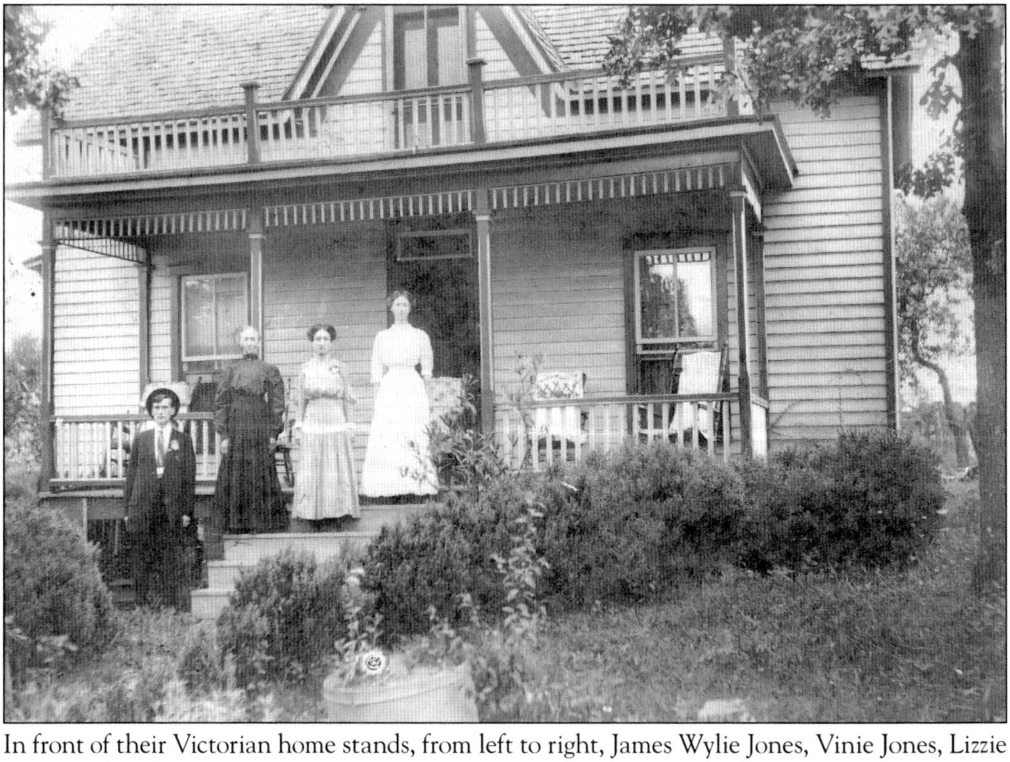

In front of their Victorian home stands, from left to right, James Wylie Jones, Vinie Jones, Lizzie Jones, and Wyline Jones.

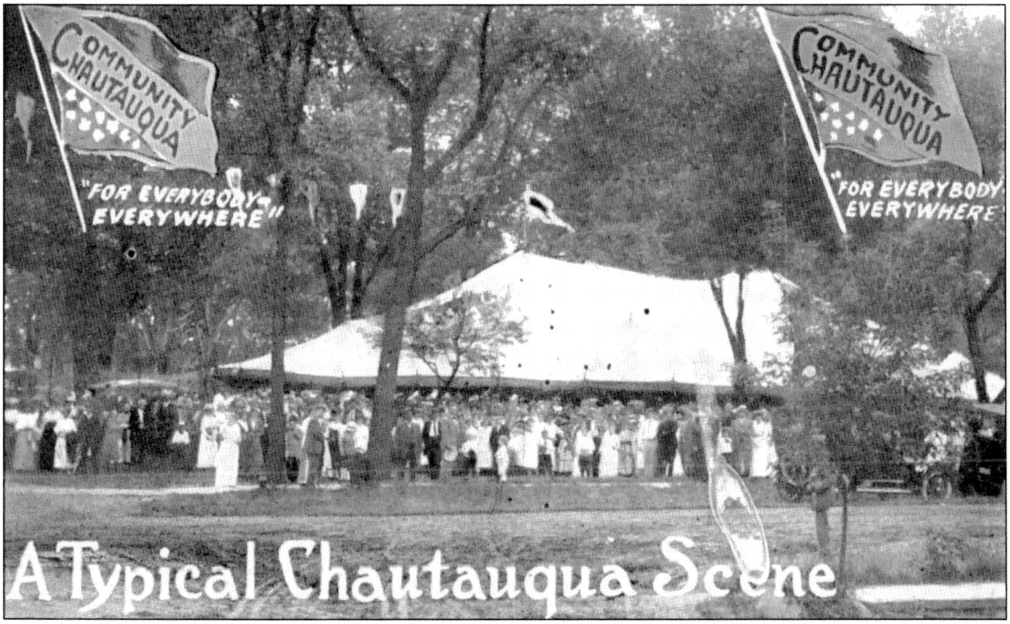

The Chautauqua Institution was established at Lake Chautauqua in New York in 1874 by the Reverend John Heyl Vincent and Lewis Miller as a summer school for Methodist Sunday school teachers. The demand for culture in rural America prompted the development of tent Chautauqua weeks that could be sponsored in smaller towns such as Benton, Etowah, Charleston, and Cleveland.

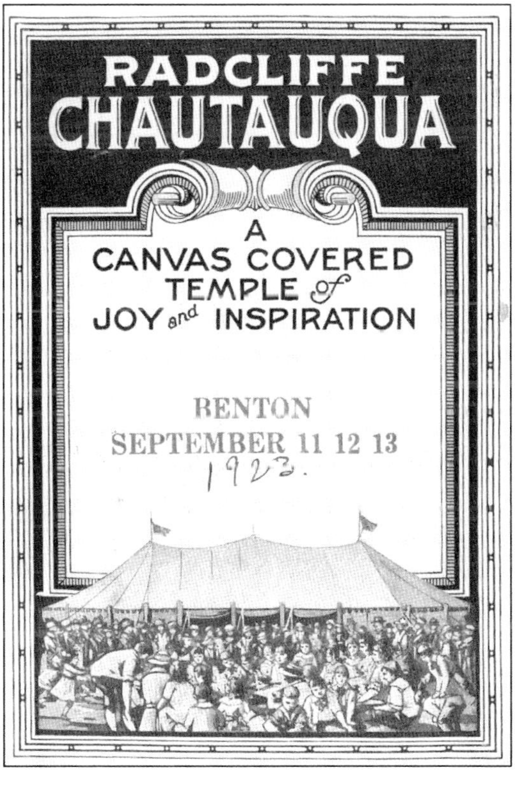

Chautauqua Week was held for 17 years in Cleveland, from 1914 to 1930. Attendance was high, with the tent being set up on the spacious grounds of Centenary College. Tickets were pre-sold by local sponsors such as the Kiwanis Club. Ticket holders heard such great speakers as William Jennings Bryan and Russell H. Conwell, author of *Acres of Diamonds*. Other acts included Edgar Bergen with Charlie McCarthy, Opie Read, and the Mikado Company. Shown is a program from the Chautauqua event held at neighboring Benton in 1923.

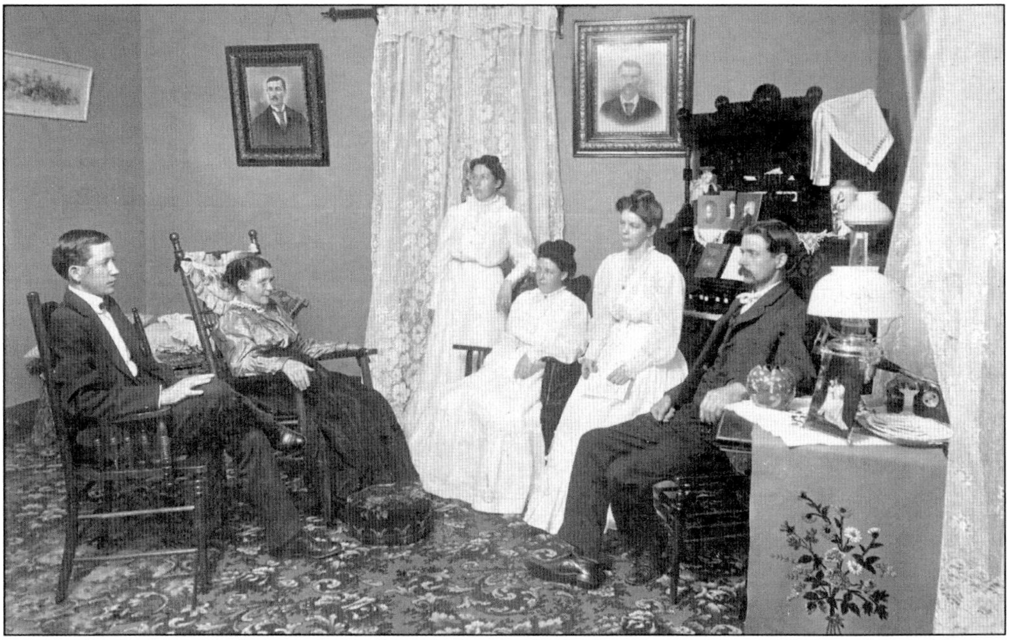

The Haggard and Grigsby families are enjoying a visit in the parlor. During Victorian times, this was the room in which families entertained their guests.

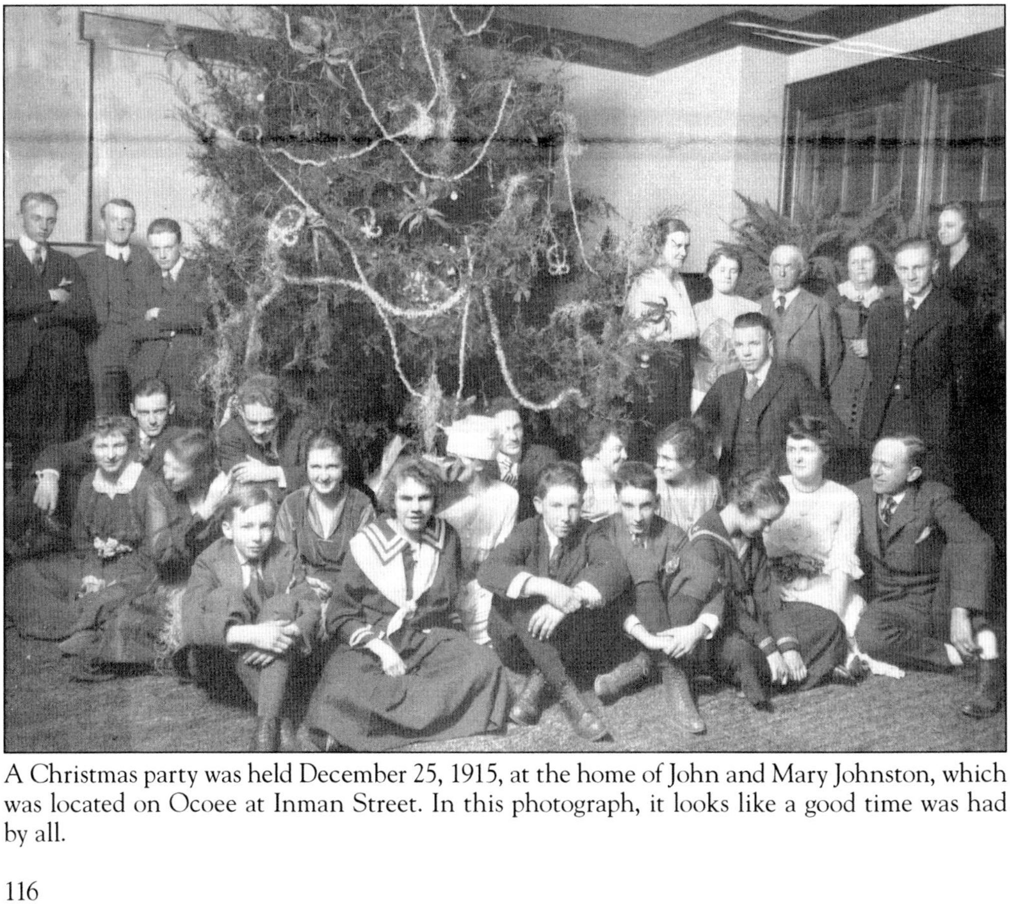

A Christmas party was held December 25, 1915, at the home of John and Mary Johnston, which was located on Ocoee at Inman Street. In this photograph, it looks like a good time was had by all.

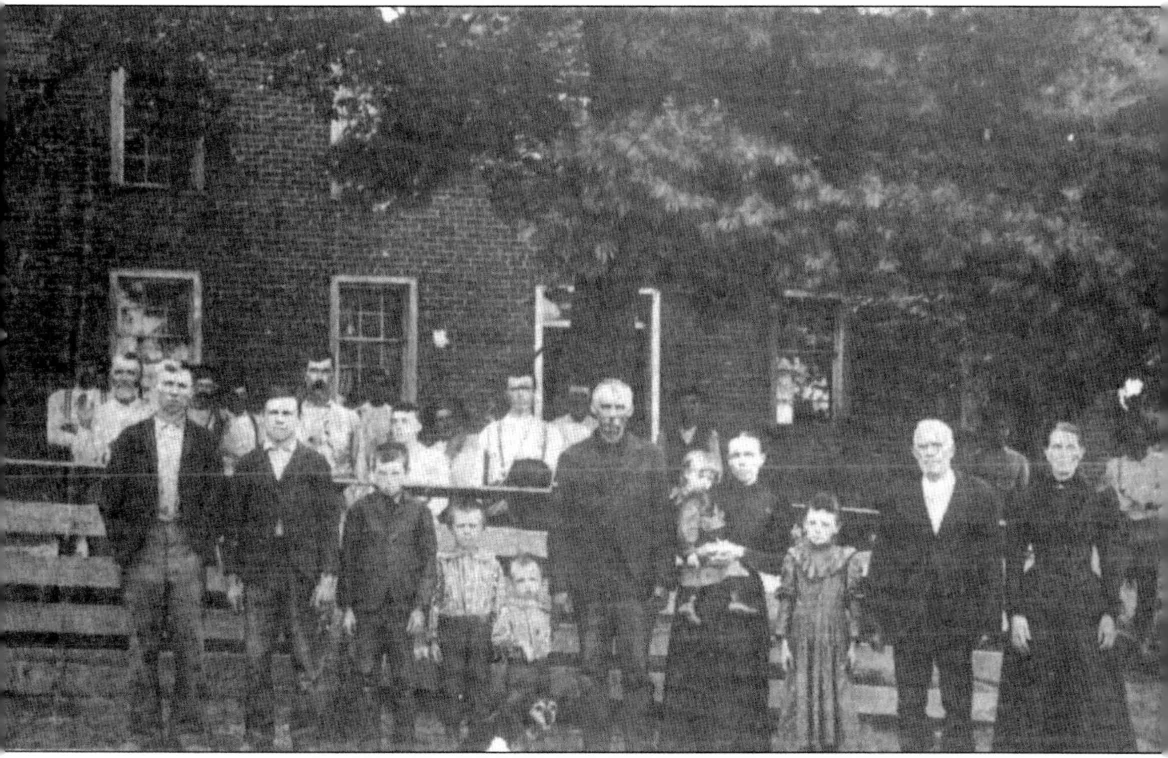

The Grief community was located 10 miles east of Cleveland on Benton Pike. This photograph made in 1894 at the Howard homestead depicts the Grief residents. From left to right are (first row) Charles Howard, Oscar Howard, Tom Howard, Walter Howard, Sumter Howard, John R. Howard, Mamie Howard, Elizabeth Wann Howard, Sallie Howard, Walter Howard, and Minerva Howard; (second row) Cam Kirkpatrick, Larkin Johnson, Lewis Armer, and Ernest Broyles. The large, two-story house was built in 1858 by the Wann family. During the Civil War, a minie ball was fired through the front door and an occupant killed. The bullet hole is visible in the door today. When this photograph was made, the Grief Post Office was located in the Howard home, and Elizabeth Wann Howard was postmistress. After the rural route system, RFD, was inaugurated, most of the small rural post offices were abolished. With this blow, the Grief community gradually lost its identity. This home was owned by Marvin Kirkpatrick from 1942 until his death in 1971.

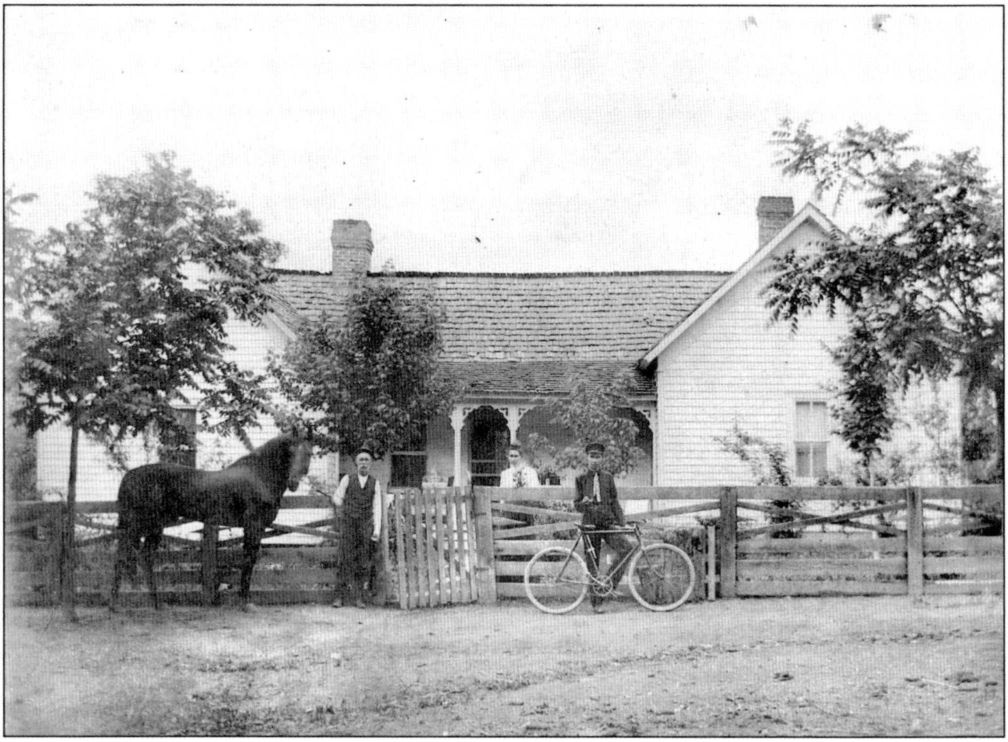

This photograph shows the Cunnyngham home off South Lee Highway.

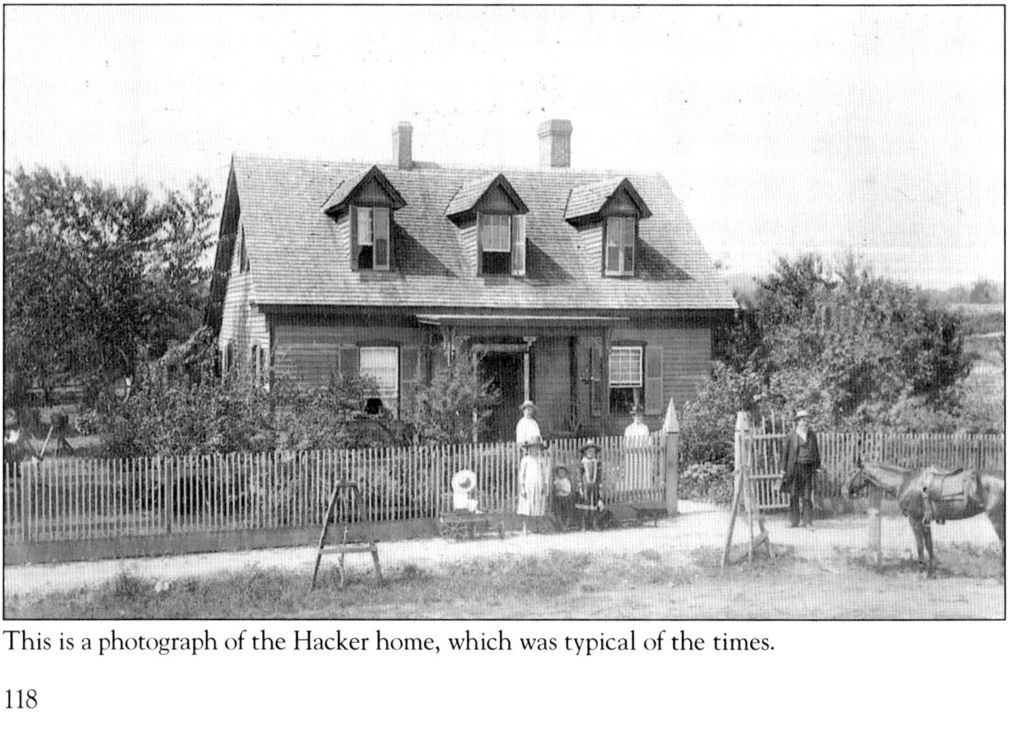

This is a photograph of the Hacker home, which was typical of the times.

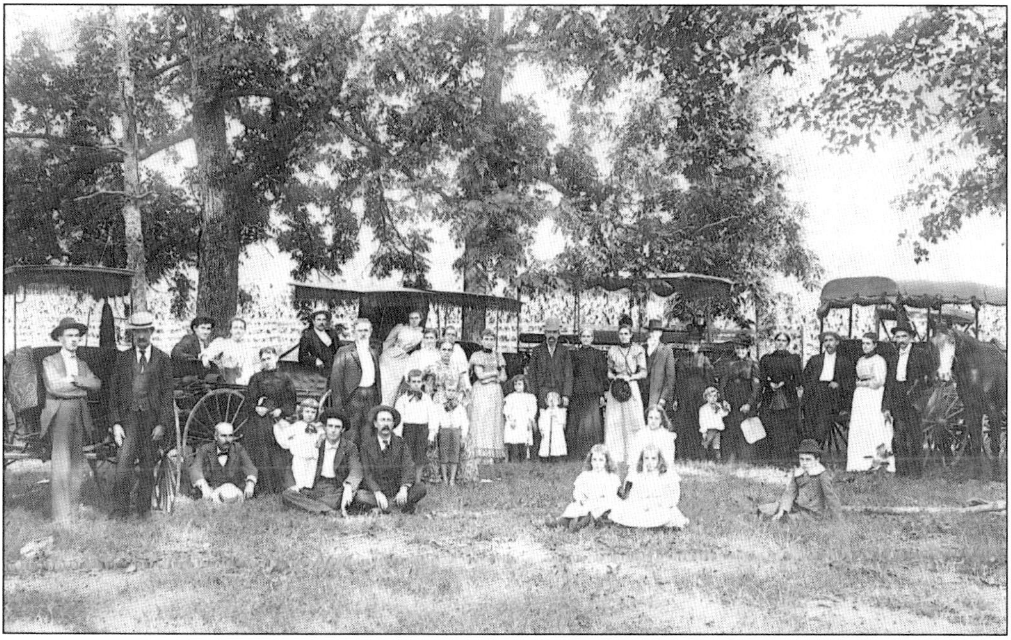

The Knox family is shown on an outing about 1908. From left to right are (in vehicles) F. U. Harle, Mary Knox, Dr. Thomas J. McKamy, and Ophelia Knox; (standing) H. M. Knox, Joe Smith, Mrs. R. L. Knox, Henry H. Knox, Minnie McKamy, Mrs. H. Knox, Knox Smartt, Harold Smartt, Una Camp, Mrs. J. McKamy, Annie Lea McKamy, James M. McKamy, James Knox McKamy, Julia Knox McKamy, Annie McKamy, Thomas J. Knox, Mr. T. J. Knox, Mrs. Tennessee S. Knox, B. Nixon, Nancy A. Knox, G. M. Smartt, Mrs. G. M. Smartt, and Walter Knox; (seated) R. L. Knox, Henry Knox, Ebon Knox, Ernie Nixon, Shelley Nixon, Florence Lee Nixon, and Knox Nixon.

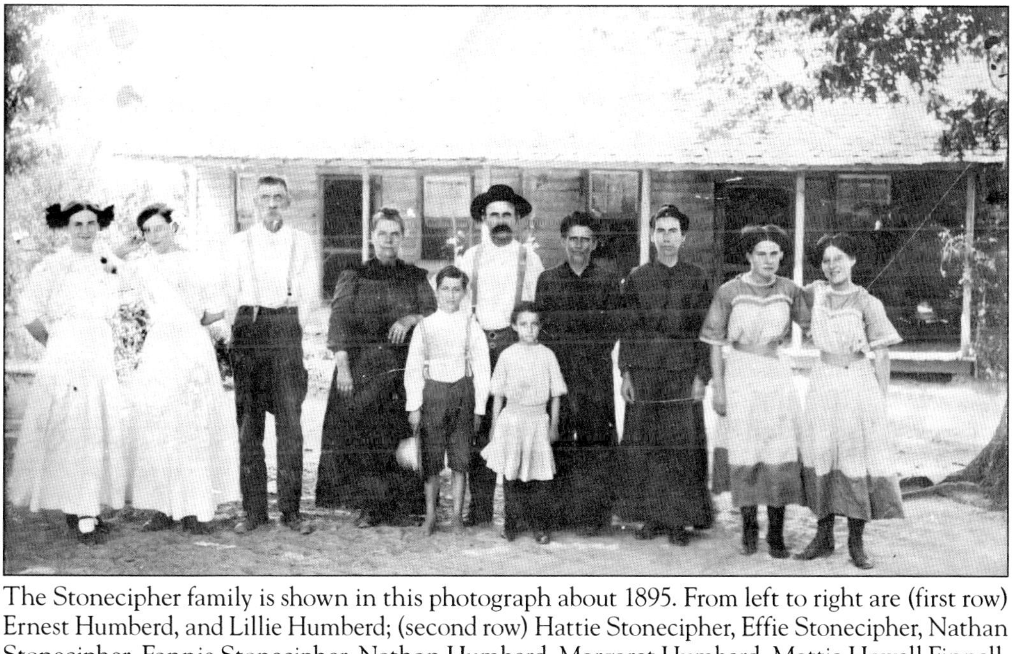

The Stonecipher family is shown in this photograph about 1895. From left to right are (first row) Ernest Humberd, and Lillie Humberd; (second row) Hattie Stonecipher, Effie Stonecipher, Nathan Stonecipher, Fannie Stonecipher, Nathan Humberd, Margaret Humberd, Mattie Howell Finnell, Nettie Stonecipher, and Ettie Stonecipher.

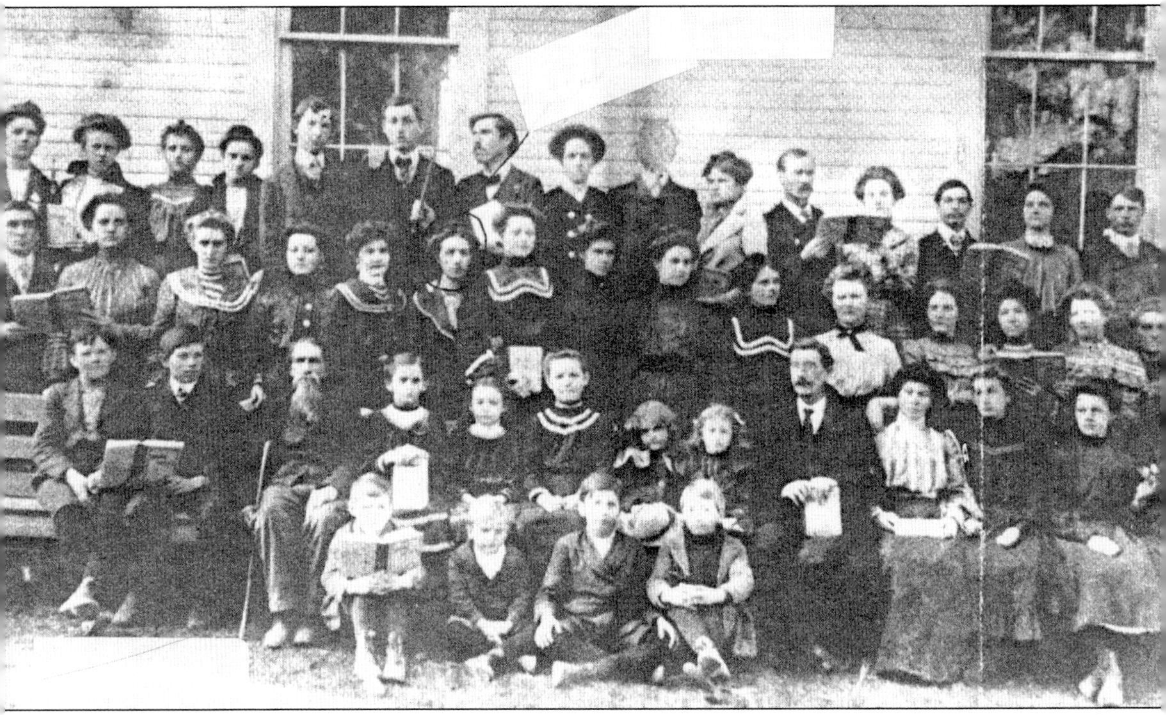

Robert Emmett Winsett (1876–1952) wrote his first song at age seven. Eventually he composed and authored over 1,000 gospel songs. He founded R. E. Winsett Music Company in 1903. A true pioneer of gospel music, his paperback songbooks appealed to Free Will Baptists, General Baptists, Holiness, and Pentecostal congregations because the songs were so spirited. As shown above, singing schools were held in Bradley County to train persons in music theory and application using shape notes.

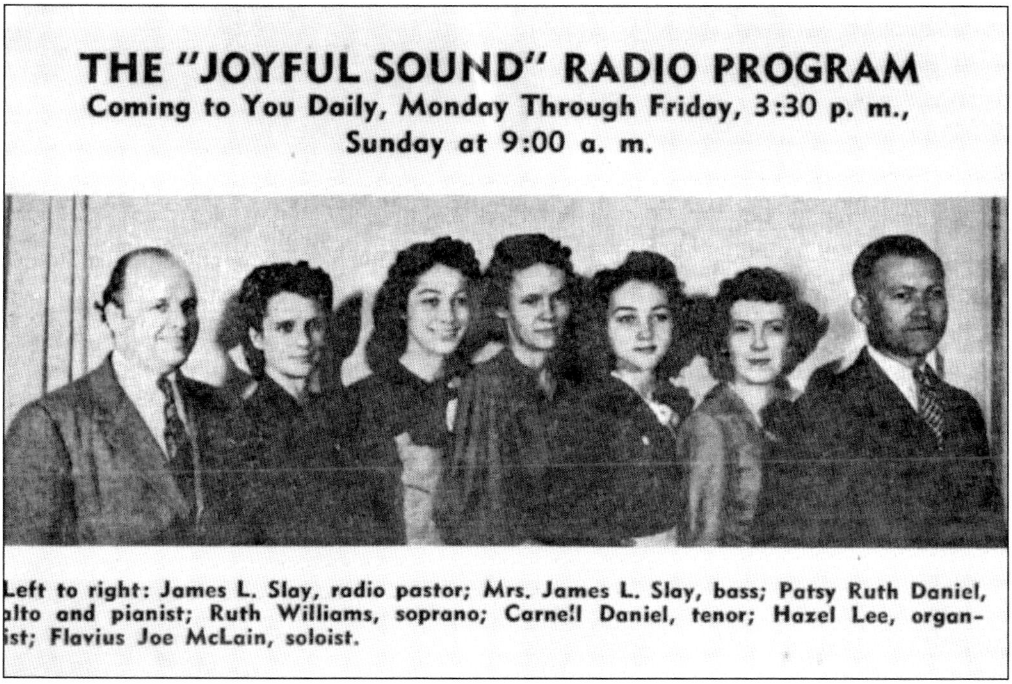

THE "JOYFUL SOUND" RADIO PROGRAM
Coming to You Daily, Monday Through Friday, 3:30 p. m.,
Sunday at 9:00 a. m.

Left to right: James L. Slay, radio pastor; Mrs. James L. Slay, bass; Patsy Ruth Daniel, alto and pianist; Ruth Williams, soprano; Carnell Daniel, tenor; Hazel Lee, organist; Flavius Joe McLain, soloist.

The *Joyful Sound* radio program was a daily broadcast by members of the North Cleveland Church of God. Pictured from left to right are James L. Slay, Mrs. James L. Slay, Patsy Ruth Daniel, Ruth Williams, Carnell Daniel, Hazel Lee, and Flavius Joe McLain.

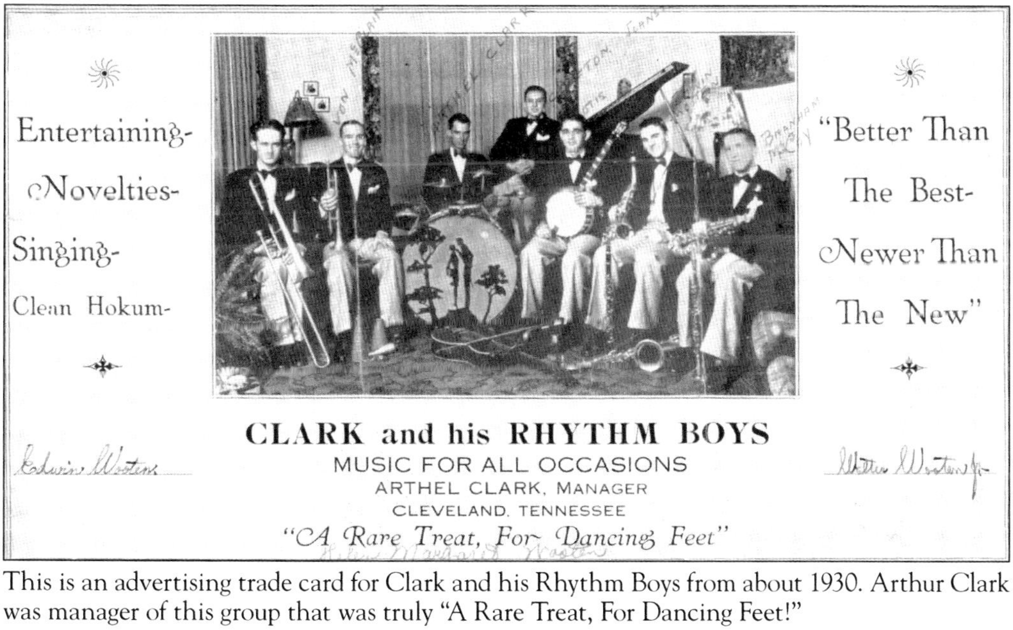

This is an advertising trade card for Clark and his Rhythm Boys from about 1930. Arthur Clark was manager of this group that was truly "A Rare Treat, For Dancing Feet!"

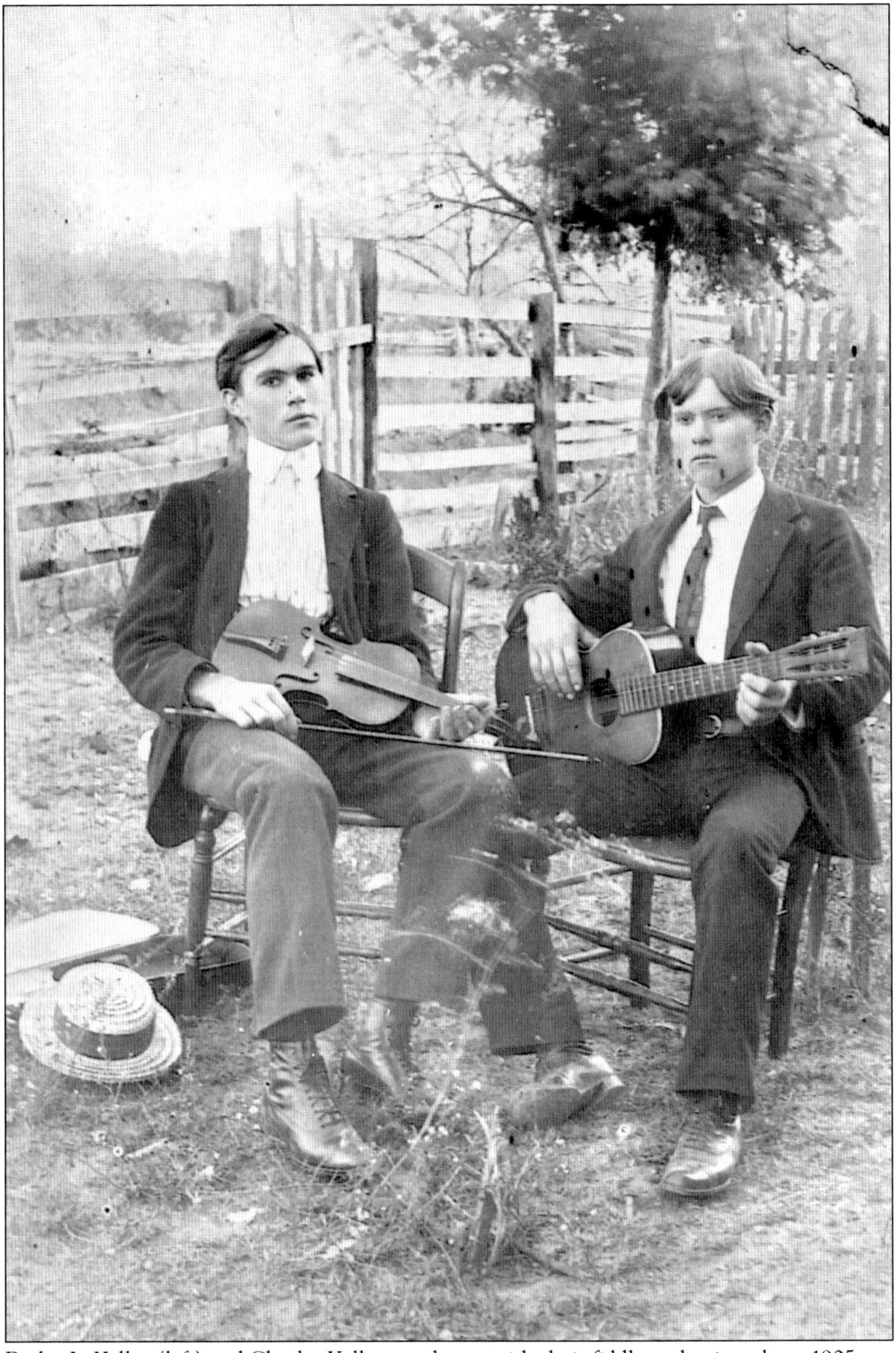

Dailey L. Kelley (left) and Charles Kelley are shown with their fiddle and guitar about 1905.

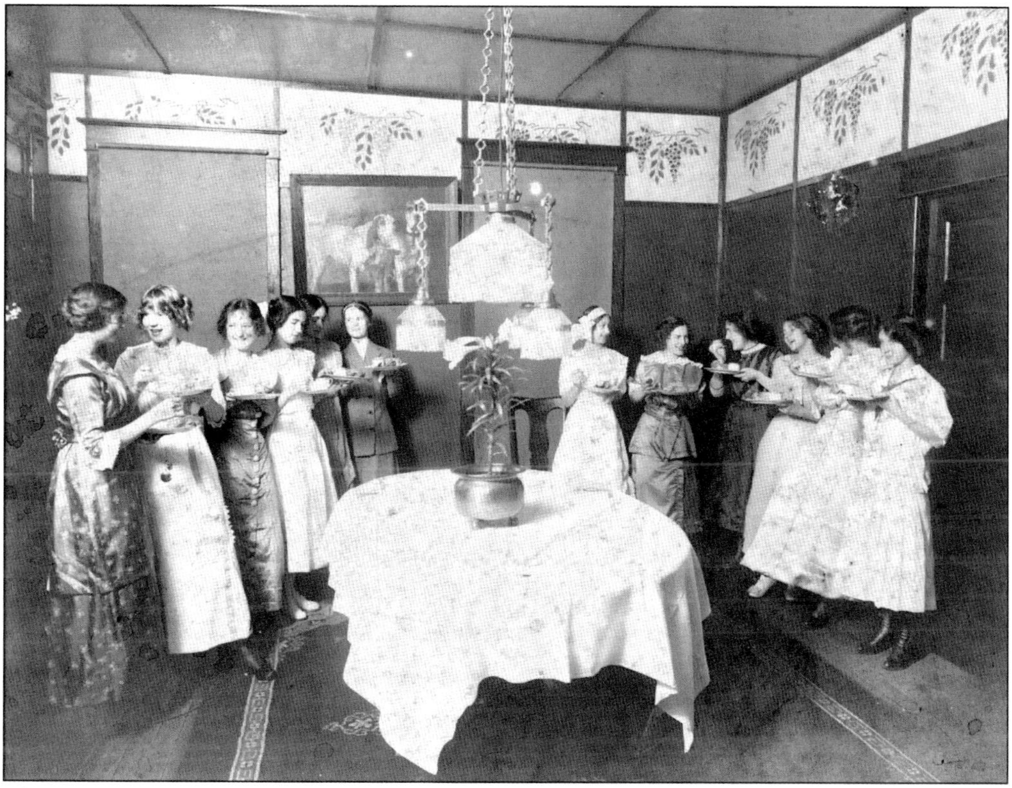

This photograph shows a party held at the Ocoee House in 1916 by the "W" Club. From left to right are Annie Templeton, Pauline Fletcher, Ethel Milne, Evylin Hannah, Grace Milne, Gertrude Steed, Charlie Taliaferro, Mary Knox, Louise Harle, Blanche Hearring, Willie Knox, and Rhoda Johnston.

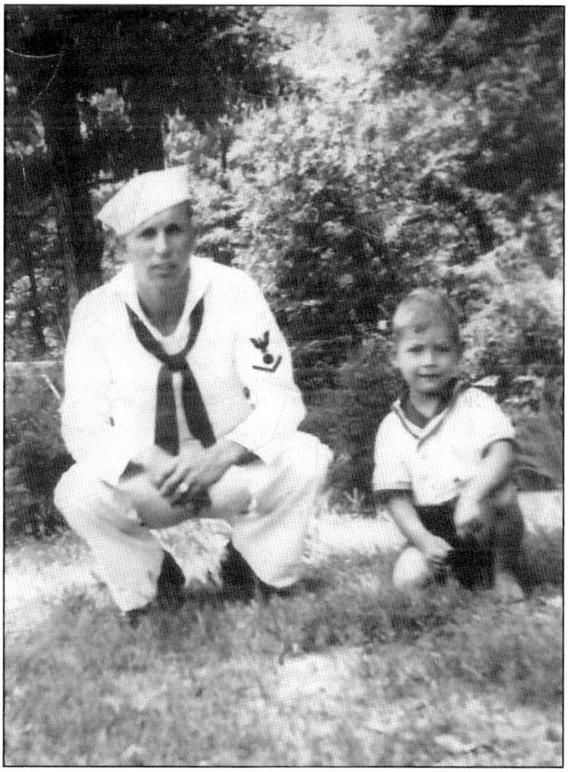

Charles LeGarde (left) and Phillip Newman enjoy some time together in the midst of World War II. Charles LeGarde was later killed in action in the European theater.

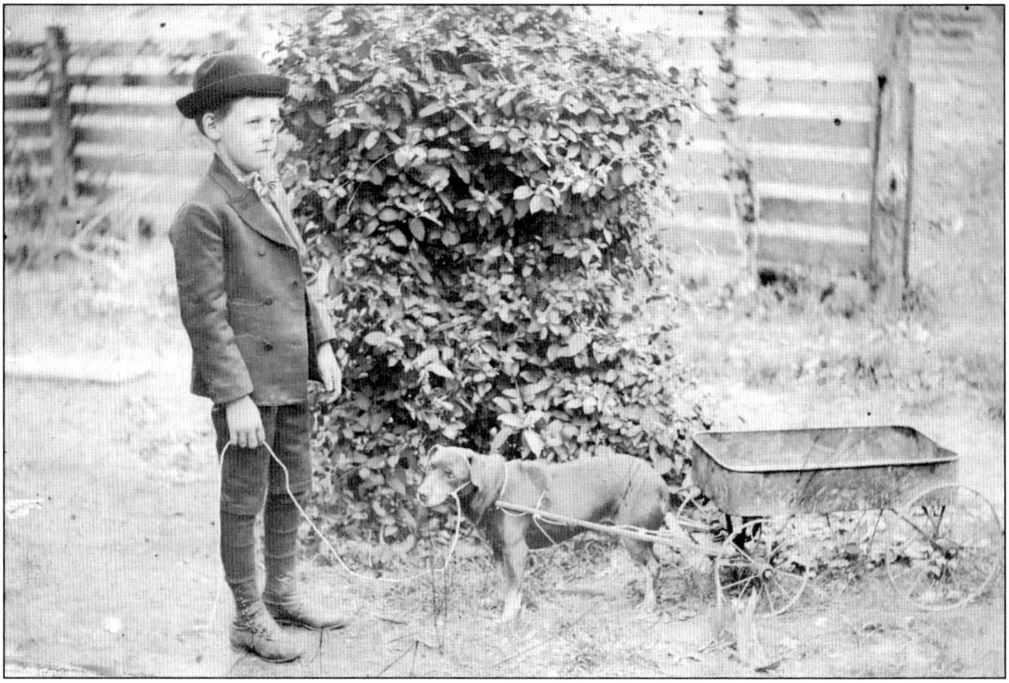

R. Clifford Johnson was born April 25, 1888, and lived in the Charleston area his entire life. He looks like he is enjoying walking his dog pulling the little wagon. Johnson later operated a blacksmith shop at the south edge of town.

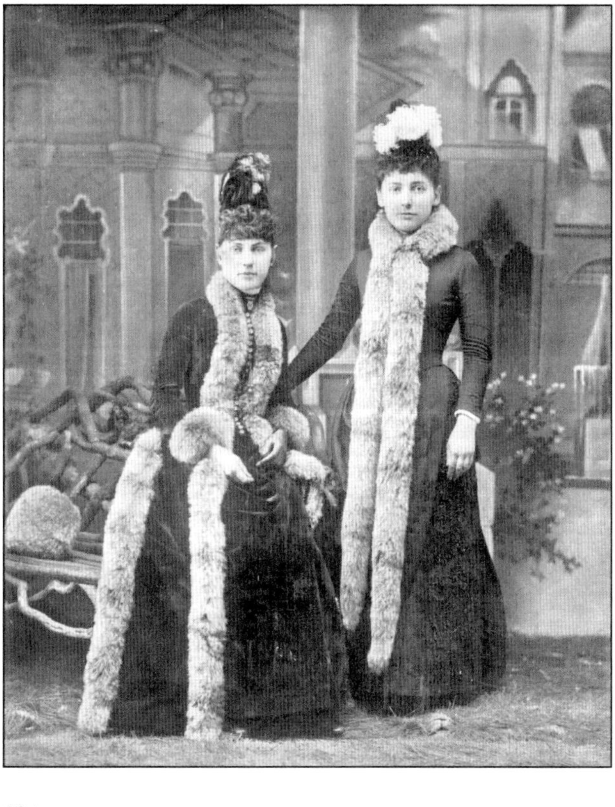

Shown in this photograph in the 1880s wearing such stunning apparel are Adelia Campbell Tipton and Agnes Hartdegen Hebert.

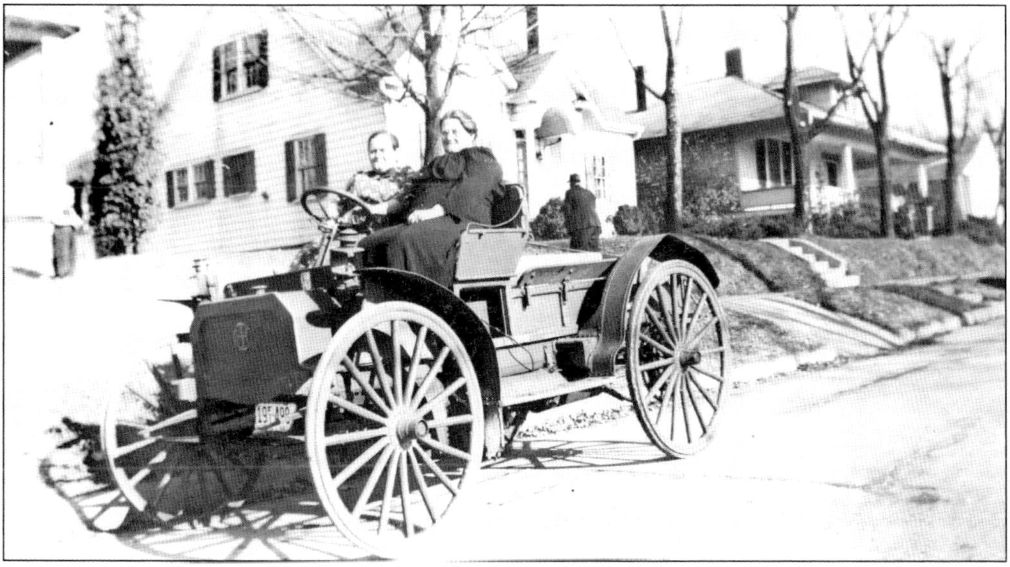

Amanda Ingram and Mae Murray are out for a drive in an early automobile in the 1940s. Note the state-shaped license plate with "19," which at that time represented Bradley County.

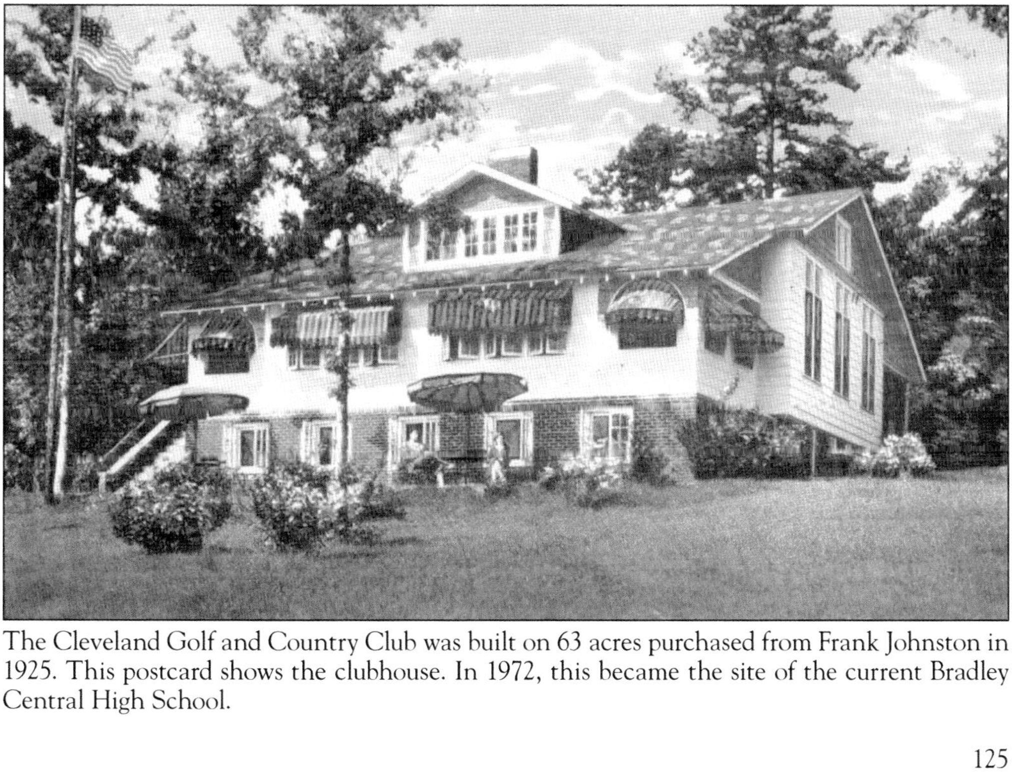

The Cleveland Golf and Country Club was built on 63 acres purchased from Frank Johnston in 1925. This postcard shows the clubhouse. In 1972, this became the site of the current Bradley Central High School.

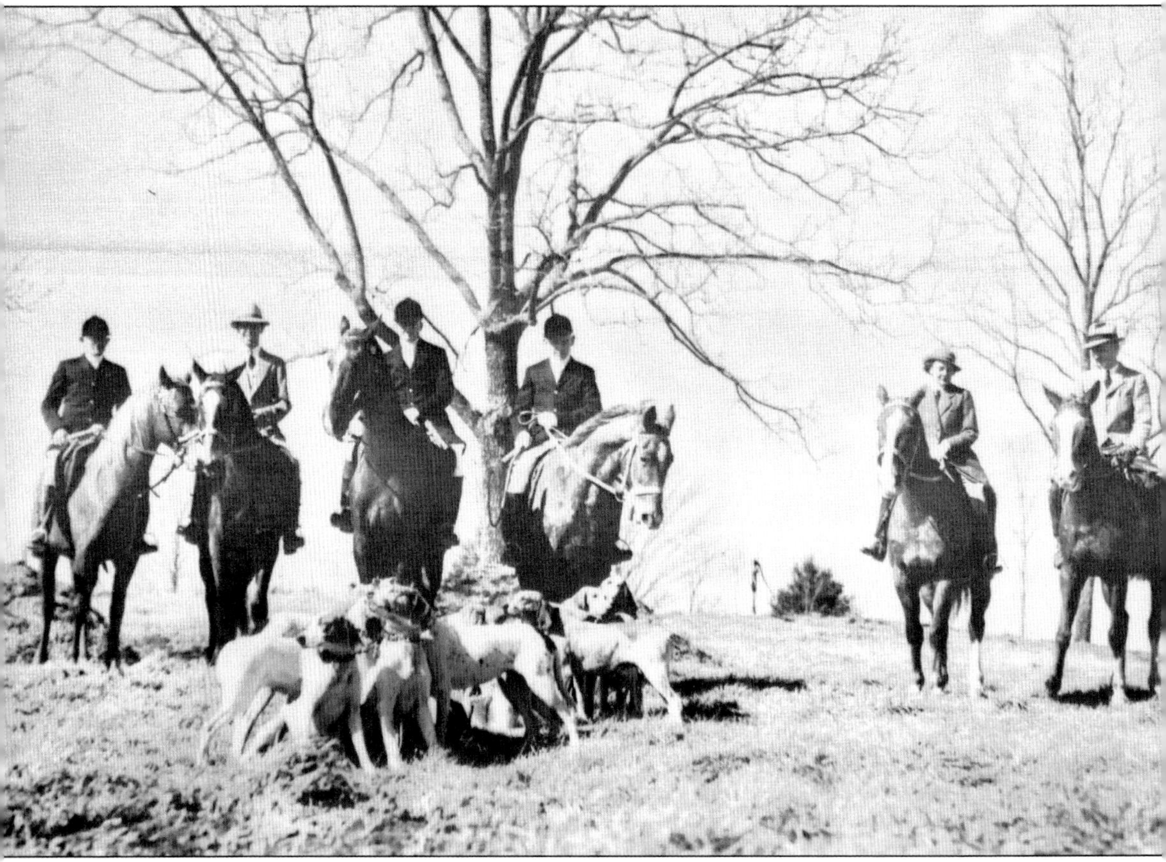

Foxhunts have often been held at Bendabout Farm in south Bradley County.

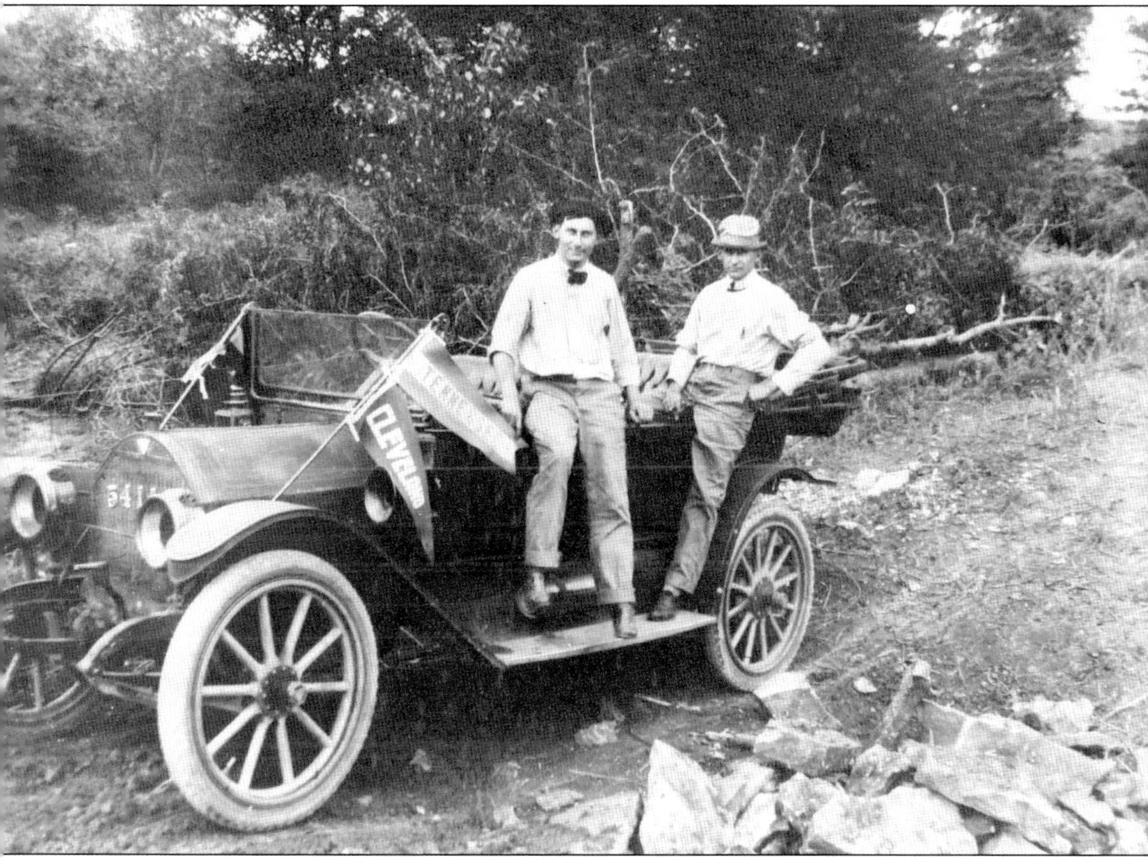

Two unidentified gentlemen are enjoying their drive on unpaved roads in Bradley County. Note "Cleveland" and "Tennessee" on the pennants.